FAMILY STRESS, COPING, AND SOCIAL SUPPORT

FAMILY STRESS, COPING, AND SOCIAL SUPPORT

Edited By

HAMILTON I. McCUBBIN

A. ELIZABETH CAUBLE

JOAN M. PATTERSON

Family Social Science
University of Minnesota

CHARLES C THOMAS • PUBLISHER

Springfield • Illinois • U.S.A.

Published and Distributed Throughout the World by

CHARLES C THOMAS • PUBLISHER

2600 South First Street

Springfield, Illinois, 62717, U.S.A.

© *1982 by* CHARLES C THOMAS • PUBLISHER

ISBN 0-398-04692-1

Library of Congress Catalog Card Number: 82-3382

Printed in the United States of America
CU-R-1

Library of Congress Cataloging in Publication Data

Main entry under title:

Family stress, coping, and social support.

    Bibliography: p.
    Includes index.
    1. Family--Addresses, essays, lectures.
2. Stress (Psychology)--Addresses, essays, lectures. 3. Stress (Physiology)--Addresses, essays,
lectures. 4. Life cycle, Human--Addresses, essays,
lectures. I. McCubbin, Hamilton I. II. Cauble,
A. Elizabeth. III. Patterson, Joan M.
HQ734.F2419   306.8'5   82-3382
ISBN 0-398-04692-1   AACR2

CONTRIBUTORS

Ronald J. Burke is Professor of Organizational Behavior and Industrial Relations, Faculty of Administrative Studies, York University.

Wesley Burr is Professor of Child Development and Family Relationships and Professor of Sociology, Brigham Young University.

Gerald Caplan is Chairman, Department of Child Psychiatry, Hadassah University Hospital, Ein Karem, Jerusalem.

A. Elizabeth Cauble is a Research Associate in Family Social Science, University of Minnesota.

Sidney Cobb is Professor of Community Health and of Psychiatry at Brown University.

Joan K. Comeau is a Research Associate in Family Social Science, University of Minnesota.

Andrea Larsen is a Research Associate in Family Social Science, University of Minnesota.

Harriette P. McAdoo is Professor, School of Social Work, Howard University.

Hamilton I. McCubbin is Professor and Head, Department of Family Social Science, University of Minnesota.

Elizabeth Menaghan is an Assistant Professor in the Department of Sociology at Ohio State University.

Phyllis Moen is an Assistant Professor in the Department of Human Development and Family Studies at Cornell University.

Robert S. Nevin is an Assistant Professor in the School of Social Work, Indiana University.

David H. Olson is Professor in the Department of Family Social Science, University of Minnesota.

Joan M. Patterson is a Research Associate in Family Social Science at the University of Minnesota.

Leonard I. Pearlin is a Research Sociologist in the Laboratory of Socio-Environmental Studies of the National Institute of Mental Health.

Lois Pratt is Professor of Sociology at Jersey City State College, New Jersey.

Carmi Schooler is a Social Psychologist in the Laboratory of Socio-Environmental Studies of the National Institute of Mental Health.

Denise A. Skinner is an Assistant Professor of Family Relations at the University of Wisconsin — Stout.

Tamara Weir is a Research Associate, Faculty of Administrative Studies, York University.

PREFACE

WE have designed this anthology to reflect our commitment to research, which extends beyond a focus on family stress alone to an understanding of how families succeed in managing life's hardships. Thus, coping and social support are major complementary themes of this book.

In an effort to bring this ever expanding domain of family stress research into sharper focus, we have underscored the central importance of basic concepts, propositions, and theory, which represent the foundation upon which future research, education, and clinical interventions might be based. We have selected chapters on a range of stressors experienced over the life span, along with chapters on coping and social support, particularly as they apply to family health. This book is the result of an extensive review of research from which critical pieces of writing were selected, which could serve as reference points for professionals in the field and particularly future investigators. The degree to which we have rendered clarity and integration to these very complex domains of family life will be determined in the family stress research of the future.

Needless to say, this edited volume would not have been possible without the support of numerous individuals and institutions who shared our commitment. Particularly, we would like to acknowledge the contribution of Regents Professor Reuben Hill who reviewed numerous versions of various chapters and who offered his personal wisdom in guiding our efforts. Certainly the numerous references to his classic studies and theoretical formulations reflect his central role in laying the foundation for past and present research in the study of families under stress. We are deeply indebted to Reuben Hill for his patience and kindness, which were so important in motivating us to examine the literature and seek out and prepare chapters that would bridge important dimensions of family stress research. Our thanks go to Diane Felicetta, and our editor in residence, Catherine Davidson who managed the numerous administrative tasks and correspondence associated with this volume, to Jane Schwanke and Gloria Lawrence for their patience in retyping drafts of numerous chapters and to Sharon Bassett, Alida Malkus, and Kay Lapour for their assistance in the manuscript preparation.

We are grateful for the assistance extended to us by our department of Family Social Science and our administrative secretary, Emma Haugan and senior secretary, Dorothea Berggren, which enabled us to concentrate energy and time at critical phases of the writing and editing. We owe much to Dean Keith McFarland of the College of Home Economics, who allowed the senior editor those important moments of administrative calm in order that he might focus his concentration upon writing and editing. This total volume would not have been possible without the funding and support of Dr. William Hueg, Dean of the Institute of Agriculture, Forestry and Home Economics, Dr. Richard Sauer, Director of the Agriculture Experiment Station, and Dr. Signe Betsinger, Assistant Director of the Station and Associate Dean of the College of Home Economics, all of whom recognized the value of this book and committed resources to ensure its completion.

H. I. M.
A. E. C.
J. M. P.

INTRODUCTION

IN comparison with the long and continuous history of research in the general area of stress and coping (Lazarus, 1966; Levine and Scotch, 1968; Coelho, Hamburg, and Adams, 1974; Dohrenwend and Dohrenwend, 1974; Janis and Mann, 1974; Moos, 1976; Monat and Lazarus, 1977), theoretical and clinical interest in *family* stresses, hardships, and coping styles is a recent phenomenon. Family behavior in response to predictable and unpredictable life events has gained respect as an important area of theory building, research, and intervention.

In response to the increasing number of systematic investigations on family stress and coping, this volume attempts to bring together both the classic theory and research efforts and a sample of normative and nonnormative stress studies. It will provide the interested student, researcher, scholar, and practitioner a sound, basic introduction to historical and contemporary thought on family life in response to stress. Since the arena of family stress and coping has its origin in landmark empirical studies (Angell, 1936; Koos, 1946; Hill, 1949) and the field has continued to develop through systematic research, this integrated volume also reveals meaningful examples of research strategies, methods, and a reliable and valid instrument for the systematic assessment of stress, coping, and social support.

Family Stress Over the Life Span

Family scholars in the area of stress research appear to agree with the philosophy presented by Lazarus (1966) and other stress scientists, who argue for using stress as a general label for a large, complex, and interdisciplinary area of interest and study. In reviewing the research conducted to date Lazarus concluded: "It seems wise to use 'stress' as a generic term for the whole area of problems that includes stimuli producing stress reactions, the reactions themselves, and the various intervening processes. Thus we can speak of the field of stress and mean the physiological, sociological, and psychological phenomena and their respective concepts" (p. 27).

Under the general rubric of "stress," family social scientists have made a concerted effort to document the normative and nonnormative stressor events and their specific hardships that impact on family functioning throughout the life span.

Normative events include predictable developmental changes over the life span in individual members of the family unit and in the family unit as a whole. Erik Erikson and other developmental psychologists have identified the major stages of human development: (a) prenatal to infancy, (b) infancy to childhood, (c) childhood to puberty and adolescence, (d) adolescence to adulthood, (e) adulthood to middle age, (f) middle age to old age, and (g) old age to death. Concomitantly, sociologists Reuben Hill, Evelyn Duvall, and Joan Aldous have described the normal transitions of the family unit over the life cycle. The most commonly referenced stages of family "careers" are (a) establishment of the marriage, (b) birth of the first child, (c) entrance of the first child into school, (d) families with adolescents, (e) families in the launching stage, (f) families without the children — empty nest, and (g) retirement. The family unit is called upon to adapt to individual changes (human development) and family system changes (roles, relationships, organization, etc.) as a natural consequence of performing its function of evolving a family unit *over time*. Operating together, family and individual changes may create psychological and interpersonal disturbances that call for coping and adaptation. The more commonly referenced developmental stressors include transition to parenthood, raising adolescent children, launching children, and retirement.

Nonnormative events include unanticipated situational family experiences, which usually place the family in a state of instability and which call for some creative effort to cope with the situation. Since they are often unforeseen, families generally are not prepared to cope and may not have available the social, psychological, or material resources needed to manage such events. Common situational events include accidental injury to a member, illness in the family, hospitalization of a family member, or loss of employment.

It is possible that family members struggling with these stressor events may emerge less healthy and more vulnerable than before.

However, it might be argued conversely that changes during family crises may move members toward increased health and maturity, and in this sense, provide an opportunity for growth through morphogenesis. By identifying family changes and transitions over the life span and trying to define the stresses and strains associated with each, we can begin to grasp the paradox of family stress. They present the family unit and its members with the opportunity for personal and family system changes and growth, while also creating increased vulnerability to the emotional well-being of family members and the stability of the family unit.

The Emergence of Family Stress, Coping, and Social Support

Family stress has gained prominence in the literature as a result of four lines of research that have the importance of family life as their common denominator. The first area of research points to the association between life stress and illness. In his most recent review of life change and mental illness research, Richard Rahe (1979) concluded that

> Subjects' recent life change buildup can be used in an epidemiological fashion to identify populations at high risk for the development of physical and/or mental illllness. . . For the majority of physical illnesses the etiological mechanism of recent life changes appear to be that of lowering the bodily resistances to disease entities which an individual is prone to develop. . .Thus, recent life change buildup results in a precipitation of clinical symptoms. . . In the case of psychological depression and neurosis, however, etiological mechanism may be broader than precipitation. That is. . . recent life change events. . . appear to exert an influence on symptom formation (p. 9).

Family life events are integral features of all measures of recent life changes (Holmes and Rahe, 1967; Dohrenwend, Krasnoff, Askenasy, and Dohrenwend, 1978) and therefore appear to be contributors to the onset of illness (Rahe, 1979).

The second body of research points to the family unit as the context in which potentially dysfunctional coping strategies may be developed, taught, and reinforced. The "pile-up" of family events and the family's difficulty in managing life strains may contribute to members' abuse of alcohol, drugs, and tobacco, as well as physical abuse (Duncan, 1977; 1978). Family norms and expectations may contribute to the members' beliefs that physical and psychological symptoms should be ignored or minimized. That is, family members may choose to interpret illness symptoms by neglecting medical attention when it may be crucial. Monat and Lazarus (1977) point out that avoidance of doctors or of medical regimens can come about as a defense mechanism such as denial, or merely because the individual is a member of a culture or subculture that values stoicism. Hackett and Cassem (1975) indicate that such avoidance can be fatal in certain instances, as in the case of heart attack victims who delay seeking medical attention. It is disquieting to note that families have been or will be abandoning health maintenance practices, e.g. regular health care checkups, dental care, in order to cope with inflation (General Mills, 1979).

The third line of research focuses on the fact that not all individuals and family units become victims of stress. Most families appear to have the ability to manage change and the resulting strains through successful coping strategies. Recently, researchers have attempted to delineate the coping strategies individuals and families employ in successfully managing stress (Coelho, Hamburg, and Adams, 1974; Moos, 1976; Boss, McCubbin, and Lester, 1979; McCubbin, 1979). Coping refers to the cognitive and behavioral efforts to master conditions of harm, threat, or challenge when a routine or automatic response is neither readily available nor a natural part of the individual's or family's basic repertoire (Hill, 1949; Lazarus, 1966; McCubbin, Dahl, and Hunter, 1976).

Coping in the family field involves the integration of at least two basic frameworks — psychological and sociological. Lazarus's (1966) psychological taxonomy of coping emphasizes two major categories — direct actions and palliative modes. Direct actions are behaviors, such as fight or flight, that are designed to alter a troubled relationship in one's social or physical environment. Palliative modes of coping refer to thoughts or actions, the goal of which is to relieve the emotional impact of stress. The term *palliative* is used because these methods do not actually alter the threatening or damaging events but make the person feel better. The latter coping strategy includes defense mechanisms such as denial, the use of tranquilizers, biofeedback, and relaxation. The sociological perspective of coping underscores the importance of individual and family resources in the management of stress. The classic work of Reuben Hill (1949) and the theory building efforts of Wesley Burr (Chapter 1) emphasize the importance of family resources, such as cohesion and adaptability directed at maintaining family organization and functioning in the face of stress. Recent studies of family coping (Boss, McCubbin, and Lester, 1979; McCubbin et al., Chapter 9) have underscored the importance of self-reliance, maintaining family unity, and the use of social support. Family coping is an active process. It not only deals with the stressor event by eliminating it or reducing its impact, but also with the simultaneous management of other equally critical aspects of family life. Family coping with life brings to the forefront the realization that coping strategies change as time passes and as circumstances surrounding the problem change.

Although social support, the fourth line of study, is used by numerous individuals in many and varied fields, its value to families and individuals in the management of stress has only recently received empirical support. Gerald Caplan and colleagues at the Harvard Laboratory of Community Psychiatry (Caplan, 1964; Caplan, 1974) have advanced the important thesis that we need to learn to "appreciate the fortifying potential of the natural person-to-person supports in the population and find ways of working with them through some form of partnership that fosters and strengthens nonprofessional groups and organizations" (p. 20). In a recent community psychiatry publication, Caplan (Chapter 11) sheds light on a particular aspect of the functioning of family life — the family as a support system. Sidney Cobb (Chapter 10) points to three types of social support that appear to buffer the adverse effects of stressor events over the life span. Social support is purely informational in nature and includes (a) emotional support leading the recipient to believe that she is cared for and loved (b) esteem support leading the recipient to believe that she is esteemed and valued and (c) network support leading the recipient to believe that she has a defined postion in a network of communication and mutual obligation.

Researchers have presented data revealing a strong relationship between social support and the ability to adjust and to cope with crises and change. Socially supported individuals appear to adapt more easily to changes and appear to be protected from the typical physiological and psychological health consequences of life stress. There is no single explanation of how support intervenes to buffer the illness response to stress, but it is widely understood that social support increases coping ability, which is what Gore (1978) calls the "etiological gate to health and well being."

Application of Family Stress, Coping, and Support

What difference will it make if professionals attempt to grasp the complexity of family stress, coping strategies, and the role of the community and its social networks in the management of stress? What would students in medicine, nursing, and behavioral science programs gain from an investment in this line of research? It would seem that if one's primary goal is the prediction of family behavior and the functioning of individual members over the life span, knowledge of family behavior in the face of normative and nonnormative stressors would be critical. If the professional seeks to understand psychological dysfunction, family conflict, and illness in an effort to prevent and treat, knowledge of family coping and adaptation and social support would be a prerequisite. Knowledge of family strains associated with stressful life events suggests that the family under stress is more amenable to influence by professionals, helping persons, and support groups than during periods of stable family functioning. Thus a relatively minor intervention may drastically change the ultimate outcome. Therefore, crisis intervention by health care and mental health professionals presents an unusual opportunity to positively influence coping ability, individual and family development, and mental and physical health. The successful mastery of family life events can constitute an important growth experience.

This book examines the fundamental nature of life changes and their impact on family life and how families call upon their internal interpersonal relationships and the community for support in coping and adaptation. This book is organized into two sections: *Family Stress and Crisis Theory* and *Stressors, Family Coping, and Social Support*. The chapters attempt to address several fundamental issues:

— What are the sources of stress in the family?
— What are the interdisciplinary conceptual frameworks that may be applied to understanding family coping behavior in response to stress?
— What types of family resources are needed to help families cope?

— What are the stressors that impact on select family groups, such as minority families, and how do they cope?
— What is the role of the family and the community as sources of social support in the management of stress?

While an attempt is made to organize the readings into a coherent theme reflecting an interrelatedness of research efforts, a sense of complete coherence is predictably lacking. This reflects the current state of the various fields in that theoretical propositions, research findings, experiences, and attempts at integration are not yet of sufficient depth to bring the entire field of family stress into sharp focus. The advancement of knowledge in this area calls for theory building, research efforts, and clinical applications beyond that of a single discipline and will involve the combination of data from experimental, field, and particularly clinical settings. This volume is intended to facilitate this indisciplinary focus.

ACKNOWLEDGMENTS

THE editors would like to thank the following authors and publishers for permission to reprint their work for use in this book (It should be noted that, in some cases, we have altered original reference or footnote formats and omitted appendices to conform to the style and purpose of this volume):

Families Under Stress, by Wesley Burr from *Theory Construction and Sociology of the Family*. Copyright © 1973 by John Wiley & Sons, Inc. Reprinted with permission of the author and John Wiley & Sons, Inc.

The Structure of Coping, by Leonard I. Pearlin and Carmi Schooler, from *Journal of Health and Social Behavior*, 1978, *19*, 2-21. Copyright © 1978 American Sociological Association. Reprinted with permission of the authors and the American Sociological Association.

Social Support and Health Through the Life Course, by Sidney Cobb, from *Aging from Birth to Death*, edited by Matilda White Riley (Boulder Colorado: Westview Press). Copyright © 1979 by the American Association for the Advancement of Science. Reprinted with permission of the author, the American Association for the Advancement of Science, and Westview Press.

The Family as a Support System, by Gerald Caplan, from *Support Systems and Mutual Help*, edited by Gerald Caplan and Marie Killilea. Copyright © 1976 by Grune & Stratton. Reprinted with permission of the author and Grune & Stratton.

CONTENTS

SECTION I.
FAMILY STRESS AND CRISIS THEORY

SECTION II.
FAMILY STRESSORS, COPING, AND SOCIAL SUPPORT

FAMILY STRESS, COPING, AND SOCIAL SUPPORT

SECTION I
FAMILY STRESS
AND CRISIS THEORY

In 1958, Reuben Hill advanced the *ABCX model* of family response to stress. This has served over the past two decades as the landmark work for family stress researchers. In Chapter 1, Wesley Burr builds on Hill's ABCX model by integrating and synthesizing diverse strands of research into a deductive theoretical model. This model identifies twenty-one variables and twenty-five propositions related to family *vulnerability* and *regenerative power* in the face of stress. This chapter is an excellent foundation for those studying families under stress, and it demonstrates the close interactive relationship between theory and research.

In Chapter 2, McCubbin and Patterson extend the theory building efforts of Hill and Burr. Their Double ABCX Model was inductively arrived at from the observations of families responding to major stressor events, primarily the absence of a husband-father as a prisoner of war, missing in action, or as a prisoner during the Vietnam War. The Double ABCX Model is a *dynamic* model that emphasizes what families do *over time* to adapt to a crisis; by looking at the *interaction of variables*, such as multiple stressors ("pile-up") family resources, and specific coping behaviors. In Chapter 9, McCubbin and his colleagues apply these variables from their theoretical model in their research of families with a chronically ill child.

3

Chapter 1

FAMILIES UNDER STRESS

WESLEY BURR

A NUMBER of research projects were undertaken in the 1930s to study the effect of an economic depression on families. The hypotheses that emerged from this research were later retested in a number of other situations where families experience stress such as bereavement, alcoholism, war separation and reunion, and unemployment. This research on how families react to and are influenced by stress has generated numerous theoretical ideas, which form an important part of the family sociology literature. This chapter is an attempt to summarize and analyze many of the ideas in this literature that can be stated as parts of deductive theory.

THE ABCX FORMULATION

One of the major formulations in the family crisis literature was developed by Hill (1949) in his study of war separation and reunion. This model was later slightly modified (Hansen and Hill, 1964; Hill, 1958), but it has remained virtually unchanged for over twenty years. Briefly, it is:

> *A* (the event) — interacting with *B* (the family's crisis-meeting, resources) — interacting with *C* (the definition the family makes of the event) — produces *X* (the crisis). The second and third determinants — the family resources and definition of the event — lie within the family itself and must be seen in terms of the family's structures and values. The hardships of the event, which go to make up the first determinant, lies outside the family and are an attribute of the event itself (Hill, 1958).

The main idea in this model is that the *X* factor is influenced by several other phenomena. The first step in reworking this model so it can be a bona fide part of deductive theory is to determine what the *X* factor is and how it varies. Hill defined crisis as "any sharp or decisive change for which old patterns are inadequate," (1949, p. 51), but he did not explain how this phenomenon of "crisis" varies. The context of his discussion seems to indicate that he views some crises as more severe than others, but this is not made explicit. Later investigators seem to have viewed this factor as a continuous variable, but none of them ever explain just what it is that is varying or how it varies. LeMasters (1957) suggested that crises vary in their severity, but he did not define this. Hobbs (1965, 1968) came closer to viewing this factor as a continuous variable when he developed an index of the difficulty of a crisis.

Since there has been no previous attempt to systematically explicate just what it is that is varying in Hill's X factor or to identify the way this variable varies, an attempt is made here to identify the phenomenon denoted in this earlier research. It seems to be implicit in the early research such as Angell (1936) and Hill (1949) and explicit in later writings such as LeMasters (1957) and Hobbs (1965, 1968) that the students of family crisis view the family as a social system in the same way Rodgers defines system in the developmental conceptual framework. Rodgers states the family is a "semiclosed system . . .which is composed of interrelated positions and roles defined by the society of which it is a part as unique to that system" (1964, p. 264). The students of family crisis also seem to view crises as disruptions in the routine operation of the family social system. The less disrupted the system is, the less severe is the crisis; the more disrupted the system is, the greater is the crisis. Thus the phenomenon that seems to be denoted is the amount of disruption in the family social system.

There are several complications in using a "social system" type of definition of Hill's X factor because there are a number of different schools of thought that make different assumptions about the nature of social systems. Hansen and Hill (1964), for example, seem to assume that systems have a number of characteristics that Allport (1960) asserted systems have, and Buckley (1967, Chapter 2) argues that there are important differences between what he terms equilibrium-seeking systems, organismic systems, and process systems. In the present context it does not seem necessary to make the assumption Hansen and Hill make, nor should it be assumed that the family social system fits only one of Buckley's three types. It is only assumed here that the family social system is an organization consisting of intricately related social postions that have complex sets of roles and norms, and that the system exists to accomplish a wide variety of objectives such as reproduction, socialization, and emotionally intimate interaction.

The X factor in Hill's ABCX formulation could be labeled with a number of different terms. The one that seems most useful is the *amount of crisis*, because the term crisis has been used so extensively in the previous literature. It denotes variation in the amount of disruptiveness, incapacitatedness, or disorganization of the family social system, and it varies continuously from no crisis to a high amount of crisis. It is probably also important to point out that when no crisis exists this does not mean there are no stresses or problems in the system. It merely connotes that the problems are of a routine rather than unusual nature.

Hill's A factor is the stressor event, but before his idea that stressor events produce crises can be stated in a proposition it is necessary to define this variable. It has been repeatedly pointed out in the literature that the same type of event produces varying amounts of crisis in different situations, yet there has been no attempt to define this "eventness" as a variable. It has been pointed out that there are many different types of stressor events, and a very elaborate paradigm has been developed that differentiates between types of stressor events (Hansen and Hill, 1964), but thus far no attempt has been found to define this variable and identify how it varies.

It is suggested here that the phenomenon that has been conceptualized in the family crisis literature as the *stressor event* is an event that produces a change in the family social system. Anything that changes some aspect of the system such as the boundaries, structure, goals, processes, role, or values can produce what has been conceptualized in this chapter as some amount of crisis in the system. Some of these stressor events or "changes" produce large amounts of crisis or disruption in the routine operation of the system, and some produce very little crisis. This variable denotes something different from the routine changes within a system that are expected as a part of its regular, routine operation. It conceptualizes events that are sufficiently unusual that the system itself changes. For example, the husband being laid off his job is a routine event in many blue-collar families, and hence, even though it is a "change," it is not the type of event that is referred to as a stressor event. However, if this husband were to become unemployed for a sufficiently long period of time that the routine activities of the family could not continue, this would be a change in the system and thus a stressor event. This variable is a dichotomy that varies between an event not changing the system and one changing the system. It is being labeled in the present context as a stressor event, and the idea in Hill's model that relates stressor events and the amount of crisis is stated in the first proposition.

Proposition 1.1:   A stressor event in a family social system influences the amount of crisis in the system, and this is a positive relationship.

The major contribution of Hill's ABCX formulation is that it identifies two variables that influence the relationship in proposition 1.1. The B factor is what Hill refers to as the crisis-meeting resources of the family. Hansen (1965) later developed a theoretical model in which he used the term vulnerability to label what seems to be the same conceptual phenomenon. Neither of these theorists define this variable, but it apparently denotes variation in a family's ability to prevent a stressor event of change in a family social system from creating some crisis or disruptiveness in the system. It is apparently a continuous variable.

Proposition 1.2:   When a stressor event occurs, the vulnerability to stress influences the amount of influence the stressor event has on the amount of crisis and this is a positive relationship.

The third major independent variable in the ABCX formulation is the definition the family makes of the event. Unfortunately, this concept is also not defined, and there is no explanation of how it varies. It is therefore necessary to infer from the context of the literature just what it is that is varying. Hill (1949) differentiates between three types of definitions and then explains that his model deals with only one of these. He points out that definitions formulated by an impartial observer, those formulated by a community, and those made by the family are very different types of definitions; and he suggests that the subjective definitions are the ones he is dealing with in his theoretical model. This does not identify just what it is about these definitions that is varying, but the context of his monograph report seems to indicate that the main difference is probably whether the family defines the change in the system as easy or difficult. If this is a correct analysis of what is varying in this variable, the best label for this phenomenon is probably the subjective definition of the severity of the change. It may be that Hill was referring to other aspects than the seriousness of the event, but it seems fairly clear that this is at least one type of definition he was identifying.

The theoretical idea that deals with the definition of the severity of changes is that the definition makes a difference in the amount of crisis. It is impossible, however, to tell whether the definition of the severity of the change (a) influences the amount of crisis directly, (b) influences the amount of crisis indirectly by influencing the family's vulnerability to stress, or (c) is just one of many specific types of resources that make up the more inclusive phenomenon of the family's vulnerability to stress. It is suggested here that the second of these three alternatives is probably the most defensible, and hence the balance of this reformulation will use this idea.

Proposition 1.3:   The definition a family makes of the severity of changes in the family social system influences the family's vulnerability to stress and this is a positive, monotonic relationship.

This idea has a long tradition in social psychology. The statement that "if something is perceived as real it is real in its consequences," and the "self-fulfilling prophecy" both seem to be more abstract statements of the idea summarized in proposition 1.3.

There is one additional idea in Hill's original formulation that was not included in later statements of the model. What he termed the "hardships of the event" (1949, p. 41) are also involved in determining whether or not a crisis occurs. Hill (1949) operationalized this variable by counting the number of changes that were required, so one way to label this variable is the *amount of change* in the system. The way this variable probably fits into the present model is by influencing the amount of crisis that is caused by stressor events in the system, and if this is the case, a further proposition can be stated.

Proposition 1.4:   The amount of change that occurs when a stressor event occurs in the family social system influences the amount of crisis that results from the event and this is a positive relationship.

The theoretical ideas in the ABCX formulation are summarized in figure 1-1. This figure attempts to show that a stressor event influences the amount of crisis. The amount of change in the system and the family's vulnerability to stress influence this relationship, and the definition the family makes of the seriousness of the change influences the vulnerability to stress.

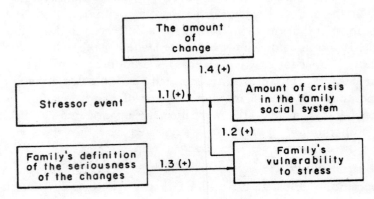

Figure 1-1. The ABCX model.

Hansen (1965) published a formulation about how several other factors influence the vulnerability families have to stress. In addition, he introduced a variable that he referred to as the *regenerative power* of families, and he developed some propositions about how this variable is influenced. Hansen suggested that difference in "influence" has an effect on both vulnerability to stress and regenerative power. He makes a distinction in the way that individuals influence the action of others by differentiating between "personal" and "positional" influence:

> The distinction arises from the insight that an individual tends to develop both a personal relationship, or the relation of ego to alter as individuals, and a positional relationship or the relation of ego to alter as status or position holders in a group. That is, there are two kinds of cohesiveness in a group: the first involves the influence members have on one another because of their personal relationship; the second involves the influence they have on another because of their position in the group structure (1965, p. 203).

Hansen argues that these two types of influence are separate variables and that each varies in amount. He does not explicitly state that they are continuous variables, but the context seems to indicate that even though he dichotomizes them in stating his hypothesis, he views them as continuous variables. His major dependent variables are family vulnerability to stress and regenerative power. Neither of these variables were defined by Hansen, but vulnerability to stress was defined in this chapter as variation in a family's ability to prevent a stressor event or change in a family social system from creating some crisis or disruptiveness in the system. Regenerative power apparently denotes variation in the ability of the family to recover from a crisis. It seems to be a continous variable varying between low and high power.

Hansen uses the term "proposition" in his paper, but his propositions are definitional statements that are used to identify several characteristics of the two variables of positional influence and personal influence. He does not summarize his theoretical ideas with the type of propositions that identify relationship between variables. It seems possible, however, to translate his ideas into propositional statements, and the following four propositions are an attempt to do this.

PROPOSITION 1.5: The amount of positional influence in a social system influences the vulnerability of families to stress and this is a positive relationship.

PROPOSITION 1.6: The amount of positional influence in a social system influences the regenerative power and this is an inverse relationship.

PROPOSITION 1.7: The amount of personal influence in a social system influences the vulnerability of families to stress and this is an inverse relationship.

PROPOSITION 1.8: The amount of personal influence in a social system influences the regenerative power and this is a positive relationship.

Hansen does not speculate on the nature of the individual relationships in these propositions other than to specify their direction. There does, however, seem to be an indication that he believes that more influence is exerted in propositions 1.5 and 1.8 than in the other two. In other words, positional influence probably makes slightly more difference in vulnerability and personal influence makes slightly more difference in regenerative power. This is diagramed in Figure 1-2.

Personal influence

		Low	High
Positional influence	High	Moderate disruption Low regenerative power	Low disruption High regenerative power
	Low	High disruption Low regenerative	High disruption Moderate regenerative power

Figure 1-2. The interaction of personal and positional influence in their relationship with vulnerability and regenerative power.

Hansen also attempts to integrate his formulation with some of the theoretical ideas that were developed in earlier research. He suggests that the type of stress, the type of reaction of the larger community, the externalization of blame, and the severity of the stress are also important variables. He seems to view the severity of stress as the amount of change that occurs in the family social system and seems to argue for the same relationship that was asserted in proposition 1.4. It is also possible to identify a proposition about the externalization of blame and family vulnerability. Externalization of blame is apparently a dichotomous variable denoting variation in whether the blame or responsibility for a stressor event is placed on a family member or on an external source.

PROPOSITION 1.9: The externalization of blame for changes in the family social system influences the vulnerability of the family to stress and this is an inverse relationship.

Hansen does not speculate on the nature of other aspects of this relationship, and the rest of this part of his model is not as clear as the earlier parts of his theory. This results in it being difficult to know just what relationships he proposes between the type of stress and the type of reaction of the community and other variables. It is possible to intergrate these last propositions with the ideas in the

ABCX model and diagram the entire formulation (Figure 1-3).

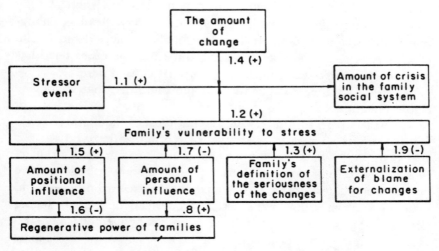

Figure 1-3. Nine propositions on families under stress.

LEVEL OF REORGANIZATION

One of the major goals in the research on families in stress has been to identify factors that are related to whether or not the families recover from the disruptive effects of stress. Unfortunately, however, the dependent variable in this research is unclear. It has had a number of different labels such as type of adjustment (Cavan and Ranck, 1938), level of adjustment (Hill, 1949), recovery from the crisis (Dyer, 1963), and level of reorganization (Hansen and Hill, 1964), but it has never been carefully defined. The context of its use in the literature, however, seems to indicate that it denotes variation whether or not the family social system is able to recover from the disruptiveness that results from a stressor event. If the system is able to recover, this apparently means that it returns to a routine pattern of operation. This does not seem to imply that the recovery eliminates such things as disorganization, change in the system, or inefficiency. It merely means that the system resumes its typical, routine level of operation after having to cope with an unusual change. If the system does not recover, this means that the system is not able to eliminate the disruptiveness introduced by the stressor event.

The most extensively used label for this dependent variable, introduced by Koos (1946), is the *level of reorganization*. This term seems acceptable if it does not eliminate the connotation that when a family social system is highly organized it is in many ways flexible, changing, inefficient, and so on. It would probably be more defensible to use a term such as level of recovery, but since the other term has been so extensively used in the literature, it is used here.

There is another complication in the literature that should be resolved before the propositions relating variables to the level of reorganization are identified. This is that most of the literature tests for a relationship between the level of reorganization and various specific factors such as amount of adaptability, integration, or affection. However, the variable Hansen (1965) refers to as regenerative power complicates these relationships. There are two different and incompatible ways that a theoretical model can be built by using both the specific factors that have been studied empirically and Hansen's regenerative power. One of the ways is to view the specific factors as variables that influence the regenerative power of families and then postulate that the regenerative power influences the level of reorganization. The other method is to view the specific factors as components of regenerative power. If the second method is used, this means that the idea that regenerative power influences the level of recovery is a more abstract proposition, and the propositions that relate the specific factors to level of recovery are more specific deductions from the general propositions.

There are unfortunately no clear-cut rules in theory building that provide a basis for making a choice between these two alternatives. In the present project, it was decided that the best alternative would be to view the specific factors as influential variables rather than as components of regenerative power. The theoretical model that is thus proposed is that the phenomenon Hansen (1965) has termed the regenerative power of families influences the level of reorganization and the various intrafamilial factors that have been found to be related to level of reorganization influence the regenerative power of families. If this is the case, the following proposition should be identified.

PROPOSITION 1.10: The regenerative power of families influences the level of reorganization after a period of crisis and this is a positive relationship.

FACTORS INFLUENCING REGENERATIVE POWER

Integration and Adaptability

Angell (1936) made the first systematic analysis of factors that were related to the ability of families to recover from crisis. His study dealt with the ability of families to recover from the disruption introduced by the economic depression of the 1930s and he found family integration and adaptability to be two important variables. He defined family integration as the "bonds of coherence and unity running through family life, of which common interests, affection, and a sense of economic interdependence are perhaps the most prominent." Hill later pointed out that this factor "is, in effect, adequacy-inadequacy of family organization" (1965, p. 144). It is apparently variation in the degree to which a family is harmoniously well organized, and it seems to be viewed as a continuous variable. Family adaptability is also a continuous variable that apparently denotes variation in the ability of a family to change its structure or way of operating with little psychic or organizational discomfort. The ideas in Angell's research seem to intensify the two following propositions.

PROPOSITION 1.11: Family integration influences regenerative power and this is a positive relationship.

PROPOSITION 1.12: Family adaptability influences regenerative power and this is a positive relationship.

There is some basis for making inferences about the amount of influence in these two propositions. Waller and Hill report that in an "unpublished restudy of the cases in Angell's study in 1942-1945 by the Social Science Research Council Committee on Appraisal of Research, the factor of adaptability was shown to be much the more important of the two" (1951, p. 461). It is premature to speculate about how much more influential adaptability is, but this does give an indication about relative differences in influence.

It should also be pointed out that Angell (1936) was not just interested in factors that were related to the family's ability to recover from the disruptive effects of stress. He was also interested in identifying factors that would assist families in avoiding the panic of a severe crisis in the stressful situation. He did not differentiate between the avoidance and the recovery variables as clearly as Hansen (1965) did later, but Angell's analysis of his data was very clearly an attempt to deal with both phenomena. His findings suggest that in addition to adaptability and integration being useful in recovering from a crisis, they also seem to be important in preventing stress from creating crisis. This leads to two additional propositions.

PROPOSITION 1.13: The amount of family integration influences the vulnerability to stress and this is a positive relationship.

PROPOSITION 1.14: The amount of family adaptability influences the vulnerability to stress and this is an inverse relationship.

Hansen and Hill also suggest that the adaptability variable differs in its impact on vulnerability according to the severity of the stressor. They suggest that low adaptability may "isolate the family from small stresses" (1964, p. 814). If this is true, a contingent proposition could be stated identifying this type of interaction. This speculation has not, however, been worked through sufficiently well that a proposition is identified here.

There are empirical data that argue for the validity of proposition 1.13. Koos (1946) and Hill (1949) both found that when the amount of "hardships" in the crisis event were held constant, those families who were less well "organized" tended to have more severe crises. Hill then tended to classify these families as more crisis-prone than other families. In a sense, Hill's crisis-proneness is another label for what has been conceptualized as family vulnerability to stress. Those families that have low vulnerability tend to be less prone to have crises when stressful changes occur, and those families with more vulnerability tend to be more crisis-prone.

Hill's Reviews of Factors Influencing Crisis Recovery

Hill has periodically reviewed the research in this area and attempted to revise and update a list of factors that have been found to be related to the ability of families to recover from crisis. He initially reviewed the literature in his study of war separation and reunion (Hill, 1949) and then again in his revision of Waller's monograph (Waller and Hill, 1951). His last review was with Hansen in the *Handbook of Marriage and the Family* (Hansen and Hill, 1964). His analysis included several variables that have already been dealt with in the present chapter — severity of the event, family's definition of the situation, externalization of blame for the stressful event, adaptability, and integration. His analysis also includes a number of other variables such as the suddenness of the event, individuated versus kinship type of community, affectional relations among family members, marital adjustment, family council type of control in decision making, participation of the wife in roles outside the home, and previous successful experience with similar types of stress. The role of each of these variables seems to deserve individual analysis.

Suddenness of the Event

Hansen and Hill (1964) argue that the more sudden or unanticipated a stressor event is, the greater the disruptiveness that will result. The conceptual phenomenon they seem to be most concerned with is not whether the change itself occurs in a short period of time, but rather whether it is anticipated for some time before it occurs. If it is anticipated for a sufficiently long period of time, then apparently preparations are usually made and there is less disruption. The variable involved seems to be the *amount of time changes are anticipated*. It can vary between no period of anticipation to long periods of anticipation.

PROPOSITION 1.15: The amount of time stressful events are anticipated influences the vulnerability to stress and this is an inverse relationship.

Individuated Versus Kinship Type of Community

Hill and Hansen (1962) developed a typology of types of communities. They created two ideal types, labeled kinship-oriented and individual-oriented communities:

> The distinction rests on the networks of relationships that connect kin to one another. In the kinship community there is a predominance of tightly

meshed families with little activity between neighbors. In the individual community, loosely knit, nuclear families predominate, and there is a great deal of activity between neighbors and friends. Many rural and mountain villages are of the first type, and most urban, industrial communities of the second (1962, pp. 200-201).

Later research and conceptual developments have refined this type of conceptualization, and it is now probably defensible to use conceptual revisions such as Winch and Greer's (1968) to replace this typology. Winch and Greer's (1968) conceptualization of what they term *extended familism*, for example, seems to conceptualize the main ideas in Hill and Hansen's typology. They view extended familism as a composite variable denoting variation in the interaction, intensity, extensity, and functionality of the kinship system. *Extensity* deals with the number of kin in close proximity. *Intensity* has to do with how closely the kin are related. *Interaction* denotes variation in the amount of activity engaged in with the kin, and *functionality* refers to the instrumental value of the interaction such as receiving goods and services. Winch and Greer's continuous variable has a number of advantages over Hill and Hansen's typology. It does not have the connotation that urban areas have low extended familism. It has been defensibly operationalized, and when continuous variables are used rather than typologies that have only two types much more can be learned about the nature of relationships.

Hill and Hansen's thesis is that low extended familism tends to better prepare families "for disaster and short-term recovery than does the kinship community (high extended familism)." But in meeting the long-term effects of disaster, it is probable that the individuated (low extended familism) community loses its advantage (1962, p. 202). What Hill and Hansen thus seem to be proposing is that the length of time of the disruption influences the effect the extended familism has on the regenerative power of families. When the stress is for a short period there is a negative relationship between extended familism and regenerative power, and when there is a long period of disruption there is a positive relationship.

PROPOSITION 1.16: The amount of extended familism influences the regenerative power of families.

PROPOSITION 1.17: The length of time a family system experiences disruption influences the relationship in proposition 1.16, which asserts that extended familism influences the regenerative power of families, and this is a quadratic relationship in which variation in short periods of time are inversely related and variation in long periods are positively related to the regenerative power.

Affectional Patterns

Hill argues that "affectional relations among family members" are related to what is conceptualized in the present chapter as the level of recovery from crisis (1958). This variable was operationalized in his study of war crisis (Hill, 1949) as the presence or absence of affectional cliques. Hill found in his study that the absence of cliques was related to the quality of adjustment to the war separation and reunion. The independent variable in this idea is thus apparently the amount of *similarity of sentiment* in a family. This then is a fairly similar sentiment felt toward all members of the family. This is a condition of high similarity, and the more differences there are between family members in their sentiment toward others, the greater is the clique formation and the less the similarity.

PROPOSITION 1.18: The amount of similarity of sentiment in a family influences the regenerative power of families and this is a positive relationship.

Marital Adjustment

One of the other variables Hill identifies in his reviews as being important is marital adjustment. This variable was defined earlier in this book in apparently the same way Hill uses it. It is a multidimensional variable designed to denote variation in overall adjustment in marriage. It includes specific dimensions such as consensus, satisfaction, happiness, and stability, and it is a continuous variable. The data Hill uses in his reviews seems to come primarily from Angell (1936), Cavan and Ranck (1938), Koos (1946), and Hill (1949); these data indicate there is a positive relationship between marital adjustment and satisfactory crisis recovery.

In the context of the present formulation, this relationship seems to be an indirect relationship, and any influence that marital adjustment has on the level of recovery from crises probably is exerted through influencing the regenerative power of families. Thus a new proposition can be stated.

PROPOSITION 1.19: The amount of marital adjustment influences the regenerative power of families and this is a positive relationship.

Power

The empirical research has investigated whether or not different types of power structure are related to recovery from crises. Unfortunately, however, there is considerable ambiguity in the conceptualization of power in this research and in the findings. In Hill's case study analysis of the subjects in his crisis study he found that what he refers to as "family council type of family control" was related to adequacy of adjustment of crises (1949, p. 325). This relationship did not appear in his statistical analysis. It is possible, however, that if some conceptual refinements are made in his analyses, the inconsistencies in these empirical findings can be resolved.

Hill's independent variable in his statistical analyses is labeled the "type of family control," but he is obviously interested in only one narrow aspect of control. His operationalization of this variable is build around the differences between husband-dominant, equalitarian, and wife-dominant distributions of power. This indicates that he is conceptually dealing with the relative *amount of power*. Conceptually this seems to be the same phenomenon that Straus (1964) argues is such a pervading factor in understanding human interaction.

Hill's independent variable in his case study analysis (1949, pp. 215-216, 223-226) seems to be conceptually somewhat different from the amount of power. It seems to have amount of power as one of its dimensions, but it also takes into account variation in the way the power is implemented. Hill differentiates, for example, between whether authority is imposed (1949, p. 216) or not, and whether or not there is consultation in the process of making decisions. His discussion of just what it is that seems to be significantly different in the adjustment to crises suggests that it may be that *"the consultive process* in the family is more important than the seat of ultimate authority" (1949, p. 224). This indicates that conceptually differentiating between the amount of power and the amount of consultation in decision making might reconcile the conflicting findings in his study. The data seem to indicate that the relative amount of power of individuals is not related to regenerative power, but that the amount of consultation is. If it is defensible to speculate that the amount of consultation actually has an influence on other variables rather than just covarying with them, the two following propositions in this analysis seem to be justified.

PROPOSITION 1.20: The amount of relative power of spouses is not related to the regenerative power of families.

PROPOSITION 1.21: The amount of consultation in decision making influences the regenerative power of families and this is a positive relationship.

Hill differentiates only between the presence and absence of a consultative process and hence does not view the independent variable in proposition 1.21 as a continuous variable. This means that there is no empirical basis for making assertions about the shape of this relationship. Intuitively, however, it seems that it would be a curvilinear relationship, as diagramed in Figure 1-4. It probably has much less if any influence when there is a large amount of consultation. In fact, it may be that excessive consultation might actually decrease the regenerative power.

Social Participation of Wives Outside the Home

Duvall (1945) found that the amount of social participation of wives outside the home was related to satisfactory adjustment to war separation. Hill (1949, p. 205) found this same factor to be positively related to both war separation and reunion crises. Rose (1955) and Deutscher (1962) also found participation in external roles to be positively related to mothers' ability to cope with the stress of launching their children. If this independent variable is defined as the amount of activity spent by wives in nonwife-mother roles, these findings seem to justify one proposition.

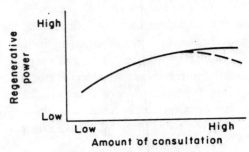

Figure 1-4. The relationship between amount of consultation and regenerative power.

PROPOSITION 1.22: The amount of social activity of wives outside the home is related to the regenerative power of families and this is a positive relationship.

There is no empirical basis for making assertions about the shape of this relationship. There is some empirical evidence in the studies referred to that this is a valid proposition, but there is also one negative finding. Hill (1949, p. 146) found a nonsignificant negative relationship between maternal employment and crisis-adjustment in his study of war separation and reunion.

Previous Successful Experience with Stress

Hill (1949) found that previous successful experience with a similar crisis was related to what has been conceptualized in this chapter as the level of recovery. This independent variable is probably valuable for predictive purposes, but it seems that its only value for theory is that it probably is an effective operationalization of the amount of anticipatory socialization for coping with changes in the family social system. The previous experience would provide an opportunity to develop skills and insights that would help cope with later changes. The conceptual phenomenon of anticipatory socialization was defined earlier as the process of learning norms of a role before being in a social situation where it is appropriate to actually behave in the role. If this variable is viewed as the important theoretical variable in Hill's idea that previous experience is related to adjustment to crises, it seems defensible to suggest the two following propositions.

PROPOSITION 1.23: The amount of anticipatory socialization for changes in the family social system influences the vulnerability of families and this is an inverse relationship.

PROPOSITION 1.24: The amount of anticipatory socialization for changes in the family social system influences the regenerative power of families and this is a positive relationship.

If Hill's variable of previous experience with crises can be viewed as operationalization of the amount of anticipatory socialization for changes, his finding that it is related to the level of recovery can be viewed as empirical support for proposition 1.24.

An attempt is made in Figure 1.5 to diagram the various relationships identified in this chapter. As can be seen in the diagram, this chapter is essentially an analysis of the factors that influence family vulnerability to stress and regenerative power, and these two variables are important because they play such an important role (a) in determining whether a family will experience a crisis when they encounter changes in the system and (b) in determining how adequately the family will be able to recover from the crisis situation.

LEGITIMACY OF POWER

One other variable may be relevant in understanding several aspects of family crises. This is the legitimacy of the power structure. Komarovsky (1940) found that the legitimacy of the power structure influenced the amount of change that a stressful event produced in the power structure. This can be stated in a proposition as follows.

PROPOSITION 1.25: The legitimacy of the power structure in a family influences the amount of change in the power structure that occurs in family crises and this is an inverse relationship.

Komarovsky operationalized the legitimacy of the power by differentiating between primary authority, instrumental authority, and a mixture of the two. Primary authority is legitimate in terms of either personal or positional factors, and instrumental power, as she defined the term, is power based on fear or coercion. She found that the most change in power occurred in the power structure with the

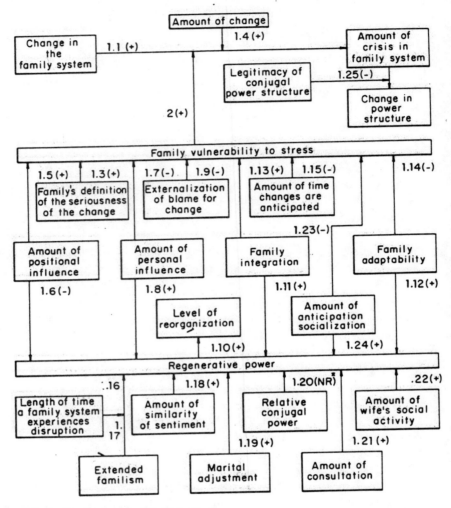

*No relationship thought to exist.

Figure 1-5. Propositions about families under stress. (NR indicates no relationship is thought to exist.)

instrumental type of power and an intermediate amount of change occurred in those families with a mixture of primary and instrumental power. This finding is consistent with the assertion in proposition 1.25 that a relationship exists between these two variables and it thus provides some empirical support. In addition, these findings provide evidence of some monotonicity in this relationship. Since these data were the data that led to the initial formulation of the idea, however, these findings should not be viewed as conclusive empirical proof of the validity of the proposition.

SUMMARY

This chapter has analyzed a number of propositions about family crises. The entire model is summarized in Figure 1.5, and it is a fairly abstract theory. The model can be extended in a number of different ways. One method would be to test the propositions in different crises to see if additional contingent variables that influence the impact of variables can be identified and to see if some of the propositions are not valid for some crises. This type of additional theoretical and empirical work should be facilitated by the modifications made in this chapter.

Chapter 2

FAMILY ADAPTATION TO CRISES

HAMILTON I. McCUBBIN AND JOAN M. PATTERSON

A MAJOR weakness of most stress studies, including family stress investigations, has been their emphasis on a three-variable research design, i.e., a family stressor event is identified, the family response to the event is described and analyzed, and the outcome of the interaction between the stressor and the response is measured. In the most common study design, families are classified in terms of the presence or absence of a particular stressor event such as a loss, separation, or illness. Another line of inquiry presupposes family exposure to a stressor and the family unit is examined in terms of its reactions, compromises, and adjustment. A third line of research has attempted to describe the dramatic, emotional, psychological, interpersonal, and systemic traumas and outcomes families experience as part of being in "crisis." While such studies have illuminated the relationship between stressors and family responses, their findings also suggest that a more comprehensive paradigm is needed to describe family behavior in response to stress. This paper sets forth such a paradigm using observations derived from a longitudinal investigation of American families responding to a prolonged war-induced stressor event of having a husband/father held captive or unaccounted for in the Vietnam War. The paradigm that emerges from these observations is an effort to expand Hill's (1949; 1958) ABCX Model of family stress.

THE BASIC COMPONENTS OF FAMILY STRESS THEORY

The foundation for a conceptual model for family stress research may be traced to Hill's (1949) classic research on war-induced separation and reunion. His ABCX formulation has withstood the

This chapter is a revision of a paper presented at the International Conference on Families in Disaster, Uppsala, Sweden, June 1980. The research was supported by the Agriculture Experiment Station, University of Minnesota, St. Paul, Minnesota.

test of time and careful assessment and has remained virtually unchanged for more than thirty years. Briefly, the family crisis framework may be stated as follows:

A (the event) — interacting with B (the family's crisis meeting resources) — interacting with C (the definition the family makes of the event) — produces X (the crisis).

Investigators have carried on family stress research with a seemingly conscious effort to render clarity and empirical support to Hill's model. Burr (Chapter 1) advanced this model in reworking the ABCX formulation into a bona fide part of deductive theory. His theoretical ideas are presented in Figure 2-1.

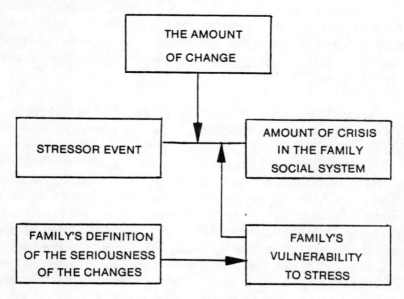

Figure 2-1. The ABCX model.

This figure attempts to show the relationship between a stressor event and the amount of crisis, i.e., where "old patterns are inadequate" and new family patterns are needed (Hill, 1949). The stressor event (Hill's *A* factor) induces a variable amount of change in the family system in terms of the number of hardships inherent in the stressor. The family's *vulnerability,* i.e., variation in the ability of a family to prevent a stressor event of change in its social system from creating a crisis, is influenced by the definition the family makes of the seriousness of the change (Hill's *C* factor). Building on this model, Burr (Chapter 1) reviewed the research and attempted to revise and update the list of independent variables (Hill's *B* factor of resources) that have been related to family vulnerability.

One of the major areas of family stress research in the past decade has been investigators' efforts to isolate those family processes and properties that are related to how well families are able to "recover" from a crisis situation. Drawing from Hansen's (1965) work, Burr (Chapter 1) gave prominence to the concept of *regenerative power*, which denotes "variation in the ability of the family to recover from a crisis."

These twin concepts of vulnerability and regenerative power have become the major reference points for scholars attempting to explain why some families are better able (a) to defend themselves against crises or (b) when stunned with a stressor event and impending crisis, recover.

WAR-INDUCED SEPARATION FOR FAMILIES OF THE MISSING AND PRISONERS OF WAR

This family stress framework was used to guide the longitudinal research efforts of the family studies branch of the Naval Health Research Center. This agency was tasked with responsibility for the study of families faced with the Vietnam War-induced separation caused by a husband/father being held captive or listed as unaccounted for in combat. The sample of 216 families consisted of wives between the ages of twenty and forty-nine with an average age of 33.2 years at the time of the interviews. The educational level of the majority of wives was in excess of twelve years; one-third had received college degrees. While the families averaged two children, one-fifth (20.5%) had no children. The 405 children ranged in age from less than one year to twenty-five years of age, with the majority (53.8%) between the ages of eight and fifteen. The majority of wives (55.2%) had been married more than ten years. Prior marriages were infrequent for both husbands (9.8%) and wives (8.4%). Religious affiliations were similar for both husbands and wives and were predominantly Protestant.

Family "Pile-Up" — The Stressor Event and Life Changes Over Time

When a family was called upon to adapt to the absence of a husband/father listed as missing or a prisoner of war, there were many family role changes and hardships which occurred as part of the natural evolution of the situation.

The length of absence for these men extended from less than one year to more than nine years. Of these absences, 139 (64.6%) were extended over a period of three to six years. The resulting strain on family relationships followed a relatively predictable course, with the number of hardships increasing as the period of absence increased. An analysis of intra-family adjustments indicated modifications in family roles with accompanying anxieties, frustrations, conflicts, and feelings of insecurity. Both the traditional and inherited responsibilities were intensified for the wives now taxed with fulfilling the dual mother-father role (McCubbin, Hunter, and Metres, 1974a). Decision making, disciplining the children, handling family finances, and managing children's health problems were cited as hardships. Family "crisis" resulted from an apparent overload of responsibilities and a pile-up of expected and unexpected life events and hardships (Table 2-1).

The observations and data from the longitudinal study revealed that the coping efforts these families used to adjust to the separation produced *additional* stressors. In addition, these families had to simultaneously adjust to the other life changes that happen in families over time and occur independent of the stressor of separation. In other words, over time and in an effort to manage a crisis situation, these families experienced a pile-up of stressors as a result of (a) the hardships inherent in the separation stressor, (b) normal change and development of family members over time, and (c) the trial and error efforts to manage the situation. Data to support these observations may be gleaned from four investigations, which focused on (a) boundary ambiguity (Boss, 1977), (b) family role adjustments and child adjustment (McCubbin, Hunter, and Dahl, 1975), (c) family legal problems (Nelson, 1974), and (d) family coping (McCubbin, Dahl, Lester, Benson, and Robertson, 1976). The observations from these investigations may be grouped into three categories: (a) member and system change over time, (b) intra-

Family Stress, Coping, and Social Support

Table 2-I

Intra-Family Adjustments

Adjustment Problems	Number of Responses*	Percentage
Psychological		
Lack of husband's companionship	120	72.3
Feelings of extreme loneliness	78	47.0
Role Strain		
Making decisions alone	66	39.8
Lack of social outlets	45	27.1
Disciplining children	31	18.7
Time for dual mother-father role	30	18.1
Handling family finances	22	13.3
Legal complications	66	39.8
Life Events: Health		
Child health problems	7	4.2
Wife health problems	18	10.8

*Number of respondents varied.

family boundary ambiguity, and (c) social ambiguity.

Member and system change over time. One of the hardships directly related to the separation of husbands from their wives was a change in wives' assessment of the marriage. The majority (79.8%) of the wives, in retrospective assessments of their marriages prior to their husbands' casualty (loss or capture), rated their marriages as being either satisfactory or very satisfactory. In contrast, less than half of the group (44.2%) felt the same degree of satisfaction with their marriages at the time of the follow-up interviews.

In order for family life to continue in some routine manner, wives typically coped with the separation by assuming a dual mother-father role. Functioning in the role as head of the household, wives appeared to become more independent and self-confident. This was especially true when they closed ranks (Hill, 1949) and developed a style of life for a family unit without a husband/father. Interestingly enough, social changes that emerged during the same period as the Vietnam War, i.e. the women's liberation movement, rendered legitimacy to the wives' effort to be self-sufficient and independent. This style of coping by wives did, in some cases, create additional stressors. Such changes in mothers' roles and strengthening of authority were often challenged and questioned by other members of the kin network, particularly in-laws who were concerned about the stability of the family unit and the possibility of a divorce. This posed a threat to the child-grandparent relationship (McCubbin, Hunter, and Dahl, 1975). Thus, wives often had to cope with disapproval from other members of the family for the way in which they were handling the separation, and this was an additional stressor.

As wives struggled to maintain a dual mother-father role while faced with the uncertainty of their spouses' return, many experienced emotional symptoms that presented a threat to the stability of the family unit. Out of twelve emotional symptoms covered by the interviewers, nearly three-fourths (73.5%) of the sample reported having experienced five or more symptoms. Additional indices of emotional difficulties included the observation that over half the group (58.2%) were taking or had taken tranquilizers during the separation period. Although almost half of the group (48.2%) were nonsmokers, a third (32.9%) of the wives reported that they now smoked more heavily than they had prior to the casualty; 23.8 percent reported that they had imbibed in alcoholic beverages more heavily than previously; 37.2 percent reported entertaining suicidal thoughts, although only 16.4 percent felt they had ever really seriously considered suicide. Furthermore, the data revealed that 31.3 percent of the wives were either receiving therapy at the time of the interview or had been in treatment at some time during the separation. For some families, emotional instability thus became another stressor adding to the pile-up.

Family life was also punctuated by life events that further contributed to the pile-up. For example, a small percentage of mothers (4.2%) reported having to cope with major illnesses in their children, which included accidental injuries and surgery. Table 2-II reveals the major childhood complications that emerged during the separation, which included emotional difficulties, conflicts with

Table 2–II

Child Health Complications

Health Complications	Number of Responses*	Percent
Common childhood diseases	166	41.0
Accidental injuries	73	18.0
Surgeries	48	11.8
Enuresis (past age 3)	31	7.6
Acute illnesses	27	6.7
Chronic illnesses	25	6.2
Special handicaps	17	4.2
Other physical problems	17	4.2

*Based on number of children in the sample n=405.

peers, and acute or chronic illnesses and special handicaps.

Intra-family role and boundary ambiguity. On the basis of systems theory and the symbolic interactionist perspective, Boss (1977) has suggested that boundary ambiguity within the family system becomes a major stressor in the case of families of the missing: "A system needs to be sure of its components, that is, who is inside system boundaries physically and psychologically, and who is outside, physically and psychologically . . . a major consequence of an ambiguous system, that is, a system that is not sure of its components, is that systemic communication, feedback and subsequent adjustment over time are curtailed."

Inherent in the stressor of having a husband/father held captive or missing in action is ambiguity as to whether he will return. Families varied in terms of whether they believed the husband/father would or would not return (Hill's *C* factor). This ambiguity also influenced family roles, especially for wives as they struggled with whether and to what degree to take over their husband's role.

Boss found that boundary ambiguity, which she operationalized as "psychological father presence," had a negative impact on family functioning, particularly mother's emotional well-being.

Family-community interface: Social ambiguity as a stressor. While Boss (1977) and McCubbin, Dahl, Lester, Benson, and Robertson (1976) at the Naval Health Research Center all point to the "ambiguousness" of the intra-family situation as a major, if not *the* major, hardship families faced, they also *implied* that resolution and adaptation were fully within the family's control. Boss (1977) argued that " . . . *it is possible for a family to perceive and act upon* the presence of a member when that member's presence is no longer a reality . . ."

The in-depth interviews (McCubbin, Hunter, and Metres, 1974a) and particularly the legal case studies (Nelson, 1974) revealed that families *did* make a concerted effort to render clarity to the situation, but in the absence of legitimate paths and procedures for resolution, families faced major roadblocks. *Social ambiguity,* that is the absence of appropriate norms and procedures for managing this stressful situation, created an additional stressor on family life and may have been the major contributor to the hardship of intra-family boundary ambiguity recorded by Boss.

As Hansen and Hill (1964) and Mechanic (1974) have pointed out, the *fit* between the family and the community may well be the major determinant of successful adaptation to stress. The family's ability to manage stress may depend on the efficacy and/or adequacy of the solutions the culture, community, or the organization provide. However, these "community solutions may lag far behind the times and offer little to families struggling to manage a difficult situation." Social ambiguity emerges when society's blueprints for family behavior under stress are being challenged or are inappropriate and the problem-solving guidelines for family postcrisis behavior are not adequate.

Not only were society's perceptions of this stressor (the war) ambiguous, but the resources (Hill's *B* factor) available to these families were also ambiguous. For example, the laws enacted to assist families in this type of situation appeared to be unclear. The federal government had enacted legislation, which was intended to protect the "soldier" against inability to adequately defend a suit because of his military commitments and provide for status determination of those missing or within enemy control.

It is only reasonable to assume that the prolonged absence of the head of a household would call for the remaining spouse to move forward with all transactions on behalf of the family system. But wives' efforts to assume this responsibility were fraught with legal problems, which emerged on a frequent and recurring basis in even the most mundane daily routines. For example, powers of attorney, executed by many servicemen to enable their wives to sell jointly held property, expired during the prolonged absence. Families were then left without legal support for their transactions and without guidelines as to how legal power could be achieved.

Wives who wished to move ahead and create a new life by remarrying faced the risk of a bigamy conviction since declaration of death had not been confirmed. The social stigma of divorce, coupled with the potential loss of military privileges and the possibility of forfeiture of benefits under a husband's estate, made this option less desirable. While a wife may actively have sought a death determination, parents of the husband strongly resisted this alternative, viewing such a course of action as abandonment of their son and possible loss of grandchildren (McCubbin, Hunter, and Metres, 1974a; Nelson, 1974). Further, while such an approach would facilitate remarriage and distribution of the husband's estate and insurance settlement, it would have no impact on the military's release of the serviceman's accrued pay and allowances. This fund, which often represented the single most important asset in the estate, could only be released by the Service Secretaries' declaration of death. Thus, many wives were pushed to await an official clarification of this ambiguous situation to realize the full benefits of their husband's estate.

In examining family behavior in response to stress over time, these families were faced with a pile-up of stressors resulting from (a) the hardships of the initial stressor event, which increased over time, (b) the consequences of family efforts to cope with the separation, and (c) additional life changes and events in the family. A significant contributing factor to these stressor events was ambiguity — both within the family regarding father's return and within society regarding norms and prescriptions for family behavior in this situation.

Family Resources and Perception: Coping and Social Support

Increasingly, the critical question for researchers in the area of family stress is not whether the stressor event causes a crisis, but rather what factors combine with the stressor event to increase its impact or to mitigate its effect. Areas of research that have received attention in the prisoner of war and missing in action studies have been coping and social support. These lines of inquiry have underscored the importance of both family "resources" and the family's "perception" of the situation that Hill (1958) labeled as the *B* and *C* factors in the ABCX model. Although family resources, such as cohesiveness and adaptability, and family member perceptions of the situation can be studied independently and give us a sense of what families have going for them, a better understanding of family behavior in response to stress involves examining the *interaction* of resources and perception. This does cause analytic difficulties, however. A reasonable compromise adopted for this longitudinal investigation was to work with both variables simultaneously through the examination of coping strategies.

Family coping as a resource. In an effort to examine what coping behaviors these families found *helpful* to them in overcoming or enduring the hardships engendered by the separation, the *Coping with Separation Inventory,* (McCubbin and Dahl, 1975) was constructed. Three coping patterns emerged as being of paramount importance:

Coping I: *Maintaining Family Integrity* — wives' efforts to maintain family stability through investing in family life and the children;

Coping II: *Establishing Independence through Self-Development* — wives' efforts to develop independence and self-sufficiency;

Coping III: *Seeking Resolution and Expression of Feelings* — wives' efforts to be involved in collective group activities in an effort to resolve the problem and to gain social support from other families.

In chronic and prolonged stress situations, the family unit is called upon to devote an effort to maintain family integrity; the more severe the stress the higher the probability that family stability will be disturbed by the stressor event (McCubbin, 1979). Both wives and children assumed new role responsibilities and modified the family's internal organization in an effort to maintain stability and unity. Wives, assuming the leadership role in the family unit, were called upon to become more self-reliant, more independent, and at the same time to do things that would enhance their self-esteem.

The most unique and complex coping pattern is evident in wives' efforts to seek resolution and express feelings. This pattern is composed of behavior items describing the collective efforts of families to establish a competing form of social organization and, through *social action*, change existing military policies and decisions that were seen as inadequate or as threatening to the family unit. Increasingly, it became clear to these families that coping with these major hardships required organized cooperative efforts that transcended those of any individual family, in order to obtain partial control over the situation and promote resolutions (laws, services, programs, benefits) that would reduce the impact of the stressor upon family life.

These collective group efforts also appeared to provide wives and family members with an important resource called social support. Cobb (1976) defines social support as the exchange of information that provides families with (a) emotional support, leading them to believe they are cared for and appreciated (b) esteem support, leading them to believe they are valued and (c) network support, leading them to believe they have a role to play in the organization and that there is a mutual obligation. Family members pointed out that the collective group, called the National League of Families, offered them a social network through which they could obtain understanding, empathy, encouragement, problem-solving information, material assistance, and a sense of belonging (Powers, 1974).

Family coping through perception. The findings from this longitudinal study suggest that religion and/or religious beliefs enabled these families to ascribe an acceptable meaning to their situation. This, in turn, contributed to the maintenance of family unity, the enhancement of member self-esteem, and also served as a source of norms and guidelines for family behavior in this ambiguous situation (Hunter, McCubbin and Metres, 1974).

While families struggled, they also appeared to reach a level of adaptive or functional stability, an outcome that could be attributed in part to wives' *redefining the situation*. For example, Boss' (1977) data revealed that not all of the consequences of boundary ambiguity were negative. It was positively associated with the interviewer's assessment of child adjustment and the family dimensions of achievement orientation, expressiveness, and organization. Wives appeared to define the ambiguity of father's absence differently for instrumental versus expressive needs: "Although it is financially functional for her (wives) to keep the father present in the instrumental role which offers satisfying financial security, it is at the same time functional for her to psychologically expel him from the emotional support role" (Boss, 1977). Wives appeared to redefine the situation by endowing father's role with some value and meaning, i.e. as financial provider, and at the same time legitimate their effort to establish a new life for themselves, i.e. by developing new ways to meet expressive needs.

In examining the interaction of family resources and perception through the study of family coping, we begin to see a range of factors families found beneficial to them in managing the crisis and working towards adjustment. The family's coping resources identified in this longitudinal study were (a) self-reliance and self-esteem, (b) family integration, (c) social support, (d) social action, and (e) collective group supports. The factors associated with the family's perceptions were their (a) religious beliefs and (b) ability to redefine the hardships and endow the situation with meaning.

BEYOND FAMILY CRISIS: FAMILY ADAPTATION

Hill's X factor (1958) the amount of "crisis" in the family system, generally has been adopted as the major outcome variable describing disruptions in family routines in response to a stressor. Burr (Chapter 1) conceived of "crisis" as a continuous variable, denoting variation in the "amount of disruptiveness, incapacitatedness, or disorganization of the family." Given this definition, it might be concluded that the purpose of postcrisis adjustment or the goal of "regenerative power" (Hansen, 1965) is primarily to reduce or eliminate the disruptiveness in the family system and restore homeostasis. It might be argued, however, that family disruptions potentially help to maintain family relationships and even stimulate desirable changes in family life. Hansen and Johnson (1979) called attention to the restrictive focus of "crisis" and noted that "families are often observed 'accepting' disruptions of habit and tradition not so much as unwelcome problems, but more as opportunities to renegotiate their relationships" (p. 584). Systems theorists (von Bertalanffy, 1968; Hill, 1971) point out that it is characteristic of living systems to evolve toward greater complexity, and consequently, families may actively initiate changes to facilitate such growth. It is questionable then, whether "reduction of crisis" *alone* is an adequate index of a family's postcrisis adjustment.

Adaptation: System-Environment Fit

Observations reviewed in this chapter suggest that *family adaptation* would be a useful concept for describing the outcome of family postcrisis adjustment. Family adaptation is defined as the degree to which the family system alters its internal functions (behaviors, rules, roles, perceptions) and/or external reality to achieve a system (individual or family) — environment "fit." Adaptation is achieved through reciprocal relationships where (a) system demands (or needs) are met by resources from the environment and (b) environmental demands are satisfied through system resources (Hansen and Hill, 1964; Mechanic, 1974; Melson, 1980).

Demands, which change over time, include the normative and nonnormative life changes and events and needs *of individuals,* e.g., transition to adolescence, need to achieve independence, and need for intimacy and close relationships, *of family units,* e.g., transition to parenthood, the launching of children from the home, the need for social contacts and support, and the loss of a parent due to war, and of *social institutions and communities,* e.g., war and its demand for young men and women, and requirements that families and individuals abide by rules and norms.

Resources are the psychological, social, interpersonal, and material characteristics of individual members, the family unit, and the community that may be brought into play in reducing tension, managing conflicts, and in general, meeting demands and needs. Individual resources include education, psychological stability, the capacity to be nurturing, the ability to manage the home, the ability to function independently, and the ability to manipulate various resources to one's advantage. Family resources could include integration, cohesiveness, flexibility, organization, moral religious values, and expressiveness. Finally, environmental resources might include social support networks, medical and psychological counseling services, and social policies that enhance family functioning and protect families from financial disaster.

Family adaptation is directed at achieving a satisfying level of stimulation complemented by resources needed to bring the family unit into equilibrium. Family adaptation is achieved by simultaneously bringing *two levels of family interaction into a "fit."* At the first level, a fit is sought between individual family members and the family environment, e.g., family meeting individual needs for autonomy and the individual meeting family needs for help on specific family tasks. At the second level, a fit is sought between the family unit and the social environment, e.g. family provides soldier-father and the military provides medical and social services, as well as financial security. Family adaptation is achieved when the *discrepancy* between the demands on the family unit (from within and from the environment) and the resources (from within and from the environment) are at the absolute minimum (Melson, 1980). Figure 2-2 depicts the two level interactional and transactional nature of family adaptation. Certainly, family members interact with the social environment and some degree of "fit" must also be achieved. However, this level of interaction is not the focus of this "family" chapter (*see* French, Rodgers, and Cobb, 1974).

As discussed, family adaptation is distinctly different from family adjustment (Melson, 1980). Adjustment is a short-term response by a family, which changes the situation momentarily, but is not intended to have any long-term consequences. Adaptation, however, implies a change in the family system, which evolves over a longer period of time and is intended to have long term consequences involving changes in family roles, rules, patterns of interaction, and perceptions.

Family Processes in Adaptation

What family processes appear to be involved in family adaptation? In negotiating family hardships associated with the crisis of a husband/father missing or unaccounted for in combat, the families in this study revealed three interrelated processes: stimulus regulation, environmental control, and balancing. *Stimulus regulation* (Melson, 1980) involves family efforts to selectively "let in, delay, or shut out" demands with the intention of minimizing family disrup-

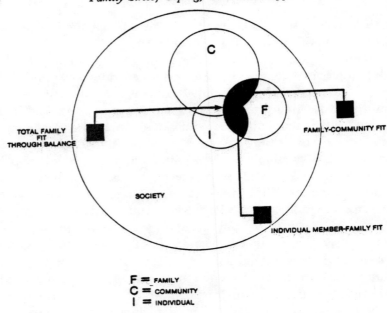

Figure 2-2. Two levels of "fit" between family and members, family, and community.

tion and exhaustion of resources. Stimulus regulation also involves family efforts to prioritize which of the numerous competing demands will receive attention, in what order, and involving what resources. Through regulation, families also permit themselves time to strengthen their resources and, if needed, to develop or gain additional resources to manage the situation. Families in this investigation made a concerted effort to regulate the impact of numerous demands such as attending to the ever changing needs of the children, to discrepancies in information regarding their husbands, to in-laws' efforts to provide help and to seek help, and to the wives' personal needs (for education, for emotional support) to prepare themselves for a life without their husbands.

Environmental control, (Melson, 1980), the second of the family adaptation processes, involves efforts to influence the type and quality of both the demands to which the family may be exposed and the resources needed to facilitate adaptation. This is an "active" process motivated by the family's desire for self-direction and autonomy. As Mechanic (1964) noted, the family's ability to adapt may depend on the efficacy of the solutions that the community provides. To the extent that the community is inadequate to the hardships these families face, family disruption may be inevitable no matter how strong the family's interpersonal capacities. Similarly, the ability of families to maintain interpersonal stability and psychological comfort will depend not only on their cohesiveness and adaptability (Olson and McCubbin, Chapter 3) but also on the social supports available or absent in the environment. The community not only offers solutions, but also imposes new challenges. As already discussed, the community may be ambiguous about its solutions — unclear as to what courses of action families may take and which of these will be "legitimated." Communities may also impose penalties (cutting back on family benefits and finances) for certain family actions as well as be exceedingly slow to modify policies and practices to assist families in need.

The longitudinal observations of these select military families revealed that collectively these families sought to change the community's (military's) approach to them. Families sought more information about their husbands, demanded access to all information, insisted on regular personal contacts with military officials, and demanded additional counseling for families in need. In approaching the U.S. Congress, these families sought changes in legislation which would ensure them of benefits to their children (preferential selection of qualified children to the Service Academies) as well as continued financial benefits and support, e.g., tax breaks, husband's continued pay and promotions. The importance of family efforts to control the environment to which it is exposed cannot be overstated. As solutions to family crises become more complex, the family's adaptation is less likely to be resolved solely by individual family initiatives and internal changes. Families are likely to depend on collective efforts with other families and the community to work out organized solutions and resources.

The third family adaptation process involves *balancing* the components of family interactions and transactions in an effort to maintain equilibrium or to achieve another more functional level of equilibrium. Because the family is a system composed of unique individuals with ever-changing and often times competing needs, it is a continuous challenge of family life to maintain a balanced needs-resources ratio at both the member-to-family and family-to-environment levels. Balancing involves the management of various dimensions of family life simultaneously, such as: (a) the maintenance of family bonds of coherence and unity, (b) the maintenance of satisfactory internal conditions for communication, (c) the promotion and enhancement of member independence and self-esteem, (d) the maintenance of family flexibility and autonomy, and (e) the development and maintenance of social supports and other resources in the community (McCubbin, Dahl, Lester, Benson, and Robertson, 1976; McCubbin, 1979). Family efforts to achieve a "fit" at one level are likely to precipitate additional strains and demands in another part of the system. To bring the totality of family interactions and transactions into balance simultaneously, families appear to engage in three additional family processes of *assimilation, accommodation,* and *compromise.*

In adapting Piaget's concepts of cognitive development to the family situation, we would argue that families readily *assimilate* new experiences or environmental or system demands, e.g., father's absence due to war separation, for which they already have the resources or ways of perceiving and interacting which "fit" such demands. Concomitantly, families *accommodate* to new changes or demands, e.g., father's prolonged absence in war, for which they lack resources and functional patterns of behavior by making changes in structure, roles, goals, and perceptions to fit the new reality, e.g., closing out husband-father's role. In other words, assimilation involves making the "new" demand fit existing family structures and functioning; accommodation involves changing the family dynamics to fit the "new" experience or demand.

For some families, the experience of crisis may be due to their "over" responsiveness and reactive style of changing behavior patterns quickly in response to every new demand. This creates instability in the family system with a sense of losing control along with a loss of family identity and coherence. Postcrisis adaptation for these families involves slowing down their efforts to change and consolidating their *existing* resources to create stable roles, rules, and interaction patterns. In other words, these families need to accommodate less and assimilate more. Conversely, for other families, the crisis may be exacerbated by their rigidity — their resistance to change existing roles and patterns of interaction to meet the new changing demands pressing on their system. Adaptation for the rigid family would involve accommodation wherein new roles, rules, and patterns of behavior are developed and shaped to fit the new demands. These two types of families represent the extreme family types, i.e. chaotic versus rigid, on the adaptability dimension of the Circumplex Model (*see* Olson and McCubbin, Chapter 3).

A family's effort to balance assimilation and accommodation is not a clear cut course of action with predictable, conflict-free-outcomes. Because the family faces a host of competing alternatives in what it assimilates (expectation of father's return versus belief in father's death) and how it accommodates (temporary shift in roles versus permanent "closing out" of father's role), each of which brings on additional hardships, the best solution is likely to be a difficult one involving the process of family *compromise*.

As evident in the studies reviewed in this chapter, numerous intra-family, e.g., child health, and social conditions, e.g., military policies and practices, limit the likelihood of the family's achieving optimal adaptation. When a family accommodates to a new reality by changing its structure, e.g., mother's effort to obtain a divorce, it is likely to involve subsequent changes in family functioning as a consequence, e.g., living on less income, and interactive effects on relationships with other members in the family system, e.g., child's withdrawal or anger towards mother. Predictably, difficulties in effecting multiple individual to family fits and a family to environment fit simultaneously, along with normative pressures to maintain the status quo of the system require economizing of efforts and compromise, which limit the family's attainment of a strictly optimal adaptation. Compromise, therefore, involves the family's arrival at and tolerance of a less than optimal solution. Families develop a sense of satisfaction in achieving quasi-equilibrium even if the adaptation is far from initial expectations or family ideals.

To be sure, the concept of adaptation may be useful in describing the dynamic processes of family postcrisis behavior, but the question remains, "what is 'successful' adaptation?" In moving from adaptation as a dynamic "process" to family adaptation as an "outcome" there is a need to attach qualitative adjectives, e.g., functional, dysfunctional adaptation, or prefixes, e.g., maladaptation, to reflect the continuum of possible outcomes. The conceptualization of adaptation as an outcome requires further clarification beyond the scope of the data discussed in this chapter. Towards this end, we would be inclined to draw concepts from the economics and management frameworks, which appear to have direct applications to our efforts to operationalize and measure family adaptation.

For example, when the family's demands-resources ratio is calculated at various points over time, and we observe the variations in both demands and resources, we may also visualize the social, psychological, interpersonal, and economic *cost* and *benefits* families incur as a result of negotiating a family-environment fit. Adaptation may therefore be viewed as an outcome to be assessed in terms of a ratio of costs to benefits. Functional adaptation may be defined as a favorable cost-benefit ratio and conversely, dysfunctional adaptation would emerge in those situations where costs exceeded the benefits. It is reasonable to expect that the systematic assessment of family adaptation as a process and as an outcome will be targets for future research and theory building.

THE DOUBLE ABCX MODEL

We appear to be at the same crossroads psychologists faced when they attempted to identify the factors that caused schizophrenia. In the study of mental health, the two-variable design was inadequate. For every individual faced with a family history of schizophrenia, a notable percentage do not develop pathology. Similarly, among family stress situations, we struggle to explain why some families with so little appear to do so well, while families with apparent resources appear to deteriorate in the face of hardships.

The previous discussion of observations and findings made of families faced with a prolonged war-induced separation suggest that the original ABCX Model might be strengthened by the addition of postcrisis variables, which could facilitate our understanding of which familes are better able to achieve satisfactory adaptations to crisis. A brief summary of findings discussed earlier would be useful in introducing a Double ABCX Model for future research and theory building.

Stress and Change: The Double "A" Factor

There appear to be at least three types of stressors contributing to a pile-up in the family system in a crisis situation. The first is the *in-*

itial stressor event with its inherent hardships, which played a part in moving the family into a "crisis" state. The second are family life changes and events, which occur irrespective of the initial stressor. The third are stressors, which are consequences of the family's efforts to cope with the hardships of the situation.

Family Resources: The Double "B" Factor

The family's resources appear to be of two general types. The first are those *resources* that are already available to the family and that minimize the impact of the initial stressor and reduce the probability of the family entering into crisis. The second are *those coping resources* (personal, family, and social) strengthened or developed in response to the "crisis" situation. The coping resources identified in this longitudinal research included (a) self-reliance and self-esteem, (b) family integration, (c) social support, and (d) collective group supports, which include social action.

Family Perception: The Double "C" Factor

Family perceptions appear to take on two different forms depending on whether we are referring to the family's response before or after a crisis. The first is the *family's perception of the stressor event,* the family's view of how stressful the event may be or is. The second is the *family's perception of the crisis,* which involves not only the family's view of the stressor and related hardships, the pile-up of life events, but also the meaning families attach to the total family situation. The family's perceptions postcrisis appear to involve (a) religious beliefs, (b) a redefining of the situation, and (c) endowing the situation with meaning.

Family Crisis and Adaptation: The Double "X" Factor

Family *crisis* appears to be but one phase in the continuum of family adjustment to stress over time. The concept of *family adaptation* is introduced as one possible outcome for the family course of adjustment following a crisis. Adaptation involves the processes of stimulus regulation, environmental control, and balancing to achieve a level of functioning, which preserves family unity and enhances the family system and member growth and development.

Balancing the various dimensions of family life is a difficult process involving assimilation, accommodation, and compromise.

Assuming that family adaptation is useful for describing the process of family postcrisis adjustment and as an outcome criterion, we can envision a prediction-type model that includes Hill's ABCX model as its foundation and attempts to lay out those critical dimensions of family postcrisis behavior that are involved in adaptation. The Double ABCX model is introduced at this point (*see* Figure 2-3). Table 2-III outlines the basic variables, symbols, and modifications in the Hill Model.

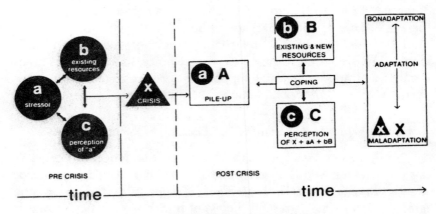

Figure 2-3: The double ABCX model.

SUMMARY AND CONCLUSIONS

In an attempt to build on Hill's (1958) ABCX model and the theory building efforts of Burr (Chapter 1), the authors have examined the results of longitudinal research on families faced with a war-induced hardship of a family member captured or unaccounted for in action. The prolonged absence and ambiguous dismemberment made the hardship unique. The analysis of nearly a decade of research findings revealed a range of postcrisis family variables that appeared to explain why some families were better able to adapt to the hardships than others. When placed in a prediction type model, these postcrisis variables suggest an extension of Hill's original ideas into what has been labeled the Double ABCX Model. Certainly the concepts and propositions advanced in this chapter need further

Table 2-III. Dimensions of the Family Crisis Framework: Double ABCX Model

FAMILY PRECRISIS FACTORS		FAMILY POSTCRISIS FACTORS	
A	Stressor event and related hardships	AA	Family "Pile-Up" - Unresolved aspects of the stressor event - Unmanaged hardships associated with the stressor event - Intra-family role changes precipitated by stressor - Changes in the family and its members over time - Residual hardships and demands precipitated by family efforts at coping - Social ambiguity
B	Family resources available	BB	Family resources—modified, strengthened, or developed as part of family adaptation - Coping by managing resources within the family to facilitate adaptation - Coping by developing, stimulating, and controlling resources outside of the family - Social support
C	Family perception of the stressor and available resources	CC	Family perception of the crisis situation and resources - Redefining the situation - Endowing the situation with meaning

X	Family crisis	XX	Family adaptation—system-environment fit through process of:
			 - Stimulus regulation
			 - Environmental control
			 - Balancing:
			     Assimilation
			     Accommodation
			     Compromise

development. The tools to measure family postcrisis behavior leading to adaptation need to be further concretized. The concepts need to be defined more precisely and operationalized for measurement. The propositions need to be expanded, formalized, and validated. Nonetheless, even in their current form, they offer some promise of encouraging additional formulations and research of the impact of stressors and of family adaptation over time. The Double ABCX, an inductively derived model, appears to have value in light of the studies reviewed and merits consideration and testing in future research on families under stress.

Chapter 3

CIRCUMPLEX MODEL OF MARITAL AND FAMILY SYSTEMS V: APPLICATION TO FAMILY STRESS AND CRISIS INTERVENTION

DAVID H. OLSON AND HAMILTON I. McCUBBIN

T HE research and theory building efforts of Hill (1949; 1958), Burr (Chapter 1), and others reveal that a plethora of concepts and propositions has emerged to describe marital and family dynamics in the face of stress. While general systems theory (Buckley, 1967; von Bertalanffy, 1968) has provided a central underlying base for many of these formulations, few attempts have been made to integrate these concepts within a systematic model that may also be applied to clinical work with families under stress.

The purpose of this chapter is to delineate two dimensions of marital and family behavior — *cohesion* and *adaptability* — that appear as underlying components for the multitude of concepts in the family field and as central concepts in family stress theory. Family cohesion and family adaptability have been organized into a circumplex model that facilitates the identification of sixteen types of marital and family systems. The circumplex model provides a viable framework for bringing together theorists, researchers, and practitioners involved in the analysis, study, and treatment of families under stress.

CONCEPTUAL DEFINITIONS OF FAMILY COHESION AND ADAPTABILITY DIMENSIONS

Family cohesion and adaptability are two dimensions of family behavior that initially emerged from a conceptual clustering of more than fifty concepts developed to describe marital and family dy-

This research was supported by the Agriculture Experiment Station, University of Minnesota, St. Paul, Minnesota.

namics.

Family cohesion is defined as the *emotional bonding that family members have toward one another and the degree of individual autonomy they experience.* Within the circumplex model, the following are some of the specific concepts or variables that can be used to diagnose and measure the family cohesion dimensions: emotional bonding, independence, boundaries, coalitions, time, space, friends, decision making, and interests and recreation. There are four levels of cohesion ranging from extremely low (disengaged) to moderately low (separated) and moderately high (connected) to extremely high (enmeshed). The operational definitions of each of the cohesion concepts at these four levels are indicated in Table 3-I.

It is hypothesized that *balanced* levels of moderately low to moderately high cohesion are most viable for family functioning. The extremes of being disengaged or enmeshed are seen as problematic, and most couples and families who come for treatment often fall into one of these extremes. When cohesion levels are extremely high (enmeshed systems), there is over-identification so that loyalty to and consensus within the family prevent individuation of family members. At the other extreme (disengaged systems), high levels of autonomy are encouraged, and family members do their own thing with limited attachment or commitment to their family. It is the central area (separated and connected) of the model where individuals are able to *experience* and *balance* being both independent from and connected to their family.

The salience of the cohesion dimension is underscored by the wide range of social science disciplines that have used the dimension or concepts related to it. Psychiatrists, family therapists, family sociologists, small group theorists, group therapists, social psychologists, and anthropologists have utilized the concept in their work. They have been highly creative in developing concepts to describe high or low levels of cohesion. Extremely high cohesion has been called pseudomutuality (Wynne et al., 1958), undifferentiated family ego mass and emotional fusion (Bowen, 1961), binding (Stierlin, 1974), enmeshment (Minuchin, 1974), extraordinary mutual involvement (Scott and Askworth, 1967), and consensus sensitive families (Reiss, 1971a, 1971b). Extremely low cohesion has been described as emotional divorce (Bowen, 1961) schism and skew (Lidz, Cornelison, Fleck, and Terry, 1957), disengagement

Table 3-I

Family Cohesion Dimension: Clinical and Research Indicators

	DISENGAGED (Very Low)	SEPARATED (Low to Moderate)	CONNECTED (Moderate to High)	ENMESHED (Very High)
Emotional Bonding	Very Low	Low to Moderate	Moderate to High	Very High
Independence	High independence of family members.	Moderate Independence of family members.	Moderate dependence of family members.	High dependence of family members.
Family Boundaries	Open external boundaries. Closed internal boundaries. Rigid generational boundaries.	Semi-open external and internal boundaries. Clear generational boundaries.	Semi-open external boundaries. Open internal boundaries. Clear generational boundaries.	Closed external boundaries. Blurred internal boundaries. Blurred generational boundaries.
Coalitions	Weak coalitions, usually a family scapegoat.	Marital coalition clear.	Marital coalition strong.	Parent-child coalitions.
Time	Time apart from family maximized (physically and/or emotionally).	Time alone and together is important.	Time together is important. Time alone permitted for approved reasons.	Time together maximized. Little time alone permitted.
Space	Separate space both physically and emotionally is maximized.	Private space maintained; some family space.	Family space maximized. Private space minimized.	Little or no private space at home.
Friends	Mainly individual friends seen alone. Few family friends.	Some individual friends. Some family friends.	Some individual friends. Scheduled activities with couple and family friends.	Limited individual friends. Mainly couple or family friends seen together.
Decision Making	Primarily individual decisions.	Most decisions are individually based, able to make joint decisions on family issues.	Individual decisions are shared. Most decisions made with family in mind.	All decisions, both personal and relationship, must be made by family.
Interests and Recreation	Primarily individual activities done without family. Family not involved.	Some spontaneous family activities. Individual activities supported.	Some scheduled family activities. Family involved in individual interests.	Most or all activities and interests must be shared with family.

(Minuchin, 1974), pseudo-hostility (Wynne et al., 1958), expelling (Stierlin, 1974), and scapegoating (Bell and Vogel, 1960). There are fewer terms to describe the more balanced and moderate areas of cohesion but some of the terms reflecting this are differentiated self (Bowen, 1961), interdependence (Olson, 1972), and mutuality (Wynne et al., 1958).

Family adaptability is the second dimension and is defined as *the ability of a marital or family system to change its power structure, role relationships, and relationship rules in response to situational and developmental stress.* In order to describe, measure, and diagnose couples on this dimension, a variety of concepts have been taken from several social science disciplines with heavy reliance on family sociology: family power (assertiveness, control, discipline), negotiation styles, role relationships, relationship rules, and feedback (negative and positive). The four levels of adaptability range from rigid (extremely low) to structured (low to moderate) and flexible (moderate to high) to chaotic (extremely high). The operational definitions of each of the concepts for these four levels is presented in Table 3-II.

As with cohesion, it is hypothesized that central levels of adaptability (structured and flexible) are more conducive to marital and family functioning, with the extremes (rigid and chaotic) being the most problematic. Basically, this dimension focuses on the ability of the marital and family system to *change*. Much of the early application of systems theory to families emphasized the rigidity of the family and its tendency to maintain the *status quo* (Haley, 1962; 1963; 1964). *Morphostasis* is the systems term used to describe the pattern of rigidity to change, and *morphogenesis* is the potential to develop and grow as a system. Until the work of recent theorists (Speer, 1970; Wertheim, 1973; 1975), the importance of potential for change was minimized. They helped to clarify that systems need both stability and change and that it is the ability to change when appropriate that distinguishes functional couples and families from others. In line with this thinking, the circumplex model postulates that *balance* is critical and that problematic families often function at either the extreme of continual change, leading to chaos, or no change, which results in rigidity.

CIRCUMPLEX MODEL OF MARITAL AND FAMILY SYSTEMS

Once the two dimensions of family cohesion and adaptability

Table 3-II

Family Adaptability Dimensions: Clinical and Research Indicators

	Assertiveness	Control	Discipline	Negotiation	Roles	Rules	System Feedback
CHAOTIC (Very High)	Passive and Aggressive Styles.	Limited leadership.	Laissez faire. Very lenient.	Endless negotiation. Poor problem-solving.	Dramatic role shifts.	Dramatic rule shifts. Many implicit rules. Few explicit rules. Arbitrarily enforced rules.	Primarily positive loops; few negative loops.
FLEXIBLE (High to Moderate)	Generally Assertive.	Egalitarian with fluid changes.	Democratic. Unpredictable Consequences.	Good negotiation; good problem-solving.	Role making and sharing. Fluid change of roles.	Some rule changes. More implicit rules. Rules often enforced.	More positive than negative loops.
STRUCTURED (Moderate to Low)	Generally Assertive.	Democratic with stable leader.	Democratic. Predictable Consequences.	Structured negotiations; good problem-solving	Some role sharing	Few rule changes. More explicit than implicit rules. Rules usually enforced.	More negative than positive loops.
RIGID (Very low)	Passive or Aggressive Styles.	Authoritarian leadership.	Autocratic. Overly strict.	Limited negotiations; Poor problem-solving.	Role rigidity. Stereotyped roles.	Rigid rules. Many explicit rules. Few implicit rules. Strictly enforced rules.	Primarily negative loops; few positive loops.

were independently identified as being important conceptually and empirically, the two dimensions were combined to form a Circumplex model. Figure 3-1 illustrates the two dimensions and the four levels of each dimension. Combining the dimensions enables one to identify and describe sixteen distinct types of marital and family systems. Although it is assumed that it is possible to conceptually identify, empirically measure, and clinically observe all sixteen types, it is also assumed that some of the types occur more frequently than others. As with any circumplex model, the more central types are the most common, but it is hypothesized that couples and families experiencing problems are more likely to represent the extreme types. The sixteen types can be organized into three groups: one group has scores at the two central levels on both dimensions (four types); another group is extreme on both dimensions (four types); and the third group is extreme on only one dimension (eight types). These groupings within the model comprise regions that correspond to some of the recent theoretical work by Kantor and Lehr (1975) and Wertheim (1973; 1975), who describe marital and family systems as being *open, closed,* and *random* (*see* Figure 3-1). A more complete discussion of open, closed, and random systems and the clinical application of the circumplex model with chemically dependent families is described in a paper by Killorin and Olson (1980).

Hypotheses Derived From the Circumplex Model

One of the assets of a theoretical model is that hypotheses can be deduced and tested in order to evaluate and further develop the model. The following are hypotheses derived from the model, some of which have been or are currently being tested and others of which can be tested.

The first general hypothesis postulates a *curvilinear* relationship between the dimensions of cohesion and adaptability and successful or effective family functioning in the face of stressor events. The exception to this general hypothesis is indicated in hypothesis 1c where the normative expectations in the family support extreme behavior on these dimensions.

1. *Couples/families with balanced (two central levels) cohesion and adaptability will generally function more adequately than those at the extremes of these dimensions.*

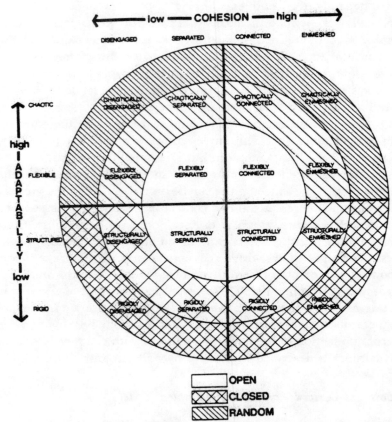

Figure 3-1. Sixteen possible types of marital and family systems derived from the Circumplex Model.

   a. Couples/families without serious problems will tend to have more balanced scores on both of these dimensions.

   b. Couples/families with serious problems will tend to have more extreme scores on one or both of these dimensions.

   c. Couples/families with normative expectations that support behaviors extreme on these dimensions will *not* develop problems as long as *all* the members accept these expectations.

An important issue in the Circumplex Model relates to the definition of *balance*. The model postulates that a *balance* on both dimensions is related to more adequate family functioning. Even though a balanced family system is placed at the two central levels of the model, it should not be assumed that these families always operate in a moderate manner. Being balanced means that the system can experience the extremes on the dimensions when appropriate, but that they do not typically function at these extremes for long periods of time. For example, families in the central area of the cohesion dimension allow family members to experience being both independent from and connected to their family. Both extremes are accepted and expected, provided an individual does not continually function at the extreme. Conversely, extreme or unbalanced family types tend to function *only* at the extremes and are not expected or able to change their behaviors. As a result, the more balanced family types will develop and maintain a larger behavioral repertoire and are more able to change compared to extreme family types.

Although a curvilinear relationship is generally predicted, some important qualifications must be made in terms of the *normative expectations* and *cultural bias* in this hypothesis. The normative expectations in our culture provide two conflicting themes that can create double and often confusing messages. One theme is that family members are expected to do things together as a family; yet, the second theme encourages individuals to do their own thing. This second theme becomes more prominent as children approach adolescence and has taken on greater importance for increasing numbers of women in our culture. As a result, many American families find that a balance of these two themes has become a personal issue.

Families in our culture still vary greatly in the extent to which they encourage and give support to individuals to develop in ways that may differ from the family's values. While parents would prefer their children to develop values and ideas similar to theirs, most parents can enable their children to become somewhat autonomous and differentiated from the family system. A sizeable minority, however, have normative expectations that strongly emphasize family togetherness, often at the expense of individual development. Their family norms emphasize emotional and physical togetherness and they strive for high levels of consensus and loyalty. Some ethnic groups in this country such as Slovak-Americans (Stein, 1978), Puerto Ricans (Minuchin, Montalvo, Guerney, Rossman, and Schumer, 1967), Italian families (Goetzl, 1973), and religious groups such as the Amish (Wittmer, 1973) and Mormons (Schvaneveldt, 1973) have high expectations regarding family togetherness. These expectations are also common, but less predominant, in many American families regardless of their ethnic or religious orientation. Many of these families could be described as extreme on the cohesion dimension, that is enmeshed, and they will not necessarily have problems in their families as long as all family members are willing to go along with those expectations (*see* hypothesis 1c).

In general, the hypothesized curvilinear relationship between effective family functioning and the cohesion-adaptability dimensions primarily applies to families that accept the current cultural norms that support both family togetherness and individual development. The general hypothesis would *not* apply, however, for families that have very high expectations for family togetherness.

Another important qualification of the hypothesis relates to our definition of problem families. We tend to define problem families as those that voluntarily or involuntarily are involved in some treatment program. There is a body of clinical evidence that those couples or families in such programs are often extreme in one or both of these dimensions. However, there are many families that are extreme in the dimensions that do function well and never seek professional assistance. There are also families extreme in these dimensions that do have problems but never choose to seek treatment. Unfortunately, most studies have relied on problem families that seek or are placed in treatment and, hence, we know very little about those that do not. Hopefully, future studies will attempt to gather data from families not seeking or receiving professional counseling and ones with extreme normative expectations so that these hypotheses can be more adequately tested.

2. *Couples/families will change their cohesion and adaptability to deal with situational stress and life changes in the family life cycle.*
   a. Couples/families without serious problems will change their cohesion and adaptability to an adjacent level (type) to deal with situational, transitional, or developmental stressors.
   b. Couples/families with serious problems will either not change their cohesion and adaptability or will flip to an opposite extreme (on one or both dimensions) to deal with situational, transitional, or developmental stressors.

The second general hypothesis deals with change in the family system to deal with stress or to accommodate changes in family members, particularly as members change their expectations. The circumplex model is *dynamic* in that it assumes that individuals and family systems will change, and it hypothesizes that change can be beneficial to the maintenance and improvement of family functioning. When one family member desires change, the family system must deal with this request. For example, increasing numbers of married women want to develop more autonomy from their husbands (cohesion dimension) and also want more power and equality in their relationships (adaptability dimension). If their husbands are unwilling to understand and change in accordance with these expectations, the marriages will probably experience increased amounts of stress. Another common example of changing expectations is when a child reaches adolescence. Like the wife in the previous example, adolescents often want more freedom, independence, and power in the family system.

3. *Positive communication skills will facilitate couples and families to balance cohesion and adaptability.*

   a. Couples/families with balanced scores (two central levels) on cohesion and adaptability will tend to have more positive communication skills than those at the extremes of the dimensions.

   b. Couples/families at the extremes of the cohesion and/or adaptability dimensions will tend to have more negative communication skills than those not at the extremes.

Positive communication skills include sending clear and congruent messages, empathy, supportive statements, and effective problem-solving skills. Conversely, negative communication skills include sending incongruent and disqualifying messages, lack of empathy, nonsupportive (negative) statements, poor problem-solving skills, and paradoxical and double binding messages (Olson, 1972). Although many studies have investigated communication and problem-solving skills in couples (Vincent, Weiss, and Birchler, 1975; Sprenkle and Olson, 1978) and families (Alexander and Barton, 1976; Guerney, 1976; Patterson, 1976), these studies have not specifically tested the relationship of these skills to the hypotheses derived from the circumplex model.

In general, positive communication skills are seen as helping marital and family systems facilitate and maintain a balance on the two dimensions. Conversely, negative communication skills prevent and minimize marital and family systems from moving into the central areas and thereby increase the probability that extreme systems will remain extreme. Carlfred Broderick (personal communication) proposed that communication was the critical dimension missing in the circumplex model and has recently developed specific hypotheses that relate family communication and system processes to child behaviors (Broderick, Williams, and Krager, 1979). There is a need for research that will more adequately assess the relationship between communication skills, types of marital and family systems, and the extent to which positive skills facilitate movement within the model.

Circumplex Model and Family Development

The Circumplex Model also allows one to begin an integration of general systems theory with the family developmental framework, a proposal advanced several years ago by Reuben Hill (1971). Building on the family development approach as described by Hill and Rodgers (1964), it has been observed that families must change and adapt to normal transitions in the family over time (Rapoport, 1962). It is expected that the stage of the family life cycle and composition of the family will influence which of the sixteen types characterizes a family system. Although there will always be variability in marital and family systems at the same stage, it is hypothesized that many of them will cluster towards similar types at certain critical stages or transition points because they are dealing with similar developmental tasks (*see* Table 3-III). For example, it would be predicted that premarital couples would tend toward the high range on cohesion (enmeshed and connected) and toward the lower range on adaptability (structured to rigid). In other words, they would fall into the lower right quadrant of the circumplex model (*see* Figure 3-1).

Table 3-III indicates the levels of family cohesion and adaptability that are expected at critical stages of the family life cycle and indicates how distressed and nondistressed families will differ. Unfortunately, there is not sufficient space to elaborate on all the predicted changes that may occur at critical transitions in marriage and family relationships. Future papers will elaborate on these ideas and hypotheses, and, hopefully, future studies will evaluate and refine them.

TABLE 3–III. Typical Types of Systems at Critical Stages of Family Life Cycle

	COHESION	ADAPTABILITY	QUADRANT OR MODE
Premarital	Connected & Enmeshed	Structured & Rigid	Lower Right
Newlyweds	Connected	Flexible & Chaotic	Upper Right
Early Marriage	Separated & Connected	Flexible & Structured	Central Area
Later Marriage	Separated &	Flexible &	Central Area
(a) Nondistressed	Connected	Structured	
(b) Distressed	One or both spouses	One or both spouses	
	Disengaged or Enmeshed	Disengaged or Enmeshed	Extreme Areas
Birth of First Child	Connected & Enmeshed	Initially Chaotic; later Structured & Rigid	Initially Upper Right; Later Lower Right
Child-Rearing			
(a) Nonproblem Families	Separated & Connected	Flexible & Structured	Central Area
(b) Problem Families	Disengaged & Enmeshed	Chaotic & Rigid	Extreme Area
Adolescent in Family			
(a) Nonproblem families	Primarily Separated; some connected	Flexible and Structured	Central Area
(b) Problem families	Enmeshed or Disengaged	Rigid or Chaotic	Extreme areas
Older Couples w/o children			
(a) Nondistressed	Separated & Connected	Flexible & Structured	Central Area
(b) Distressed	Disengaged or Enmeshed	Rigid	Lower Left or Right

CLINICAL APPLICATION OF THE CIRCUMPLEX MODEL

One of the major goals in developing the Circumplex Model was to provide a conceptual framework that could be used by marital and family therapists. More specifically, the Model was designed so that it could be used in diagnosis, in establishing treatment goals, and in assessing the effectiveness of the treatment program. The Model assumes that the circumplex types are dynamic, can be changed, and are not as static or stable as personality types.

Diagnosis of Marital and Family Systems

There are basically two ways of making a diagnosis using the Circumplex Model: the clinical approach and the empirical approach.

Clinical approach. In a clinical assessment, the therapist would first need to interview and observe the couple or family to obtain information on the variables or indicators of cohesion and adaptability. In terms of cohesion, the therapist would determine how the system dealt with the following variables indicated in Table 3-I: emotional bonding, independence, boundaries, coalitions, time, space, friends, decision making, interests, and recreation. In terms of adaptability, the therapist would identify the variables indicated in Table 3-II: assertiveness, control, discipline, negotiation style, role relationships, relationship rules, and system feedback.

In the assessment, the therapist would need to look at how each member, each dyadic unit, other member combinations, and the entire system functions. As family size increases, the number of combinations (dyads, triads, tetrads, pentads, etc.) of family members makes the system even more complex (Lindsay, 1976). For example, while a three-person family has only three dyads and one triad, a six-member family would have fifteen dyads, twenty triads, fifteen tetrads, and one pentad — fifty-six total combinations.

It should be emphasized that not all combinations of family members within a family will be classified in the same manner. In fact, the unique groupings of members are rich sources of clinical information that can be used later in treatment.

Another factor that influences the complexity of marital and family systems is that they may function differently depending on the situation and kind of problem. In a *post hoc* analysis of conflict resolution styles in couples, Craddock (1977, 1978) found that one couple's predominant style changed when they dealt with religious issues. The couple was highly religious, and, in these areas, both partners felt that the husband should be the authority. Their general style of dealing with problems reflected a democratic form of power structure and role sharing. They also had balance on the cohesion dimension between autonomy and togetherness. As a result, they typically functioned as a *flexibly-connected* couple (central area of model). However, when dealing with religious issues, such as their child's attendance at Sunday school, the husband became the authority, and they demonstrated an extreme level of cohesiveness. They then functioned as a *rigidly-enmeshed couple*. Because of the potential changes in systems in some situations, it is therefore important to learn of family interaction in a wide variety of situations.

Once the clinical observation is completed, the therapist needs to determine the *general system functioning* of the various combinations of family members on *each* of the *nine* variables of cohesion and the *seven* variables of adaptability. This more global assessment is used to classify the system at one of the four levels of cohesion (disengaged, separated, connected, enmeshed) and one of the four levels of adaptability (rigid, structured, flexible, chaotic). Basically, if four or more of the seven ratings on adaptability fall on the *same* level, this would be considered the *modal* pattern for that system. It should be remembered, however, that this more global assessment might conceal some of the clinical richness revealed by the ratings. This additional information should be retained and used in the clinical intervention.

The therapist's assessment is certainly important, but this assessment might differ from each family member's own perception of their system. Also, these assessments might differ from a more empirical assessment using a self-report scale or behavioral task. There is considerable evidence that insider's and outsider's views of the same relationship may differ in both systematic and unsystematic ways, but these differences can be clinically and empirically useful (Olson, 1977).

Empirical approach. Although a variety of self-report and/or behavioral instruments can be used to do an *empirical assessment,* a self-report scale was specifically developed to measure each of the sixteen variables related to the cohesion and adaptability dimensions. The *Family Adaptability and Cohesion Evaluation Scales* (FACES) is a self-report instrument recently developed by Olson, Bell, and Portner (1978). There are six items for assessing each of the sixteen variables related to the model and a fifteen item social desirability scale, making a total of 111 items in FACES. Each family member completes FACES in terms of his or her perception of the marital and family system. Each member, therefore, has a score on each of the sixteen variables, a total score in the two dimensions, and a social desirability score. These individual scores can then be plotted so that it is possible to compare family members. Couple or family scores can be obtained by summing individuals, and discrepancy scores can also be obtained between individuals.

As mentioned earlier, the complexity of diagnosis and placement of *all* family members within a type becomes more difficult as the number of family members increases. Also, as different sources and methods are used for the diagnosis, e.g., therapist's ratings, family members' perceptions, scores on objective measures, the richness of the diagnosis increases, but the degree of agreement on the *type* of system decreases. Unfortunately, there is no easy solution to this dilemma. However, it is maintained that this multimethod approach to diagnosis is generally advantageous since it enables the therapist to more adequately assess the richness and complexity of marital and family systems that have so often been elusive.

Common Problems in Marital and Family Systems

The Circumplex Model enables one to focus on two central themes in marital and family dynamics that go beyond presenting symptoms. One theme (cohesion) is concerned with how much individual members want to be connected to each other versus how much they want to maintain their autonomy. The second theme (adaptability) relates to how much they would like the system to change. Trying to handle or balance these two themes to satisfy all family members is one reason couples and families have problems. No matter what *type* of system within the Circumplex Model best describes the couple or family, if one person has highly discrepant expectations or behaviors from others in the system, there is strong likelihood that problems will develop.

One frequent problem with couples coming for counseling is that each spouse is at an *opposite extreme* on the *same* dimension. On the cohesion dimension, one partner might want more cohesion in the relationship, while the other person might want more autonomy and freedom. On the adaptability dimension, one partner might want more change in the system while the other wants it to stay the same. In this example, both are at opposite poles on each dimension and are unable to balance the extreme differences in their expectations and/or behaviors. McCubbin, Dahl, Lester, Benson, and Robertson (1976) described in greater detail the struggle that wives of returned American prisoners of war had in dealing with their conflicting needs for closeness and autonomy.

A second type of problem encountered by couples is when *both* partners are at the *same extreme* on one or both dimensions. On the cohesion dimension, they may both be disengaged or enmeshed. Disengaged couples spend so much energy doing their own thing that they have little to give each other. On the other hand, enmeshed couples are so invested in each other that they have little autonomy. Neither of these couples will necessarily have problems unless it is discrepant from what they want in the relationship.

Setting Treatment Goals and Treatment Strategies

Once the diagnosis is completed, the therapist is then ready to begin setting the treatment goals. Therapists vary in the extent to which they involve the couple or family in deciding on the goals of treatment. From the perspective of the Circumplex Model, several general guidelines are suggested. First, the couple or family should be consulted about how they would like to change in each dimension. Second, if a couple is extreme in one or both dimensions, it is suggested that the goal of treatment be to move them only *one* level toward the central area. It has been found that if a shift is attempted through more than one level in the dimension, the couple will either resist, change, or flip to the opposite extreme.

The therapist then needs to decide with the couple or family what dimension and what specific variables related to the dimension to work to change. The setting of the intervention *goals* is critical and often neglected. As Feldman (1976) stated: "In many ways, the most important initial task for the family therapist is goal-setting. Unfortunately, this process is often not carried out. In too many instances, family therapists (especially being family therapists) start to "intervene" before having formulated (in conjunction with the family) a clear set of goals for the therapy. As a consequence, the therapy often gets bogged down, meanders aimlessly, or is precipitously terminated" (p. 111).

While the Circumplex Model is designed to assist the counselor in making a diagnostic assessment and choosing goals for intervention, it does not indicate what intervention techniques to use. Techniques are for the most part atheoretical and can be used regardless of the counselor's theoretical orientations. The counselor must, therefore, choose the techniques from his/her repertoire that seem most appropriate for achieving the specific goals.

Intervention With Families Under Stress: A Case Analysis

In order to illustrate the application of the Circumplex Model in the diagnosis and intervention of family units faced with a stressful situation, a case analysis will be presented on a family struggling with the strains of the family developmental event of becoming parents for the first time.

This case analysis is one of several ongoing examinations conducted by Clinical Nurse Practitioners in the School of Public Health, University of Minnesota, who were challenged with the task of conducting systematic analyses of families faced with either a developmental, transitional, or situational stressor event. Specifically, they were asked to (a) select two families who had recently experienced the same stressor event, (b) select one family under stress who had presented indices of psychological and/or interpersonal strain and had sought professional help, and (c) select another comparison family who would be comparable on some basic demographic characteristics, e.g. age, education, family configuration, etc., who faced the same type of stressor event, but had not indicated strain nor the need for professional intervention in coping with the situation.

The case analysis presented here focuses on the family under stress. Information on the comparison family is also displayed to highlight certain clinical findings and to underscore the value of the circumplex model for clinical evaluation and intervention with families in crisis situations.

The transition to parenthood may be classified as an intra-family stressor event involving accession of a new member. Aldous (1978) describes transition to parenthood as a "change in the plurality patterns," which may create strain in the marital relationship due to the changes in family roles; a couple moves from a dyad to a triad, creating new tasks and responsibilities and alternative ways of interaction.

The two couples selected for analysis were both parents of male infants (first child) under one year of age (nine months and eleven months). These families were selected for study because (a) they had both experienced the same developmental event, (b) they appeared to differ in the amount of strain associated with their transition to parenthood resulting in a stressed family and a comparison family, and (c) they had similar backgrounds and were of the same socioeconomic status. They were matched on the basis of age, education, community in which wives grew up, and church affiliation. Both couples owned their own home and had been married for approximately the same length of time (5 years). Both couples had taken childbirth classes.

The couples were asked to complete two self-report inventories: *FACES — Family Adaptability and Cohesion Evaluation Scales* (Olson, Bell, and Portner, 1978), to measure the two dimensions of the Circumplex Model, family cohesion and adaptability, and *FILE — Family Inventory of Life Events* (McCubbin, Wilson, and Patterson, 1979). *FILE* is an 171 item self-report instrument that is designed to record the life events and changes experienced by a family during each six-month period of the past year.

Family circumplex profile. Table 3-IV indicates the scores for the two couples on all the subscales of FACES. On the cohesion dimension, both couples obtained primarily balanced scores, although the stressed couple was more separated. On two scales, *space* and *decision making*, their low scores indicate the desire for separate space both physically and emotionally and a pattern of individual rather than shared decision making.

On the adaptability dimension, there is greater variance between the two couples. The stressed couple obtained very low scores on four of the seven scales, which placed them on the "rigid" extreme of the adaptability dimension. The low scores suggest that the stressed couple has difficulty being assertive with each other and probably exhibit passive or aggressive styles, poor problem-solving skills characterized by limited negotiations, primarily negative communication with few positive loops in the system feedback, and stereotyped, rigid roles. In contrast, the comparison couple had balanced scores on all but two of the adaptability scales, placing them in the "flexible" quadrant of the circumplex model.

Both couples may be classified as one of the sixteen types on the circumplex model. In examining Figure 3-1 and considering the aforementioned profiles we would place the comparison couple in the upper right quadrant and describe their family system as being *flexibly connected*. This is the type of system predicted for a family at the stage of the life cycle when the first child is born (*see* Table 3-III). In contrast, the stressed couple would be placed in the lower

Table 3–IV

Couple Comparison on "FACES"—Family Adaptability and Cohesion Evaluation Scales

	SUBSCALES	COMPARISON COUPLE (FLEXIBLY CONNECTED)	STRESSED COUPLE (RIGIDLY SEPARATED)	FAMILY INTERVENTION COMMENTS FOR STRESSED COUPLE
COHESIVENESS	Emotional Bonding	Moderate to High	Low to Moderate	
	Independence	Moderate to High	Low to Moderate	
	Family Boundaries	Moderate to High	Low to Moderate	
	Coalitions	Moderate to High	Low to Moderate	
	Time	Moderate to High	Low to Moderate	
	Space	Very Low	Very Low**	**Work on promoting the sharing of physical space
	Friends	Moderate to High	Low to Moderate	
	Decision Making	Very Low	Very Low**	**Work towards joint decision making
	Interests & Recreation	Moderate to High	Low to Moderate	
ADAPTABILITY	Assertiveness	High to Moderate	Very Low**	**Work towards improved general assertiveness
	Control	Very Low	Moderate to Low	
	Discipline	Very Low	Moderate to Low	
	Negotiations	High to Moderate	Very Low**	**Work towards more structured negotiations & problem solving
	Roles	High to Moderate	Very Low**	**Work on improving role making and sharing
	Rules	High to Moderate	Moderate to Low	
	System Feedback	High to Moderate	Very Low**	**Work on more positive communication

left quadrant and described as being *rigidly separated,* which is atypical of family systems when the first child is born. The lower amount of cohesiveness in the stressed couple's system may have contributed to their difficulties with the transition to parenthood.

In addition, results from FILE — *Family Inventory of Life Events* reveal that the stressed couple experienced a recent (past six months) pile-up of family life changes in the areas of work and the family, family communication, recreational outlets, and unanticipated events, all of which appear to add to the family's vulnerability and strain. Specifically, the husband had recently acquired a second job. Even more recently he made a significant job change. Prior to that he had been experiencing increased conflict with his supervisor as well as co-workers. This situation was encumbered by an increase in work load. The couple's communication was hampered by increased expression of anger and marital conflict. They passed up an expected and desired vacation opportunity. Additionally, they experienced the unanticipated events of an automobile accident and their infant's hospitalization for eye surgery. Mother, in this case, experienced a loss of status and independence when she withdrew from her valued and responsible job with a resulting loss of income. In adapting to the situation, father's additional employment also meant a decrease in the amount of time he was available to his wife and family as well as minimal involvement in child care. Presumably, the stress resulting from the couple's difficulty in coping with this pile-up of life changes led to rigidity in their family system.

Goals and plans for crisis intervention. Attempts to intervene with this stressed family system could be made on several dimensions. It would seem most therapeutic to focus on those family issues and specific life changes about which the family had already expressed some concern and had indicated some effort toward resolution. The experienced pile-up of family life changes would seem to call for family efforts at *stimulus regulation* (*see* McCubbin and Patterson, Chapter 2). The family could be encouraged to direct attention to the changes in family life precipitated by the husband's second job and how they might bring their situation back into balance. First, they would do well to *regulate* any additional life changes that would add to their already overtaxed system. Second, the couple could be encouraged to restore sources of social support and family strength that were lost or severely taxed by this pile-up of life changes. For example, the wife's termination of her employment meant a loss of support for her. She might be encouraged to seek outside activities that would enhance her self-esteem and provide new sources of support. They might also be counseled regarding the cohesion and adaptability dimensions of their marital relationship. On the *cohesion* dimension, a goal would be to increase their awareness and appreciation of their strengths, particularly in the areas of emotional bonding, coalitions, time, friends, interests, and recreation. The treatment goals could include working on minimizing the physical and emotional gaps that appear to have been exacerbated by father's extra work commitments. Reducing the seemingly excessive distancing of father from child care routines and the development of opportunities for husband-wife relationships would be central themes for marital counseling. Concomitantly, there needed to be a concerted effort to work towards increased joint decision making on child care and routine family events.

Adaptability also would become a primary focus of intervention. There appeared to be very basic issues the couple needed to address to facilitate their successful transition to parenthood. As the Family Intervention Comments in Table 3-IV indicate, the adaptability goals for this family could be to work towards improved general assertiveness, more structured negotiations, and a concerted effort towards problem solving, improved role making and sharing, particularly in the area of child care, as well as enhancement of couple communication to include more positive feedback between parents. Because the family occupies an extreme postition along the adaptability dimension, helping the family system to move to a central level toward "structural connectedness" would presumably increase its ability to function and adjust to the hardships associated with the transition to parenthood.

CONCLUSIONS

The circumplex framework adds in an appreciable way to our understanding of and work with families under stress. Certainly, the model offers the theorist, researcher, and clinician a meaningful way to analyze, study, and influence families faced with normative and nonnormative life crises. This chapter underscores our need to understand family processes in adjusting to stress and calls attention to the impact of life change and stress on family systems.

Of equal, if not greater, importance in our work with families under stress, is the need to focus on not only intra-family adjustments, but also upon how the community may be used to provide support and facilitate family adaption to stress.

SECTION II
FAMILY STRESSORS,
COPING,
AND SOCIAL SUPPORT

Social and behavioral scientists have just begun to understand the highly complex manner in which families prepare themselves for life's stressors and hardships and the coping strategies they employ in recovering from the impact of life changes upon family stability and development (McCubbin et al., 1980). Recent investigations have shed light upon how internal family properties such as family cohesiveness and expressiveness serve to buffer and diffuse the penetrating impact of stressors. Lois Pratt (Chapter 4) has made a concerted effort to document what family characteristics are fundamental to "energized families," that is those most capable of promoting physical and emotional health. By describing her research and salient findings about family strengths she sets the stage for the remaining chapters, which attempt to document in greater detail the nature of stressors, the importance of active coping, and the supportive role family members play and the community plays in facilitating family adjustment and adaptation to transitions, stressors, and social change.

There is a considerable body of stress research focused on how families adjust to normative events and changes they experience over the life cycle. Transitions such as the birth of the first child, a child starting school, the launching of the youngest child and so on, have all been viewed as potential periods of family disorganization affecting overall family functioning. In Chapter 5, Elizabeth Menaghan reviews the theoretical and empirical literature regarding the effect of family transitions on marital experiences and presents findings from her own research on these supposed effects. Menaghan calls for a more rigorous approach to defining complex variables, such as transitions, in family stress research.

Chapter 6 also focuses on normative family stress, specifically on the hardships associated with the roles of spouse, parent, economic provider, and employee. Pearlin and Schooler attempt to delineate the normative coping responses men and women use to manage the persistent strains associated with these four roles. They distinguish between the *psychological* resources people have, such as self-esteem, and the *specific coping actions* they take, between what people *are* and what people *do*. Both of these must be studied, the authors argue, to understand the range of responses people make to manage their life strains.

The importance of this chapter lies in the careful conceptual groundwork the authors lay for further examination of the repertoire of responses to stressors and strains. Although they do deal with individuals, and not specifically with families, the strains and coping patterns they uncover have obvious relevance for family stress theorists and researchers. The reader should note, too, that the authors pointedly exclude the social resources, including family support from the purview of their study. By focusing specifically on other ways of coping, this chapter complements later chapters, such as Cobb's (Chapter 10) or Caplan's (Chapter 11), that look only at the role of social support. It is interesting, however, that, in their conclusion, Pearlin and Schooler return to the "collective" response to stress, reaffirming the need for social support, and social or political action to deal with the "failure of social systems in which individuals are enmeshed."

The dual-employed family has emerged as a very common life-style in the United States since 1970, partly in response to the cycle of inflation and recession in our economy and partly in response to the changing roles of women. Families are struggling to cope with the new "normative" stressors this life-style brings, as members balance their commitments to their work, to their families, and to themselves. In Chapter 7, Denise Skinner looks at *dual-career* families, where both spouses have strong commitments to their work. In reviewing the literature on this issue, she summarizes the specific stressors and hardships these families face. She outlines five coping patterns dual-career families may employ to cope with this life-style. The concept of a pattern or related groups of coping behaviors, which Pearlin and Schooler outlined in Chapter 6, is taken up again here and is an important idea for family stress researchers. Skinner also makes suggestions for family counselors who will be working with more such dual-career families in the coming years.

In Chapter 8, Phyllis Moen examines how families cope with the financial stressors of unemployment. She looks specifically at how families avoid economic vulnerability by relying on economic resources in their families, such as having a second-wage earner, and in the community, such as unemployment compensation or Aid to Families with Dependent Children. Her findings are of particular interest to those concerned about the effects of government social policies and programs on alleviating family stress.

In Chapter 9, social and behavioral scientists of the Minnesota Family Stress and Coping Project make an effort to link the Double ABCX family stress framework (Chapter 3) to the study of families with handicapped children. This chapter calls attention to the disturbing and disruptive effects of pile-up of stressors, the importance of both mother's and father's coping strategies, and the salient role the community plays in offering social support to families of handicapped children.

The role of the social network and the potential support it offers was touched on by Skinner, Moen, and McCubbin et al. in Chapter 7, 8, and 9 as part of the coping pattern families use. Indeed, this concept of social support has emerged as one of the most significant domains for research, theory building, and clinical application. Sidney Cobb (Chapter 10) sets forth the most widely used definition of social support: "information . . . leading a person to believe that she is loved, . . . esteemed and valued, . . . [and] has a defined position in a network of communication and mutual obligation." Cobb reviews the relevant literature to show how these different aspects of social support directly affect the health and development of individuals throughout the course of their lives. This review suggests that social support has both an *ameliorative* effect (in helping persons recover from stress) and a *buffering* effect (in protecting persons from experiencing stress).

In Chapter 11, Gerald Caplan expands on the concept of social support by clarifying the many ways a family is the primary source of support for individuals. He reviews the various ways in which a "healthy" family supports its members and how it has a "health-promoting and ego-fortifying effect" on children, youth, parents, and grandparents. Caplan's work has very clear implications for both public policy and professional practice. He has specific recommendations for legislators, educators, physicians, and other care givers that will enhance and augment the role a family plays in helping its members cope with stress.

Caplan and Cobb have defined the family as an important provider of social support and thus an aid in managing stress. In Chapter 12, Burke and Weir present findings from two studies that show what role the spouse plays in providing such support and what traits or behaviors enrich this aspect of marriage. At a time when the *quality* of married life is becoming more important for many people, the social support or therapeutic function of marriage is a timely subject for both family stress researchers and counselors.

Caplan outlined the ways in which families provide social support for individual members. He noted that the extended family — grandparents, aunts, cousins, and even friends — is very much alive today as a source of social support. The ideas Caplan identifies are played out in Harriette McAdoo's study of a group of black middle-class families under the extraordinary stressors in racism (Chapter 13). She shows how much they continue to rely on their extended family and kin network for support of various kinds. McAdoo's work is important for policy makers and counselors, who should, she argues, be sensitive to the role of kin support in black families.

Chapter 4

FAMILY STRUCTURE AND HEALTH WORK: COPING IN THE CONTEXT OF SOCIAL CHANGE

Lois Pratt

T HE prevailing cultural conceptions of how to maintain health and control disease influence what health responsibilities are assigned to families, and the nature of the responsibilities influences how successfully families will be in coping with health work. We are in the process of changing our beliefs about how to maintain health and control disease and are coming to believe that personal life-style is the crucial factor in health and disease, not medical care. Our changing view will significantly increase the family's responsibility for caring for their own members' health and preparing children to care for their health. It will also require families to view health from a longer time perspective and to plan over the course of a lifetime. There is evidence that families are tending to respond to these new interpretations of disease by modifying their living habits and their orientation to the medical care system. It is hypothesized that the emerging health responsibilities of families call for a family structure with capabilities that are different from those of the traditional form. The energized family appears to have these capabilities.

THEORIES ABOUT DISEASE

The belief system that has prevailed in science and popular thought during this century was a single-cause theory of disease (Dubos, 1959). These are the elements of that theory:

The evidence reported here is based on the study reported in: Lois Pratt, *Family Structure and Effective Health Behavior: The Energized Family.* Boston: Houghton Mifflin Company, 1976. The study was based on detailed personal interviews conducted in a northern New Jersey city of about 150,000 people, with a cross-sectional sample of families having a husband and wife in residence and at least one child aged nine to thirteen. Separate interviews were conducted with the husband, wife, and child. The final sample consisted of 510 families.

1. Each disease has its own particular cause;
2. The task of science is to isolate this pathogenic agent causing the disease;
3. Medical science will discover, one after another, the cause of each disease;
4. A drug will then be developed to conquer each;
5. It is the task of clinicians to focus on a particular organ or organ system that is diseased and treat the specific disease with a drug or surgical procedure that cures it;
6. Medical science has been the principal source of control over disease, and the medical practitioner has the specialized training to protect the health of the nation.

Our emerging theory of health and disease is a multiple-factor theory, (Engel, 1962; 1977; Lee and Kotin 1972) and the following are its elements:

1. Rather than the result of an infectious agent alone, disease occurs as a result of a complex interweaving of genetic factors in the host, the social and physical environment, a microorganism, and the agent that carries it.
2. Nothing remains unchanged. The pool of genes is constantly changing; man creates new noxious agents; the physical environment is modified; and microorganisms mutate.
3. We cannot expect to develop a drug to control each disease, for the causes of disease are too complex. Even if a drug does kill an offensive microorganism, the disease will not be controlled unless the underlying causes are controlled — the features of the social and physical environment that foster disease.
4. Medical science will not in the future be the major source of control over disease. Major improvements in health will have to be sought through modifying the environment and personal habits.
5. We can no longer hope to conquer all diseases or to achieve mastery over human health, for the causes of ill health are too complex to comprehend or to control.

What concerns us here is not the scientific validity of either of these theories in accounting for the cause and control of disease, but rather, the force of a particular set of beliefs in molding and justifying our health behavior and assigning responsibility for health care. In the past, our theory of disease justified the building of a vast medical technology and our reliance on medicine to protect our health. The emerging theory calls for the individual and family to assume responsibility for health.

FORCES FOR CHANGE IN THE THEORY OF DISEASE

New scientific evidence, as well as economic, political, and other social forces, are converging to bring about this reformulation of disease theory. Many medical scientists now conclude that medical science has very limited tools to control disease and to improve human health. They cite historical evidence that medical science was not the principal source of control over disease in the past. The major microbial diseases (plague, leprosy, and typhus) had all but disappeared before scientific medicine was an effective force. The gain in life expectancy was due more to better nutrition of children and to sanitary developments than to drugs and medical care. Others point out that medical technology does not now offer significant help for the major diseases found in contemporary society. There is no decisive technology for cardiovascular disease, which accounts for two-fifths of deaths (except for rheumatic and congenital heart disease); for cancer, which accounts for one-fifth of deaths; for stroke, which accounts for one-tenth of deaths; as well as for many other diseases ranking lower on the list (Thomas, 1977). Others cite the actual harm done by medicine — disability due to unnecessary surgery, adverse drug reactions, disease and death associated with hospitalization, and various other forms of iatrogenic disease.

A crucial form of evidence is research that shows that "control of the present major health problems in the United States depends directly on modification of the individual's behavior and habits of living" (Knowles, 1977). This is the so-called preventive life-style interpretation of disease. The supporting evidence emphasizes the effects of smoking, diet (especially high cholesterol and caloric intake), alcohol consumption, and lack of exercise on risk of cancer, stroke, heart disease, liver disease, and on overall life expectancy (Belloc and Breslow, 1972; Belloc, 1973); the effects on maternal and infant health of unplanned pregnancies and faulty prenatal health behavior; and the personal and social causes of accidents (such as failure to use seat belts), suicide, and homicide.

Social science research did not have much bearing on the old theory; its only work considered relevant were some practical studies on how to get the public to make regular visits to doctors and dentists and to comply with professional instructions. But the social sciences are becoming a central force in the emerging theory. A basic assumption of the social sciences is that it is useful to view any kind of behavior — health, crime, sex — within the social and cultural context in which it occurs. Studies have shown that the social setting in which illness comes about and is cared for affects how illness is experienced and the meaning it has in social relations. Studies are beginning to be done on how the family affects health. Studies of family violence are readily incorporated in the new theory, for they demonstrate a direct influence of the family on the member's health.

In addition to scientific evidence, economic and political forces exert pressure for a revised explanation of the cause and management of disease. As health care developed into our third largest industry, the American image of health care as an independent physician has been replaced by the image of a large and complex business system. The burgeoning costs and the performance failures of the health care system are viewed as a major national problem.

A solution that is being formulated to this problem is to call for more preventive health care and to place greater responsibility for health on the individual and family. The call comes from various positions on the political spectrum. One extreme urges dismantling of the medical care system and return to nontechnological self-care by families (Illich, 1975). Conservative political forces urge that access to medical care be restricted because the costs have risen to levels the society cannot afford. The Right To Die or Death With Dignity movement calls for limitation of heroic medical care measures that are administered to terminally ill persons, for the right of the dying person and family to call it quits and for more dying days to be spent at home rather than in the hospital. Some, in the women's movement, are attempting to demedicalize pregnancy and childbirth and to return normal childbirth to the home. There is an organized effort to induce women to breast feed babies. The natural health movement urges that the restorative capacities of the body be encouraged, especially by natural foods.

We are fashioning from these scientific, economic, and political ideas a set of beliefs about the cause of disease and the management of health that is serving as the basis for very different health policies and programs than we have had in the past. This is how the problem is being formulated: families have failed to develop and practice healthful living habits. The solution, then, is to get families to do their job effectively.

IMPLICATIONS FOR FAMILIES: ORIENTATION TO HEALTH

The earlier view of health and disease prompted us to consider health care as consisting almost entirely of medical care. We focused the family's efforts on clear-cut parcels of medical care action, such as getting the child immunized, taking the child for a checkup, and phoning or seeing the doctor when symptoms occurred. We framed and isolated health care as a limited set of ritual acts that signified taking care of children's health. Even when medical care did not provide a cure for an illness, the dramatic and concrete rituals — drawing blood, giving an injection, taking a blood pressure reading — sustained the conviction that this form of health care produced results.

Families were encouraged to place primary responsibility for health care on the professionals and were discouraged from meddling in health matters because they lacked proper training. The professionals showed little interest in mundane living habits, such as diet and exercise, regarding these as distractions in the diagnosis and treatment of disease. Thus, families received little encouragement to manage their life-style as a means of maintaining health.

As we come to accept a redefinition of health, every aspect of life is opened up as a potential influence on health that must be evaluated and managed — job, community, home, military service, recreation, and aspects of personal conduct such as sex, diet, exercise, smoking, alcohol, stress, exposure to chemicals, and risks of accident. Rather than calling for a revised set of routine preventive practices and simple restorative formulas, this demands overall *life-style management*. While medicalizing of health meant taking a problem out of its social-psychological-environmental context and isolating it for treatment, the new life-style construction of health means that any health problem must be examined in terms of the full complexity of the person's and family's life situation and in terms of past, present, and future life situation.

The professionals' role in health care remains large but becomes more specific. Families will be required to negotiate discriminately and assertively with the health care system in order to obtain service that complements their own skills and fulfills their particular needs. The responsibility for health care shifts largely to families because they are more knowledgeable than the professionals about their own pattern of life; only they can reform their living habits when those habits are found to endanger health; and only they can be expected to sustain the long-term commitment to the person's destiny that is the basis for managing health as a lifelong enterprise. This changed time perspective on health is one of the major implications of the emerging theory of health.

LENGTHENED TIME PERSPECTIVE ON FAMILY HEALTH

The new beliefs about health and disease call for a long-term time perspective on each family member's health. First, increasing stress is being placed on how parent's own health conduct may affect the later health of their children; hence, parents must regard their own behavior as child-health behavior. For example, women are told that stilbestrol taken in pregnancy increases the risk of cervical cancer in their daughters when the latter are young women. A wide range of diseases of women during pregnancy, including multiple sclerosis, diabetes, and measles, are now recognized as dangerous to the fetus.

Next, parents are urged to recognize that the child's own very early health behavior will affect his or her health years later. The diseases that are the principal causes of death, such as heart disease and cancer, take a long time to develop, and they are also the diseases in which style of life is causally implicated. Thus, parents are called on to prevent the diseases of middle and old age by planning life-style from the outset of the child's life. Here is an example of such an admonition from a newspaper health columnist: "Parents may have it in their power to help their children avoid an early death from heart disease, a disease that remains epidemic in this country . . . The researchers have come to view childhood as the arena for the prevention of heart disease and they are urging doctors and parents to be more vigilant than they have been up to now . . . (One doctor) has found that children as young as 2 years old already have cholesterol levels as high as that of young adults" (Flaste, 1977).

Evidence on obesity brings similar pressure on parents. It is reported that people who are overweight tended to be overweight as children and that fat cells developed in early childhood are not readily dissipated by later dieting. There is also a tendency to regard consumption practices as habituating, so that if parents allow their children to engage in faulty practices — overeating, excessive use of sugar, junk foods, and cigarettes — the children will find it difficult to rid themselves of these habits in later years. Recreation experts now urge that children be encouraged to select sports and recreational forms that they can participate in throughout their lives. Moral overtones may accrue to long-term life-style planning. As venereal disease cast shame on the infected person and stigmatized the family for their failure to provide a decent upbringing, so juvenile obesity or smoking, for example, may come to taint a family that fails to provide a protective life-style.

Another time dimension of planning the life-style is making appropriate changes as the family moves through the life cycle and the members' health needs change. Examples are to move to larger quarters as the family expands in membership and to adapt the existing quarters or move to a more suitable residence when a member becomes disabled. Since each family member is at a different stage in his or her individual life cycle, the adaptations made by the family to accommodate one member need to be coordinated with the time sequences of the other members; for example, to select a community and a time to move that are appropriate to the parents' health needs as well as the children's. Then there is the need to decide how much of total family resources to invest in health support facilities that will be useful for a particular segment of the life span; for example, whether a major commitment, such as the purchase of a boat or summer recreation home, provides good value in terms of the number of years of the family life span it will be used.

There is still another dimension of this need for the family to change over time. Increasing attention is paid to the role of *individual differences* in genetic background, physical makeup, life experiences, and environmental circumstances in determining who becomes ill, the course an illness takes, and response to therapy. This obligates both professional medicine and the family to regard each person as having a different potential for disease than any other and calls for individualized regimens of health protection.

An example of the particularlized versus universalistic version of human disease is seen in the debate over whether low cholesterol diet will, indeed, reduce the risk of heart disease in a population or whether individuals vary so widely in blood composition, in lipoproteins, for example, and, therefore, in response to diet, that a massive prescription of low cholesterol diet for the population would result in relatively small gains because only those with the relevant response characteristics would benefit.

As applied to the family, this approach to health means that no "tried and true" formulas can be developed on the basis of experience with a first child. A large body of research on birth order has shown that first births turn out to be quite different types of people from later births. What is appropriate for such a child may not work well with his or her later siblings. The parent's refrain, "Why can't you be like your brother Charlie?" is outmoded when we come to believe that each body is so subtly different from others, even within the same family, that each requires a health regimen adapted to his or her uniqueness.

Each family also has to coordinate its time sequences with historical time patterns. Cultural patterns prescribe the proper age for various health-related activities, such as the age at which it is acceptable to have sexual intercourse, to independently monitor one's own excretory functions, teeth cleaning, eating, and sleeping and to bear responsibility for one's own use of drugs, tobacco, and alcohol. It is easier to live congenially in a society when one's family time patterns correspond with those approved in the era in which one lives than when one defies the cultural clock. Some failures to coordinate with historical time patterns are punished and pose serious dangers to health. For example, people who are sexually active before the approved age may be denied valuable health care, such as birth control, abortions, and prenatal care. A person who is obese in a "slim" culture may be punished for failure to conform to the health and social standards of the particular historical time.

Of course, one of the basic obligations of parents has always been to help children adapt to basic cultural patterns. The emerging belief in the influence of social and environmental factors on health will sustain this child care principle by prescribing that the child must be guided to bring his or her life into congruence with a basic cultural prescription of the era — the norm calling for lifelong practice of healthful living habits.

In a society characterized by rapid scientific and technological change, an important aspect of adapting to historical time is keeping abreast of new and revised evidence concerning health and health care and modifying family health practices accordingly. Old truths are assaulted by new evidence and by new interpretations of old evidence. Often a new piece of evidence destroys confidence in an old truth without providing a positive alternative to replace it. For example, sugar is found to be a major cause of dental caries and obesity and indirectly of the many diseases associated with obesity. Cyclamates and saccharin do not cause those health problems, but each, in turn, is implicated in cancer. It is the nature of science that evidence is produced and released piecemeal, is tentative and subject to revision from new studies, provides only partial explanations, and seldom leads directly to clear-cut measures that families can practice. According to the new theory of health, families are expected to manage their lives so as to avoid disease; hence families will be called upon to keep up with the scientific evidence as it is produced, a responsibility that even professionals are hard pressed to fulfill.

FAMILY RESPONSE TO CHANGING HEALTH CONCEPTS

If the revised approach to health and disease has indeed taken hold, we would expect to find families beginning to respond to the pressures by changing their relationship to the health care system, for example, by attempting to reduce their dependence on professionals or by using medical services more selectively; by acknowledging responsibility for their own health maintenance; and by modifying their health habits in accordance with the preventive life-style doctrine.

Relationship to Professional Medicine

Now that more emphasis is being placed on personal health habits in an effort to deemphasize technological-professional medicine, one might hypothesize that families would tend to reduce their use of professional medical services. The fact is that this has not happened so far. The average number of physician visits per person per year has risen as follows: for 1963-64 — 4.5, for 1966-67 — 4.3, for 1969 — 4.3, for 1971 — 4.9, for 1973 — 5.0, and for 1975 — 5.1 (U.S. DHEW, 1975; 1979a). The rate of use has stayed up for every age, sex, race, income group, and region.

While families' overall use of professional services may not decrease, the basis of the family's relationship to the service network may be altered. Rather that viewing and using medical services within the allopathic medical viewpoint, families may come to select services according to the preventive life-style conception of health. We might then expect families to search for supplements or alternatives to technological forms of care.

A small segment of the population (12%) has turned to spiritual disciplines, such as transcendental meditation or yoga, as a method of attaining self-mastery and integrating the care of physical health with social and spiritual health (Gallup, 1976). The successful campaigns in twelve states to legalize laetrile represent rejection of the position taken by orthodox medicine regarding this substance and suggest a growing popularity of a naturopathic concept of disease and restorative processes. Resistance to a ban on laetrile may represent an early skirmish in a broader self-care movement aimed at checking the power of the orthodox allopathic medical system and restoring power to the public (Petersen and Markle, 1977).

There is other evidence of some erosion of public confidence in the efficacy and safety of medical care. One survey (General Mills, 1979) found that 80 percent of the adults sampled agreed (strongly or partially) that "many doctors are too quick to give medication these days. You have to worry about overmedication," and 62 percent agreed that "Some of the old-fashioned remedies are more effective than all of the new wonder drugs." But this study found that, while critical of medical technology, most people do not yet envision a reliable alternative, for 79 percent said they felt technology is the only way they know to solve current health problems.

Resistance to the medicalizing of health may be part of a growing general disenchantment with technology. Over 70 percent of Americans reported in a survey that they believe we have become too dependent upon machines and other technology, and only 5 percent reported no disenchantment with technology (LaPorte and

Metlay, 1975).

Yet the same study (General Mills, 1979) that found the public critical of doctors' tendency to overmedicate also found that three-fourths had a lot of confidence in doctors, and three-fourths had a lot of confidence in their own doctors as a source of health information — a much larger proportion than reported confidence in any other source of health information. Gallup (1977) also found that 73 percent reported a great deal or quite a lot of confidence in professional medicine in 1977, although this represented a decline from 80 percent reporting confidence in 1975.

Acknowledgement of Responsibility for Health

Survey evidence indicates that the overwhelming majority of Americans now consider that personal health habits rather than medical care are the essential basis for keeping a family in good health. Very few cite professional medical care as a means of maintaining health, and, when asked what health practices are overemphasized, medical drugs are mentioned most frequently (Stolz, 1967; Litman, 1971; General Mills, 1979). Good nutrition is cited most frequently as fundamental to health, and three-fourths of one sample felt that a major reason for poor health is improper diet (U.S. FDA, 1972). Nutrition and exercise are regarded as the health practices that have been given too little emphasis.

A majority of families now believe that they must take on health care as a formal task. They do not take good health for granted, and they believe that in order to be really healthy you have to work at it every day. Most significantly, they believe it is the *family's* responsibility to care for members' health. The vast majority state that parents have the main responsibility for teaching children good health habits (General Mills, 1979).

Coping With Health by Life-style Modification

The most direct indication of the effect of the changed conception of health and disease is whether families are tending to manage their living patterns to cope more effectively with known threats to health. I shall examine evidence on two life-style issues: first, effectiveness of controlling pregnancies and births in order to protect the health of mother and child; second, control of cigarette smoking, dietary fat intake, and exercise in order to protect against lung cancer, heart disease, and other health problems.

Control over pregnancy. Women who have unwanted births as a result of not controlling fertility have significantly greater risks of illness and death than women who prevent unwanted pregnancies by employing any of the major methods of fertility control (with the exception of pill use after age forty) (Tietze, 1969; Tietze, Bongaarts, and Schearer, 1976).

Greatest health protection is achieved by using a contraceptive that is harmless even though not fully effective and backing it up by abortion (Tietze, 1969). There has been a dramatic trend toward more effective control over fertility both by preventing pregnancies not wanted at all and by delaying pregnancies till the time wanted. Marital fertility declined by almost one full birth (by .91 birth) between 1961 and 1970, and virtually all of this decline was due to reduction of unplanned fertility (Westoff, 1976). That is, the decline was not due to reduction in the number of children people wanted or changes in the proportion of women married. The proportion of unwanted pregnancies was reduced by half from the 1950s to the 1960s. By 1972, the proportion of all births that were unwanted (not wanted at that time or ever) was down to 8 percent (Weller, 1976).

The most important source of this increased success in controlling fertility is the shift to the pill from other less effective methods — this accounted for 57 percent of the improved success in preventing unwanted pregnancies and for 53 percent of the improvement in delaying the next wanted pregnancy. The other source of improved control is the greater care with which the other methods of contraception were employed (Ryder, 1973). One can conclude that there has been a revolution in family control over fertility within this relatively short period of time.

The reproductive behavior of teenage girls is of special concern, not only as daughters whose health may be affected, but also as mothers of infants whose health may be impaired. The risks to the teenager mother's health from pregnancy and childbirth are accentuated because they are more likely than older women to delay getting prenatal care and to obtain late abortions. Infant mortality is highest when mothers are aged fifteen to nineteen, and the only other age approaching their rate is women ages forty to forty-nine

(Baldwin, 1976). The younger the mother the higher the incidence of low birth weight, a major factor associated with developmental problems, such as epilepsy and mental retardation.

How adequately have teenagers protected themselves against this risk to health? About 42 percent of teenagers are sexually active (Jaffe and Dryfoos, 1976). Fewer than a fifth of unmarried sexually active teenagers consistently use some method to prevent pregnancy and an additional three-fifths use one sometimes. About a million get pregnant during a year, and two-thirds of these pregnancies are not intended. Approximately 600,000 babies are born to teenage mothers in a year, making up a fifth of all births in the United States. This teenage reproductive activity exceeds that of other industrialized countries (11 percent in England, 7 percent in Sweden, and only 1 percent in Japan) (Baldwin, 1976). But it has been the declining fertility among women over age twenty that has made teenage fertility so visible, rather than an increase in teenage fertility rates (Jekel and Klerman, 1979).

While we are repeatedly warned of an epidemic, this is a gross distortion of the actual trend. From 1966 to 1975, birth rates for eighteen and nineteen-year-olds declined sharply, a rate of decline that was just about as sharp as that for older women. Among girls aged fifteen to seventeen, on the other hand, the birth rate rose slightly from 1966 to 1975 (from 35.8 to 36.6 per 1,000) (Ventura, 1977). While the young teenagers did not show a reduced birth rate in this period, neither did they launch an ever-increasing epidemic of births.

By 1975, about half of the sexually active adolescents had seen a physician or attended a clinic for contraceptive services, although this does not indicate whether they used or how effectively they used the methods they obtained. The abortion rate has also increased for teenagers from 1971 to 1975 (Jaffe and Dryfoos, 1976). The contraception and abortion patterns for teenagers suggest that sexually active teenagers are beginning to adopt the effective control practices that were adopted by older women during the 1960s.

Modification of smoking, diet, and exercise. Individuals' smoking practices tend to reflect family practices. In families in which both parents smoke, the children are about twice as likely to smoke as in families in which neither parent smokes; and having a spouse who smokes is a major factor in the maintenance of the smoking habit, especially for women (U.S. DHEW, 1979b). Hence, reductions in cigarette smoking are likely to reflect family efforts to modify health behavior.

Between 1964, when the surgeon general of the United States warned of the health hazards of tobacco smoking, and 1978, 29 million Americans quit smoking. It is estimated that 95 percent of these individuals were able to stop smoking without the assistance of organized or professional smoking-cure programs. The prevalence of regular smoking among adult males declined from 53 percent to 38 percent, but the proportion of adult women who smoke has remained at 30 percent. The rate for boys ages twelve to eighteen has remained the same (about 15%), and the rate for girls has increased to equal that of boys (U.S. DHEW, 1979b).

The total death rate from lung cancer has continued to increase. But the reduction in smoking among adult males is apparently beginning to have a selective effect: Male cohorts born between 1935 and 1944 have lung cancer death rates below those of previous cohorts. A long-term reduction of lung cancer requires that the present cohorts of teenagers replicate the 1964 to 1978 pattern of quitting smoking when they are older.

It was also in 1964 that the American Heart Association recommended a reduction of saturated fat in the diet. Over the ten years following that warning, Americans reduced their per capita consumption of animal fats by 57 percent and increased their use of vegetable fats and oils by 44 percent (Walker, 1977).

Some people are making remarkable changes in their exercise habits. One study reported that, in 1961, only a fourth of American adults engaged in vigorous exercise of any sort on a regular basis, and, in 1978, six out of ten were doing so. This left four out of ten people doing no vigorous activity at all (Perrier, 1979). Another study (General Mills, 1979) reported that 36 percent of adults get planned physical exercise at least several times a week, while 64 percent save planned physical exercise for weekends, exercise only occasionally, or do not exercise at all. This study found that the regular exercisers were tending to increase their exercise activity, but very few of the sedentary majority were doing more planned exercise.

The death rate from coronary heart disease had risen between 1950 and 1963, and then began to decline in 1965, the year that those changes in smoking, fat consumption, and exercise began to occur. Between 1968 and 1977, mortality rates for coronary heart disease dropped by 23 percent and for stroke by 32 percent (Levy, 1979). The question arises as to whether the decline in cardiovascular deaths is simply part of the broader pattern of decline in the death rate. Apparently the cardiovascular death rate is declining independently of the overall trend, for its decline exceeded the general decline by more than 60 percent in 1975 (Walker, 1977). The evidence suggests that a sufficient number of Americans have made changes in living habits in the past dozen years to have significantly affected the death rates for these major diseases.

Family Structure and Health Care

My hypothesis is that increasing the family's responsibility for maintaining their own health, as well as selecting and using medical services appropriately, requires a family structure with capabilities that are different from those offered by the traditional form. My evidence shows that there is a family form — that I have labeled the "energized family" — that appears to have the required capabilities. Energized families develop better personal health practices in their members, utilize professional medical services more proficiently, and sustain their members' health at a higher level than other families.

Here is the type of family in which members have the best *personal health practices*. All the members interact with each other regularly in a variety of contexts — tasks and leisure, conversation and activity, both inside and outside the home. Energized families develop varied and active contacts with other groups and organizations — the whole range of medical, educational, political, recreational, and business resources of the community that can be utilized to advance family members' interests. These families actively attempt to cope and master their lives, for example, by grasping the opportunity to join a sports team, seeking out information on how to improve their diet, and weighing the advantages and disadvantages of various jobs or hospitals.

The energized family tends to be fluid in internal organization. Role relationships are flexible; for example, laundry work may be shared, and everyone may take a turn at cooking. Power is shared, each person participating in decisions that affect him or her. Relationships among members tend to support personal growth and to be responsive and tolerant. Members have a high degree of autonomy within the family. Energized families promote their members' capacities to function fully as persons and develop their capability for taking care of themselves.

Notably, it is precisely in those dimensions in which the energized family differs most sharply from the traditional family pattern that it provides its most significant contributions to members' health practices. It is when *men* are deeply involved in internal family functioning — interacting with children and engaging in health education of children — that all the members' health practices are best, rather than the traditional pattern of having women monopolize this role. It is *women's and children's* activity outside the home that contributes most to health practices of the men as well as women and children. It is not good enough to have the man active outside the home, as in the traditional pattern; the women and children must also be personally involved in the broader world if the members are to develop responsible health behavior.

Energized families use *professional medical services* more effectively and appropriately than traditional families. That is they are more likely to have preventive medical checkups and immunizations and to obtain prompt care for symptoms. As far as use of professional services is concerned, the most important aspect of family structure is the extent of the family's links with the organizations, activities, and resources of the broader community. It is particularly by having women and children actively engaged in the community that the energized family achieves its advantages over the traditional pattern. These families develop the expertise and confidence in dealing with organizations that enable them to get the care they need from the medical care system.

The central finding concerning the effect of family structure on *health and illness* is that freedom is clearly better for health than discipline and control. Giving positive support to members' moves toward independence and to their efforts to cope and function was favorable to health. Punishment of children and obstructive conflict between husband and wife were related to many health problems. Both punishment and conflict represent tendencies to block the other person's efforts to function and to act independently without offering a constructive alternative, and this appears to be the underlying element that is harmful to health.

Some analysts have stressed that the family must concentrate on training its members to conform to the requirements and standards of societal institutions. In the professional health field, great stress is laid on the need for families to utilize the services, to comply with the advice, and to adhere to the procedures laid down by the providers. Yet the author's evidence shows that traditional disciplinary families are failing to develop sound health behavior and are failing to sustain their members' health. Providing the person with freedom to develop his or her full capacities turned out to be crucial for health, not restraint. Helping the person to cope and to deal assertively with outside organizations was essential for getting good professional health services and developing responsible personal health practices, not passivity and obliging conformity.

The author's evidence also shows that only a small minority of families have the structural capability that the author called the energized pattern. Only 10 percent of the families in the study sample had the composite of characteristics of the model, and another 20 to 30 percent had some of the features of the model. On the other hand, equally few families were nonenergized, as only 8 percent fell at the opposite extreme. Yet the energized form is not restricted to an eccentric segment of the population: it was found in all socioeconomic strata. This suggests that this family form has a broad societal base. If families are pressed increasingly to assume greater responsiblity for their members' well-being and if families are provided enabling resources to assume these expanded responsibilities, then the energized family may emerge as a dominant family form.

Chapter 5

ASSESSING THE IMPACT OF FAMILY TRANSITIONS ON MARITAL EXPERIENCE

ELIZABETH MENAGHAN

INVESTIGATORS who share a life span perspective have assumed that adult development and everyday life are organized by the demands of the enduring adult roles of worker, spouse, and parent. Role transitions — events signaling the assumption of a new social position, e.g., first job or the birth of a first child, exit from a particular role, e.g., widowhood or the launching of a final child, or major changes in the demands of an ongoing role, e.g., promotion or children's entrance into school — have been expected to have deeply felt repercussions, both on people's experience in related roles and in their overall psychological equilibrium.

Yet the impact of such transitions is largely putative, and few studies have explicitly linked their occurrence to changes in role experiences or psychological functioning. In this chapter, the author shall take advantage of short-term longitudinal data from a large Chicago-area survey to examine one of the most frequently asserted linkages — that between family transitions and changes in marital experience. Before discussing the author's own study, the author shall review the theoretical arguments and empirical evidence for this linkage.

THEORETICAL BACKGROUND

Why should family transitions — such as children's births, their school entrance, their becoming adolescents, and their eventual departure from home — be expected to affect parents' marital experience? The logic for the connection varies with the theoretical persuasion of the speaker. For example, psychoanalytic theorists focus on the parents' experience of and involvement with their children's psychosexual development and suggest that such involvement propels parents to rework their own, often partial, resolutions of issues of separation and connectedness, gratification and restraint, independence, interdependence, and isolation (Benedek, 1952). Such reworking, it is argued, reverberates on all of the important interpersonal relationships in parents' lives, including that with their spouses.

In contrast, *family developmental theorists*, e.g., Hill and Rodgers, 1964; Duvall, 1971; Rodgers, 1973, have focused more explicitly on specific transitions, and have specifically delineated and studied the "family life cycle" — the typical sequence of changes in family tasks and individual experiences from the time a man and woman marry, through the birth, development, and departure of their children, until one or the other spouse dies. Because they view the family as a dynamic role system, these theorists argue that pressures, constraints, or pleasures stemming from the life cycle position of any one family member can impinge on all of the other role relationships in the family. Just as a death in the family is an event occurring to a single person but affecting all of the survivors, so are events occurring to children also thought to affect all members of the family. Thus, the marital relationship is thought to be readily affected by the regular, age-linked changes in household membership and children's activities, which constitute the family life cycle.

Researchers and *theorists in adult development and aging*, in contrast to family developmental theorists, have focused less on differences between family stages and more on the stressful potential of the transition from one stage to another. Kimmel (1974), for example, discusses the birth of the first child as "a crucial turning point that involves considerable potential for emotional crisis" (p. 207) and suggests that the high divorce rate in the early years of marriage may reflect this potential crisis point. Lowenthal and her associates (1976) examine the marital dissatisfactions of women anticipating the departure of their last child. They suggest that at this transition, husbands' desires for nurturance and relaxation conflict with wives' vague desires for independence and self-assertion. Neugarten and Hagestad (1976) question the stressfulness of family transitions in general and that any such changes will invariably affect other role relationships. They argue that major stresses are caused by unanticipated events that *upset* the expected sequences and rhythms of life. Further, they argue that changes in one role are unlikely to affect other relationships uniformly since family roles allow for "role making," improvisation, and negotiation by the role partners themselves.

Even theorists who agree that family transitions may influence other roles are often vague in specifying the direction and extent of such influences. Hill and Rodgers (1964) have predicted that transitions that produce a change in *household structure* (the addition of a new member, or the departure of an established member), causing disorganization and renegotiation of family role relationships and reciprocities, will be particularly stressful. Among the factors Burr (1973, 1976) identified that help families avoid disruption from changes and/or recover from major disruption is the *amount of prior learning* about the change (either by watching others, reading, or experiencing the same or a similar event previously). Thus, transitions involving later children may be easier to handle than those involving the first child.

While the literature on transitions does not paint a coherent picture, it does suggest that transitions experienced for the first time may be more difficult for families to manage, and so be more closely associated with disturbances in the marital relationship. It also seems likely that if change is the crucial dimension, multiple transitions, for example, the oldest child leaving home about the same time that the youngest is entering adolescence, should be more difficult than single ones. Such double transitions, however, have not been examined empirically.

THE EMPIRICAL EVIDENCE

How well has empirical research supported a relationship between family stages and marital experience? The relationship has been largely inferred from simple visual inspection of synthetic longitudinal curves constructed from large cross-sectional studies (*see* Blood and Wolfe, 1960; Rollins and Feldman 1970; and Rollins and Cannon, 1970). The observed differences among marriages of different durations have tended to follow a "shallow U-shaped curve" (Rollins and Cannon, 1970), with satisfaction highest among preparental couples, lowest among school-age and teen families, and high once more among couples whose children are no longer living at home. This generalization has been widely quoted in the literature, often in language that suggests it was based on longitudinal data. For example, satisfaction is said to "drop" when children are born and "rise again" when they depart. As Rollins and Cannon point out, however, not only have such actual *changes* never been documented, but this pattern has not been found in all studies. It seems to appear and disappear depending on the aspect of marital experience investigated, e.g., companionship, spouse's understanding, spouse's love and affection.

Moreover, these cross-sectional surveys have not controlled for potentially confounding differences in economic resources, social class, family size, or occupational involvement. And even before disentangling such confounded effects, the absolute size of the differences that have been observed is not particularly impressive. The amount of variance in marital experience usually accounted for by family life cycle differences is "in a practical sense a relatively minor and unimportant trend in terms of its predictive value" (Rollins and Cannon, 1974, p. 277).

The differences are also quite inconsistent. Spanier, Lewis, and Cole (1975), after comparing three cross-sectional studies sharing similar methodology and measurements (one in Ohio, one in Georgia, and one in Iowa), found three different family life cycle patterns — a significant curvilinear trend in one, a linear negative trend in another, and no relationship at all in the third. They comment that "claims of curvilinearity in recent articles and papers may have been premature" (p. 271).

They also caution that in all of the results reported, including their own, initial cohort differences and selective survival effects are necessarily confounded with whatever true differences may exist. Each of the groups in the cross-sectional studies was married at a different point in time and reflects somewhat different historical and socialization experiences, somewhat diverging sex-role beliefs and differing histories of childrearing vogues and prohibitions. Differences among such groups may reflect such prior enduring differences among them as much or more than they reflect recent changes in response to parental transition points. Cross-sectional differences, in short, may not tell very much about the kinds of *changes* in marital experience that would be observed if one followed couples over time as they made transitions from one stage of family life to another.

Unfortunately, there are few such direct studies of changes in the marital relationship over time, and these few are also problematic.

In most studies, baseline data on characteristics of the marital relationship was not collected; many did not focus particularly on the
quality of the respondent's marital experience, and most have studied
only one transition, without comparison to a group experiencing
either different transitions or no transition at all (*see* Menaghan
(1978) for a more detailed summary of this literature).

Prior studies have also ignored the possible confounding effects of
two other factors likely to affect how one's marital experience
changes over time: individual coping strategies and individual nonfamily commitments.

Regarding coping strategies, Burr (1973) has reviewed and summarized a range of studies that suggest that when faced with a variety of stresses, those with greater comfort and efficiency in their current family organization and those with a greater ability to modify
habits and roles and adopt new ideas stand a better chance of
avoiding or minimizing disruption. At the individual level, family
transitions often necessitate changes in parental activities or in-
terfere with previous patterns of interaction between spouses; thus,
they have the potential to cause one spouse or the other, or both, to
feel unfairly imposed upon or deprived of appropriate affectionate
rewards and opportunities for fulfillment. When such feelings are
generated, respondents with less effective ways of coping with problems or negotiating solutions should be less successful in restoring
more positive conditions. As Pearlin and Schooler (Chapter 6) have
pointed out, coping adequacy is not randomly distributed among
people, but tends to vary with age, sex, income, and education. In
assessing the impact of family transitions, then, it becomes important to separate differences in established coping strategies from differences in family transitional experience.

Regarding the influence of nonfamily commitments, family
developmental theorists agree that the impact of any one change in
family roles on marital conditions may be influenced by the role
responsibilities those same actors hold in other systems. A transition
bringing new or more demanding activities to a parent is most likely
to produce role strain in people who are already absorbed in other
activities and are unable or unwilling to reduce their total set of
demands (Burr, 1973). It may be only under such conditions that a
particular family transition provokes marital problems. Even under
these conditions, it is not clear that the marital partner will feel un-

justly treated. Sieber (1974), discussing the advantages of multiple role involvement, suggests that the more visible role commitments a person is juggling, the more role partners feel reluctant to press for better performance in any one area. Thus, the direction of effects is unclear. But it does seem important to separate the effects of family transitions themselves from any concurrent pressures arising from husbands' and wives' commitments in other role areas, especially the occupational sphere. Yet this has not been done in prior studies.

In short, while a linkage between family transitions and changes in marital experience has often been asserted as if already demonstrated, the logic for the connection remains vague; supporting evidence for the association is often weak, conflicting, and cross-sectional; and other variables modifying this relationship have not been systematically examined or controlled. The present study has attempted to avoid some of these methodological pitfalls, and thus to offer a more definitive test of the linkage between family transitions and marital experience. It compares the impact of a range of such transitions; it includes information about role conditions prior to the transitions; and it controls for factors that may confound the relationship between family transitions and marital experience, such as demographic idiosyncrasies, other role commitments, and established coping strategies.

METHOD

The Study Population and Measurement of Major Variables

Data for the findings to be discussed here are derived from a panel study of 1,106 Chicago-area adults, aged twenty-two to sixty-nine, interviewed in 1972 and 1976. Samples and procedures for the larger study, which focused on social stresses in everyday life, life events, and adaptation, are described in detail elsewhere (Pearlin and Radabaugh, Pearlin and Schooler, Chapter 6; Pearlin and Lieberman, 1979). The 1972 interview included measures of self-esteem, sense of mastery, and psychological adaptation; sources of difficulty and emotional distress associated with marital, parental, occupational, homemaking, and economic roles; reports of coping strategies used in each of these areas; neighborhood and friendship involvements; and physical health. Identical measures of role-related difficulties and dissatisfactions, coping strategies, and overall psychological adaptation were included in the Time Two (1976) survey. In addition, the interview ascertained whether any of twenty-two possible transitions or other life events had occurred in the time between interviews. (More details about the study including descriptions of questions, results and analyses are available from the author.)

This design has several important advantages. First, since identical information about marital experience was obtained at each time point, prior marital experience could be controlled in assessing the effects of the intervening transitions — an enormous advance over previous analyses of transitional impact. Second, the breadth of the study design provided information about concurrent conditions and changes in other nonfamily roles, so that effects of transitions could be separated from such changes. Specifically, four patterns of occupational change were distinguished, both for respondents and their spouses: moving into the labor force; moving out of the labor force; remaining continuously employed; and remaining out of the labor force at both time points. Finally, the Time One data provided an assessment of the individual's approaches to handling marital problems — their overall coping repertoire. This was assessed by a set of six coping factors originally identified by Pearlin (and more fully described in Pearlin and Schooler, Chapter 6) to tap three possible kinds of coping behavior: active efforts to change an undesirable situation; attempts to reinterpret the situation by denying the importance of problems or focusing exclusively on more positive aspects; and efforts to manage the anger or hurt feelings an undesirable situation might provoke. Multiple regression analyses showed that each of six coping factors had a significant, independent effect in reducing felt emotional distress, even when reported difficulties were held constant. The effective marital coper that Pearlin and Schooler found exerted effort to change his situation and used optimistic comparisons to interpret his situation positively, but he avoided emotional discharges, selective ignoring of problems, and passive endurance and did not seek help or advice from others. For this analysis, the overall effectiveness of each person's coping repertoire was measured by summing over the six subscales. In order to ensure that our measurement reflected coping strategies *prior* to the occurrence of transitions, this information was collected at the initial interview.

Before discussing the characteristics of the transitional and stable groups, the conceptualization of marital experience used here should be explained. The literature is replete with studies and measures of marital adjustment, quality, and satisfaction, some of which have been reviewed by Spanier (1976). Many of these have inferred marital quality from the frequency of specific actions — for example, the number of joint activities, the frequency of sexual intercourse, or the extent of agreement on specific topics. However, such a procedure assumes prior knowledge of the relationship between such behaviors and the quality of the respondent's experience of the marriage — knowledge that is usually uncertain or nonexistent. The approach here, in contrast, takes the participants' assessment of their marital conditions as the ultimate basis for evaluating the success of a relationship. In this view, feelings of inequity, isolation, and frustration of expectation are more important than reports of frequency of particular activities and behavior. For example, we do not ask questions about who does what, but ask whether the respondents feel that their partners expect more from them than they are willing to give in return; similarly we ask, not how often intercourse occurs, but whether the respondents feel their spouse is a good sex partner. In short, we focus on respondents' subjective experience of the relationship between themselves and their spouse.

Two aspects of marital experience were distinguished. The first, labeled equity, focuses on the perceived justice or equity in the marriage, the balance between what partners feel they give to the relationship and what they obtain. The second aspect, labeled affection fulfillment, taps issues of the spouses' love, affection, and appreciation, and the extent to which the spouse is seen as enhancing respondents' freedom to be the kind of person they wish to be.

These two aspects of marital experience were initially identified by respondents in open-ended interviews as important elements of marital experience, and each significantly influences the emotional distress people associate with their marriages; such emotional distress, in turn, is strongly related to overall depression, even when distress stemming from other roles is controlled. While these two aspects of marital experience clearly do not capture all of the complexity of marital relationships, they do seem to be important to individuals' emotional lives. Equity and affection fulfillment are also important to the continuance of marriage: Time One scores clearly discriminate respondents who subsequently divorced from those who remained married. Thus, we can be fairly confident that the measures used here capture important aspects of people's marital experience.

Because *change* in marital experience is the major dependent variable, the study population is restricted to people married to the same partner at both time points, who could be classified into one of ten transitional and four stable (no family transitions) groups. The ten transitional groups include eight who had experienced a single transition (becoming a parent for the first time, having a later child, seeing the oldest child start school, seeing the youngest start school, seeing the oldest become a teen, seeing the youngest become a teen, seeing the oldest move away from home, and seeing the youngest leave home), and two who had experienced double transitions (oldest became teen and youngest started school, and oldest started school and youngest child born). Four categories of stable groups were distinguished: childless people; parents whose children were all living at home at both time points (to be referred to as "stable full house"); parents who had already "launched" some older children prior to Time One, but had not had any transitions in the ensuing four years ("stable launchers"); and parents whose children had all left home prior to the first interview ("stable empty nest"). The total sample size, then, was 639, 259 stable and 380 transitional respondents.

The ten transitional and four stable groups differed in fairly predictable ways by age, education, number of children, and occupational patterns. For example, new parents and those whose children were just starting school were younger and somewhat better educated than those facing later transitions; they also had fewer children. Wives' movements into and out of the labor force were also related to the transitions they had experienced. Among the new parents, half of the wives had stopped working; while among those whose youngest had just started school, 31 percent had moved into the labor force. The youngest starting school seemed to be a watershed of sorts. For family stages earlier than this, fewer than 20 percent of wives were employed outside the home; while from that transition on, about half were employed. There was a downturn in wives' work participation; however, among the oldest groups, both those whose youngest had just left home and those with a stable empty nest. The presence of such group differences in demographic characteristics and occupational involvements, of course, points up the necessity of controlling for such differences when examining the impact of family transitions.

RESULTS

Family Transitions: Subjective Appraisals

One way of assessing the impact of transitions on people's lives is to ask them directly how they think they were affected. Such subjective appraisals are not necessarily related to objective changes in any one role area or even in overall well-being, but they do offer some sense of the average felt ease or difficulty of various events. Accordingly, the present study asked respondents (a) whether there was anything about the transition that bothered them, and if so, how bothered they were; (b) whether they were pleased or excited about the transition, and if so, how much; (c) whether the transition changed their life in some ways, and if so, how much; and (d) whether the transition changed the way they felt about themselves.

These four dimensions of change were only moderately interrelated for any transition. Perceptions of life change and self-change were more closely related than the two questions about affect. For most transitions, being troubled by a transition was relatively independent of reported pleasure or excitement. Respondents reporting high life change or high self-change were both more likely to be pleased and more likely to be bothered than respondents not reporting change.

Taken as a group, family transitions were not evaluated as particularly traumatic: only 17 percent of the respondents were somewhat or very bothered, 23 percent thought their lives had changed a great deal, and 17 percent thought it had changed the way they felt about themselves. Table 5-I displays the comparable percentages for a variety of other life changes; one may note, for example the rather strong impact of occupational events as a class.

Table 5-II displays the differences in appraisals by kind of transition. The transitions most frequently considered troubling, as family developmental theory predicts, were those which changed the composition of the family household: births and departures. Feelings of great pleasure, on the other hand, were concentrated among transitions coming earlier in the family life cycle, particularly births. Parents seemed more ambivalent about children becoming teens or leaving home, with increasing proportions not at all pleased by these occurrences. Contrary to expectation, there was little difference in appraisal by whether a first or last child was involved in the transition.

Appraisals of bother and pleasure were largely similar for men and women. There were two exceptions: women were more both-

Table 5-I

Appraisals of Selected Transitions in Major Roles

Event	My life changed very much	My feelings about myself changed	I was somewhat or very bothered
Parental Transitions			
First child born	78[a]	53	30
Later child born	57	36	28
Oldest started school and younger child born	18	22	9
Oldest started school	22	19	6
Youngest started school	22	20	15
Oldest became teen & youngest started school	15	18	12
Oldest became teen	4	5	17
Youngest became teen	5	5	12
Oldest left home	17	11	22
Youngest left home	21	0	21
Occupational/Economic Changes			
Entered labor force	72	62	35
Voluntary job change	67	44	20
Demoted	not asked	not asked	67
Temporary job disruption	40	16	43
Family standard of living declined	50	27	39
Marital Changes			
Got married	71	39	not asked
Became divorced or separated	88	73	84
Became widowed	81	35	90
Health Changes			
Decline in own parents	27	16	41
Problems with own health	44	36	56
Problems with spouse's health	25	not asked	56
Problems with children's health	21	not asked	61

[a]Percent of those experiencing the event.

Table 5-II

Appraisals of Family Transitions

Transitional Group	N	BOTHERED			PLEASED			LIFE CHANGED Men			LIFE CHANGED Women			SELF CHANGED
		not at all little	only a little	somewhat-very much	not at all	only a little-somewhat	very much	not at all	only a little-somewhat	very much	not at all	only a little-somewhat	very much	Yes
First child born	(32)	57	13	30	0	4	96	0	25	75	0	20	80	53
Later child born	(37)	69	3	28	3	21	76	14	36	50	16	21	63	36
Oldest started school & later child born	(33)	75	16	9	0	28	72	17	67	16	10	71	19	22
Oldest started school	(17)	94	0	6	6	38	56	71	29	0	33	23	44	18
Youngest started school	(55)	79	6	15	15	38	47	88	4	8	29	36	35	20
Oldest became teen & youngest started school[a]	(34)	68	20	12	12	67	21	36	50	14	35	50	15	18
Oldest became teen	(41)	78	5	17	42	41	17	64	36	0	69	24	7	5
Youngest became teen	(60)	81	7	12	41	29	29	86	14	0	68	22	10	5
Oldest left home	(37)	28	48	22	41	27	32	68	16	16	22	61	17	11
Youngest left home	(34)	18	62	20	47	27	26	50	38	12	33	39	28	0
Totals	(380)	65	18	17	24	32	44	54	27	19	35	36	28	18

[a]Rounded average of individuals' appraisals of the two transitions experience.

ered by births, first and later, than were men ($X^2(2) = 4.77$; p = 0.09); and women reported greater pleasure when their oldest child entered school ($X^2(2) = 6.29$; p = 0.04).

Assessments of self-change and life change did not cluster by either presence/absence of household change or oldest/youngest child involved. Only the births of the first child evoked feelings of self-change for more than half of the respondents; other births and children's school starts prompted such feelings only for some; and self-change was rare or completely absent for the teen and departure transitions. Transitions were more frequently linked with changes in their lives, especially for women. Men and women agreed about the strong impact of births, but they diverged significantly in the life change brought by children's school entrance: 44 percent of mothers, but not a single father, felt their lives changed a great deal when their oldest child started school, and 36 percent of mothers, as compared to 8 percent of fathers, associated the youngest starting school with a great deal of change. The later transitions, even children's departures, were not often appraised as highly life changing by either men or women.

Thus, neither changes in household composition nor transitions occurring to oldest children were uniformly appraised as more demanding than others. While births brought the greatest changes and some bothered feelings, they were also associated with the greatest pleasure; while children starting school brought life change, especially for women, this did not seem to arouse negative feelings or much change in sense of self. Teenage transitions did not emerge as particularly impactful one way or the other; and departures brought more bothered feelings but not much sense of change in self or life.

In short, parents' appraisals of the personal impact of family transitions do not consistently identify any one transition, or kind of transition, as either overwhelming or exhilarating. Nevertheless, there *were* differences among the transitions in appraised impact. Our next task was to examine changes in marital experience over time in order to see whether some transitions had clear repercussions, positive or negative, on married life.

Family Transitions and Marital Experience: Comparisons

We have noted that prior studies of this linkage have been flawed by a failure to control for possible group differences in demographic composition, such as social class, family size, or proportions of men and women, for differences in established coping strategies and styles, and for differences in other nonfamily commitments, particularly employment status. Most seriously, prior studies have generally lacked information about prior marital conditions and hence could not know to what extent any observed differences merely reflected differences anteceding any particular transitions. The analyses reported here incorporate these controls and thus offer a more appropriate test for effects of family transitions on subsequent marital conditions.

Two kinds of comparisons are possible. First, we may ask to what extent transitional experiences make such groups different from stable groups. Second, we may make comparisons among the transitional groups, and we can use such comparisons to address the three expectations raised by prior research and theory:

1. Changes in family household compositions will bring more negative marital changes.
2. Transitions involving the first child will bring more negative change.
3. Multiple transitions will be more disruptive of prior marital conditions.

Turning first to comparisons *between* transitional and stable groups, we discover no overall differences between the two groups taken as wholes, either in marital equity or in affection fulfillment. This lack of difference, of course, is easy to dismiss, since it could be caused by offsetting combinations of positive and negative effects or by the dilution of strong marital effects by insignificant ones. In order to assess the real impact of such transitions, we cannot lump them all together in this fashion.

As a first step in sorting out their different effects, each transitional group can be compared to its most similar stable counterpart, e.g., new parents are contrasted to the childless and to the stable full house group, and the oldest left home group is contrasted to the stable launchers. By and large, these specific contrasts are also unimpressive. Not a single transition can be distingished from a stable group on changes in affection fulfillment, and only two of ten transitions can be so distinguished on the marital equity measure. The two exceptions are a slight but significant positive shift in felt equity when the youngest child had left home and a negative shift for the transition combination of oldest turning teen and youngest starting school.

Comparisons *among* transitions are similarly inconclusive. Contrasting transitions involving household membership change with all others, we find no evidence that such transitions are more disruptive; in fact, the evidence is in the opposite direction, though failing to reach conventional levels of statistical significance. Although births are associated with more self-appraised change than are departures, these two different sorts of membership change do not have distinguishably different effects. Although household membership changes may bring more alterations, they do not bring clear shifts in marital equity or affection fulfillment.

What of the suggestion that one benefits from past experience in managing later transitions? Contrasting oldest versus youngest child for each of the four transitions fails to confirm this generalization. The effect of later births tended to be slightly more negative, in fact, and school starts and teenage transitions do not differ by marker child in their effects. Only departures follow the predicted pattern and only for changes in equity.

Finally, we examine whether transition combinations have more negative consequences than their single components. Here, the evidence is split: one combination (oldest became teen and youngest started school) is significantly more negative, while the second (oldest entering school and additional child born) is not. The generalization that such multiple changes are more disruptive to the marital dyad is not supported.

A series of tests for interaction among independent variables was also pursued, in order to discover whether the effects (or lack of them) of transitions might be conditional on certain levels of other variables, or different for men and women. However, these tests failed to suggest any modifications to the growing suspicion that the link between family transitions and marital experience would not be supported by these data.

DISCUSSION

No single study, of course, is ever conclusive, particularly one that fails to demonstrate predicted effects. Nevertheless, we are left with an uneasy feeling. The relentlessly consistent lack of explanatory power of the transitional variable in these data, coupled with the methodological problems of earlier analyses, almost forces the researcher to reexamine the basic question: Are family transitions in themselves all that important in shaping marital experience?

As the review of the theoretical underpinnings of the concept began to suggest, family transitions may be potential stressors at best. They offer points at which parental activities may shift; they offer opportunities for role reorganization for some families; and they may bring individual feelings of temporary distress and bother. For most people, however, such transition points bring no more or less disturbance to their married life than stable groups may experience over the same time span. The implicit assumption of family theorists — that such changes are stressful and that such stress tends to disrupt intimate relationships — does not seem to be supported.

As Neugarten and Hagestad (1976) have pointed out, such transitions are so thoroughly expected and anticipated and have been vicariously experienced so often in the course of an ordinary life that their stress-inducing potential may be neutralized. Similarly, Burr's (1973) suggestion that the amount of prior learning about a change increases one's ease in management, rather than predicting that a final child's transition will be easier than a first's, may in fact suggest that both kinds of transitions, because they are so heavily anticipated, are relatively easy to manage.

In some ways, however, the changes that children's births, departures, and transitions bring to adult lives, even if expected, remain quite real and palpable. Life is never quite the same again after one becomes a parent. Common sense and ordinary experience support some linkage between children's activities and parents' intimate relationships. Whether they are thought to bring spouses together, pull them apart, block the expression of affection, or satisfy needs for fulfillment, there always seems to be some enduring, if diffuse, impact. It seems premature, despite the failure of more rigorous analyses to document it, to abandon the hypothesis that such transitions will shape marital experience over time.

Why then are empirical attempts to trace such effects so inconclusive? The major reason for the absence of clear transitional effects in this study and the conflicting and minor ones shown in earlier analyses the author may lie in what some promoters of the concept claim as its cardinal virtue: its "packaging" of a broad set of typically interrelated phenomena into a single organizing concept. In identifying family life cycle stages and transition points, we are implicitly scanning across a range of career lines and mentally totalling up their separate impacts. Transition categories thus are used to imply at least three separate sets of possible changes: changes in the content of the parental role, changes in patterns of economic consumption and economic pressure, and changes in participation in nonfamily roles. To the extent that these parallel lines of change are only loosely linked to each other and to specific transitional points in actual lives, our categorizations become blurred and difficult to interpret.

In discussing changes in *parental* roles, we generally use transitional points as a sort of rough shorthand for a broad set of only loosely related variables that we think change over time. One is the sheer amount of *time and energy* expended in child care and the number of hours per day that children will ordinarily be at home and requiring supervision. The impression is that, as children grow older, time demands decline in a jagged curve from the near continuous demands of newborn children to the relatively complete autonomy of young adults. A second group of variables refers to the *psychological demands* of parenting: the degree of daily preoccupation with children's actions, problems, and general development; the effort to impart values and to shape behavior; and the feelings of parental responsibility for children's current and future lives. The author would submit that we know very little about how such variables wax and wane over the life span; certainly we do not know enough to link them with specific events in children's lives. A third set of variables embraces the *rewardingness of interaction* with one's children at various ages: the amount of parental pleasure, the frequency of parent-child struggles for control, the opportunities for shared interests and companionship, and intensity of conflict over values and behavior. Once more, there is some cultural consensus on temporal patterns here, but it is doubtful that we can generalize *a priori* with any safety. There is wide variation in "favorite ages" of children, and different parents clearly seek different rewards of interaction with their children. Can we really identify some nadir in parent-child interaction that will be the same for all parents?

Changes in *economic* pressures and consumption patterns similarly vary over time, but the pattern probably differs depending on the pace of childbearing, total family size, social class, material desires, and definitions of "necessities." The points of economic pressure that have been identified (*see*, for example, Oppenheimer's (1974) discussion of the "life cycle squeeze") tend to hold only for some occupational groups, seem gradual in their onset, and span several stable periods as well as transition points. While years married or family life cycle stage may pick up some of these shifts, the linkage ignores large variations within categories.

Similarly, family transitions have tended to imply simultaneous changes in parents' involvements in *nonfamily* roles; mothers' participation in paid employment is usually the major change envisioned. Again, there is a broad pattern of labor force exits and entrances related to children's age. Once more, however, empirical studies document a range of employment sequences of married women, and if anything, the variation may be expected to increase in the future. Not all wives leave the labor force at childbirth, not all rush in as soon as the youngest child starts school. Women in the labor force vary in the pleasure they derive, the hours per week and months per year they are on the job, and the extent to which household maintenance tasks continue to be defined as their responsibilities. Similarly, the economic and intrinsic rewards that husbands are able to obtain from paid employment shift over time, as trainee status gives way to increasing seniority, possible promotions, changes in specialization, and opportunities for supervision. Once more, however, the linkage between job experience and stage in the family life cycle is a loose and variable one.

In short, the concepts of family transitions and family stages connote a wide range of loosely associated changes over a broad span of simultaneously occupied roles. The very richness, evocativeness, and breadth of these concepts are precisely the qualities that make them inappropriate explanatory variables when we seek to understand the empirical connections between experiences in related roles. The language we customarily use to discuss family changes over time — milestones, turning points, crises, transitions — implies a degree of clarity, coherence, and discontinuity that is seldom empirically justified when attention is turned to concrete lives over time. The variation *within* the categories on each of these parental, occupational, and economic dimensions makes it unlikely that we shall find consistent differences and handicaps our understanding of whatever differences we do find. It could be argued that it is the task of the empirical researcher to disentangle the separate threads underlying family transition categories and to measure them directly if we hope to understand which among them are the critical variables shaping marital experience, or indeed other role experiences as well.

Of course, we have no guarantee that the marital relationship is particularly affected by any of these more specific variables either. Linkages between role experiences may not be as strong or as invariant as we have supposed; certainly, we have not yet formulated compelling theoretical rationales for any specific predictions. Despite the popular and critical attention devoted to marital success and failure, social scientists have learned very little about how much marital experience changes over time or how much other role experiences influence the direction or extent of such change. The author would suggest that answers will not emerge until we stop importing complex package categorizations like "transitions" uncritically into empirical research and begin working directly with the discrete continuous variables they have been combining. While the notions of family transitions and family stage have served to sensitize us to the temporal dimensions of family life and will probably continue to serve as a convenient shorthand in discussion and pedagogy, it is time to abandon them in empirical research.

Chapter 6

THE STRUCTURE OF COPING

LEONARD I. PEARLIN AND CARMI SCHOOLER

B Y coping we refer to the things that people do to avoid being harmed by lifestrains. At the very heart of this concept is the fundamental assumption that people are actively responsive to forces that impinge upon them. Since many of these impinging forces are social in their origins, the understanding of coping is a prerequisite for understanding the impact that societies come to exert on their members. Yet we know relatively little of the nature and substance of people's coping repertoires and even less of the relative effectiveness of different ways of coping. This paper deals with these issues first by specifying some of the life-circumstances that people find problematic, next by identifying an array of coping mechanisms people use in attempting to deal with these problems, and then, by assessing the efficacy of the coping mechanisms so identified. Finally, we shall examine some of the linkages between the social characteristics of people and their coping behavior.

The limited attention social science has given to coping stands in striking contrast to its long and abundant interest in circumstances that are potentially deleterious to the well-being of people. Classic examples include such circumstances as the discontinuities between early socialization and the demands confronted later in life (Benedict, 1938), the contradictions among the norms that define situations and actions (Stouffer, 1949), the disparities between different dimensions of status (Jackson, 1962; Lenski, 1954) that are frustrated by limited opportunity structures (Merton, 1957). By confining its attention largely to conditions that are possibly harmful and by ignoring ways of avoiding harm, social science has left knowledge about coping primarily to clinical workers. This has understandably resulted in a distinct tendency to regard coping as a

From Leonard Pearlin and Carmi Schooler, The structure of coping, *Journal of Health and Social Behavior, 19:*2-21, 1978. Copyright © 1978 by the American Sociological Association. Reprinted by permission of the American Sociological Association.

highly individualized defense against threats aroused in highly individualized situations. Since its focus is primarily on intra-psychic phenomena, a clinical approach to coping tends to overlook the presence of institutionalized solutions to common life-tasks (Mechanic, 1974). By contrast, the present analysis emphasizes enduring and widely experienced life-strains that emerge from social roles and, moreover, it is exclusively concerned with coping modes that are shared by people who also share key social characteristics. Our interests, therefore, lie with normative coping responses to normative life-problems.

Over the years, coping has acquired a variety of conceptual meanings, being commonly used interchangeably with such kindred concepts as mastery, defense, and adaptation (White, 1974). Because of its multiple meanings, it is necessary that we specify our own working definition. Essentially the concept is being used here to refer to any response to external life-strains that serves to prevent, avoid, or control emotional distress. Thus, we regard coping as inseparable both from the life-strains experienced by people and from the state of their inner emotional life. In order to understand coping and to evaluate its effectiveness, it is, therefore, necessary to examine it in the context of the problems with which people have to contend and the potential emotional impact of those problems. Following a brief description of the background of this inquiry, we shall specify in greater detail the strains and stresses to which coping is linked.

BACKGROUND AND METHODS

The data presented here are part of a larger investigation into the social origins of personal stress. A cluster sample of households was drawn, using techniques and procedures that are described in detail elsewhere (Pearlin, 1975; Pearlin and Radabaugh, 1976). The information was gathered through scheduled interviews with a sample of 2300 people representative of the population in the Census-defined urbanized area of Chicago. Only people between ages 18-65 were interviewed, for it was desired to have a sample weighted in favor of those actively engaged in occupational life. Where more than one person in a household satisfied these age criteria, the older candidate was systematically chosen. The sex of the person to be interviewed in each household was predesignated so that the final sample would have as equal a number of males and females as possible. This restriction was ignored only in households where all age-qualified respondents were of the same sex. Because females typically head such households, the final sample contained more women than men.

The interview schedule was designed to yield several distinct types of information. First, it asks people about potential life-strains — that is, conflicts, frustrations, and threats — that earlier exploratory interviews had revealed to be commonly experienced in major social role areas. Second, the interview includes a number of questions about the coping repertoires people employ in dealing with the strains they experience in these roles. And third, it inquires into the emotional stresses that people feel and the extent to which they experience symptoms of depression and anxiety.

THE CONTEXT OF COPING, LIFE-STRAINS AND EMOTIONAL STRESS

From a sociological perspective many of the difficult problems with which people cope are not unusual problems impinging on exceptional people in rare situations, but are persistent hardships experienced by those engaged in mainstream activities within major institutions. Whereas many studies of stress have examined people faced with extreme and somewhat unusual threats and trials, such as impending surgery (Janis, 1958) or the grim competition experienced by students seeking a Ph.D. (Mechanic, 1962), this study focuses on people engaged in very ordinary — indeed, required — pursuits. Thus, we are fundamentally oriented to aspects of structured social experiences that adversely penetrate people's emotional lives.

There is a vast array of such experiences arising within the boundaries of the multiple roles that people typically play. However, we shall confine our attentions to the persistent life-strains that people encounter as they act as parents, job holders and breadwinners, husbands and wives. By strains we mean those enduring problems that have the potential for arousing threat, a meaning that establishes *strain* and *stressor* as interchangeable concepts. The strains that are included for study here were identified from themes that surfaced repeatedly during relatively unstructured interviews with over 100 subjects. Standardized questions about these strains were gradually developed, tested, and included in the final interview schedule. The role areas around which our questions center do not by any means exhaust the sources of social strain, nor are we capturing all strains that exist within each of the roles. Those life-strains that we have succeeded in identifying, however, do represent problems that are frequently outstanding in the experiences of people in their roles as marriage partners, economic managers, parents, and workers.

Because our structured questions about life-strains were so closely developed from the progressively focused exploratory interviews, we were reasonably optimistic that our items were conceptually meaningful at the outset. Some further refinement was achieved, however, by subjecting the questions about life-strain to factor analysis, the items within each of the four role areas constituting separate pools of information. Eleven factors were delineated, three in marriage, three in the parental area, one in household economics, and four in occupation.

The second conceptual domain to which coping behavior is inseparably bound involves stress. Because stress is a phenomenon studied by representatives of several disciplines, and because it can be manifested at different levels of organismic functioning, it is understandable that there is confusion about its "real" meaning. Our treatment of the concept is constrained by the fact that it is being assessed through a household survey of a normal population, requiring that its physiological and biochemical manifestations be bypassed. Instead we rely on the reported experience of emotional upset as our indicator of stress, looking exclusively at the unpleasant feelings of distress of which people are aware.

Not all such unpleasant feelings necessarily represent what we regard as stress. Emotional stress, as we conceive of it, is primarily distinguished from other negative states by its specificity. It is specific in two related respects: by being determined by particular strainful and threatening circumstances in the environment, and by being a condition that has clear boundaries rather than an enveloping, total state of the organism. By contrast, extreme anxiety and depression, which may very well develop from intense and enduring stress, are more global and diffuse. These disturbances may cling even in the absence of specific threats; they do not vary as their hosts move from one situation to another, and they often dominate one's entire affective life. But as we are treating it, stress is primarily linked to areas of life that are problematic, with the result that one area of life may be insulated from the stresses being experienced in another.

Consistent with this view, we developed several meausures of stress, one for each of the role areas in which strains are being assessed. The measures themselves are based on adjective check-lists. These lists were presented to respondents as the last series of questions asked about a particular role. For example, following all other questions about occupation, respondents were told: "I want to know now the kinds of feelings you get when you think of your day-to-day job — your daily working conditions, your pay, and other benefits, and the people you work with. Adding up all the good and bad points about your job, how — — — do you feel?" The interviewer would repeat the last part of the question, using a different adjective each time — bothered, worried, tense and so on. There were four intensity categories from which subjects chose their response to each adjective and the responses were then factor analyzed. The same format was employed to construct separate stress measures in each of the role areas.

DIMENSIONS OF COPING

Coping needs more detailed specification than either strains or stresses, both because it is pivotal to our analysis and because of the bewildering richness of behavior relevant to it. We shall outline some of the broad dimensions of the concept and at the same time describe the more concrete aspects of coping that have been selected for study here. Following this the issue of coping efficacy will be taken up.

At the outset a fundamental distinction needs to be made between *social resources, psychological resources,* and *specific coping responses.* Resources refer not to what people do, but to what is available to them in developing their coping repertoires. Social resources are represented in the interpersonal networks of which people are a part and which are a potential source of crucial supports: family, friends, fellow workers, neighbors, and voluntary associations. The configurations of these networks in the lives of people, the conditions under which they can be drawn upon, and the obligations and costs their use incur are all somewhat complex issues and are outside the scope of this paper.

The general psychological resources of people, on the other hand, are very much in the purview of the present analysis. Psychological resources are the personality characteristics that people draw upon to help them withstand threats posed by events and objects in their environment. These resources, residing within the self, can be formidable barriers to the stressful consequences of social strain. Three have been incorporated into this analysis: self-esteem, self-denigration, and mastery. Self-esteem refers to the positiveness of one's attitude toward oneself and is a factor formed from items in the Rosenberg (1965) scale. Self-denigration, an independent factor derived from the same original pool of items, indicates that extent to which one holds negative attitudes toward oneself. Mastery, finally, is assessed by a measure constructed for this study and concerns the extent to which one regards one's life-changes as being under one's own control in contrast to being fatalistically ruled. Other aspects of personality that represent potential psychological resources for coping were also examined. These include measures of denial, general tendencies toward escapism, and dispositions to move toward or away from people when troubled. They will not figure into our analysis of efficacy because, as measured here, they were found to have no coping functions.

In distinction to general psychological resources are the specific coping responses: the behaviors, cognitions, and perceptions in which people engage when actually contending with their life-problems. The psychological resources represent some of the things people *are*, independent of the particular roles they play. Coping responses represent some of the things that people *do*, their concrete efforts to deal with the life-strains they encounter in their different roles. Such responses may indeed be influenced by the psychological resources of individuals, but they are conceptually and empirically independent.

Questions concerning coping responses were developed in the same manner as those dealing with role strains. That is, in the open-ended exploratory interviews people were asked not only to identify the problems they face, but also to describe how they attempt to deal with them. Thematic examination of these interview materials suggested a number of coping patterns, and questions tapping these patterns were gradually developed, tested, and standardized. Responses to these questions, thus, yielded a body of information about coping within each role area; they were then factor analyzed and scored to proved the measures of coping that we shall be using. There is a total of 17 such factors, some of the factors containing many items.

It needs to be recognized that the 17 coping responses captured by this single study constitute but a portion of the full range of responses people undoubtedly call upon in dealing with life-exigencies. But although the specific coping responses under consideration here are by no means exhaustive, they can be viewed as a sampling of three major types of coping that are distinguished from one another by the nature of their functions. These are: (1) responses that change the situation out of which strainful experience arises; (2) responses that control the meaning of the strainful experience after it occurs but before the emergence of stress; and (3) responses that function more for the control of stress itself after it has emerged. We shall describe each of these coping functions in greater detail below, suggesting at the same time where among these each of our 17 coping factors falls.

It would seem that *responses that modify the situation* represent the most direct way to cope with life-strains, for they are aimed at altering or eliminating the very source of strains. In fact, however, such responses were not among the types of response frequently mentioned by people in the exploratory open-ended interviews. Thus, on prima facie ground only three out of the 17 factors have this as a primary function: *negotiation in marriage,* the use of *punitive discipline* in parenting, and the *optimistic action* factor in occupation, while two other responses, the *seeking of advice* in both the marital and parental roles, may be seen as responses potentially preparatory to acting on the situation.

Given the many conceivable ways that people may act to modify or eliminate situations productive of strain, it is surprising that it is not a more commonly used type of coping than it apparently is. There are several possible reasons for this. First, people must recognize the situation as the source of their problem before they can mobilize action toward modifying it, and such recognition is not always easy. Next, even when the sources are recognized, people may lack the knowledge or experience necessary to eliminate or modify them. Third, actions directed at the modification of one situation may create another unwanted situation, resulting in an inhibition of the coping action. Finally, some of the most persistent strains originate in conditions impervious to coping interventions, thus discouraging individual ameliorative coping efforts. Clearly, then, there are several conditions that can deflect people from directing their efforts toward the modification of a problematic situation, regardless of how reasonable this kind of coping action might appear on the surface.

In circumstances where coping does not succeed in changing the situation, and thereby fails to eliminate the problem, the stressful impact of the problem may nevertheless be buffered by *responses that function to control the meaning* of the problem. The way an experience is recognized and the meaning that is attached to it determine to a large extent the threat posed by that experience. Thus, the same experience may be highly threatening to some people and innocuous to others, depending on how they perceptually and cognitively appraise the experience (Lazarus, 1966). By cognitively neutralizing the threats that we experience in life-situations, it is possible to avoid stresses that might otherwise result.

There are many devices that function in this way. Indeed, it is by far the most common type of individual coping, encompassing most of the responses identified by this study. One such frequently used coping mechanism involves the making of *positive comparisons*, a device captured in such idioms as "count your blessings," "we're all in the same boat," an so on. Thus conditions appearing to an outside observer as very difficult may be experienced by people as relatively benign when they judge the conditions to be less severe — or no more severe — than those faced by their significant others. Misery truly loves company. Comparisons may entail a temporal frame of reference as well as one formed by significant others. Thus, if hardship is evaluated either as being an improvement over the past or as a forerunner of an easier future, its effects will be tempered.

Another perceptual device that functions to control meaning, also measured in each of the role areas, is *selective ignoring*. Selective ignoring is typically attained by casting about for some positive attribute or circumstance within a troublesome situation. Once found, the person is aided in ignoring that which is noxious by anchoring his attention to what he considers the more worthwhile and rewarding aspects of experience. One's ability to ignore selectively is helped to trivializing the importance of that which is noxious and magnifying the importance of that which is gratifying. There are other devices similar to selective ignoring, these involving the hierarchical ordering of life-priorties. The *substitution of rewards* in occupation and the *devaluation of money* in the area of household economics are instances of this. In both cases people are attaching a differential importance to different areas of their lives. They may succeed in avoiding stress to the extent that they are able to keep the most strainful experiences within the least valued areas of life. When confined to life-areas defined as of secondary importance, strains are less likely to result in stress because they are less likely to threaten the self. The hierarchical ordering can, thus, function to shrink the significance of problems and, in this way, minimize the resultant stresses.

The third type of coping functions neither to alter the situation generating the stress-provoking strains nor to create congenial perceptions of problematic experiences within the situation. This type of coping functions more for the management of stress than for its vitiation. Such coping mechanisms essentially help people to accommodate to existing stress without being overwhelmed by it. The open-ended exploratory interviews revealed a variety of sentiments, some of them quite familiar, that potentially function in this manner: try not to worry because time itself solves problems; accept hardship because it is meant to be; avoid confrontation; those who are good-naturedly forebearing will be rewarded; take the bad with the good; just relax and difficulties become less important; everything works out for the best. These kinds of themes suggest that out of the beliefs and values in the culture people are able to create a strategy for manageable suffering, a strategy that can convert the endurance of unavoidable hardships into a moral virtue.

Clearly, this strategy brings together a number of orientations to life-problems: denial, passive acceptance, withdrawal, an element of magical thinking, a hopefulness bordering on blind faith, and belief that the avoidance of worry and tension is the same as problem solving. The actual identification of concrete coping responses having stress management functions is somewhat difficult, however, for there is often nothing intrinsic to behavior that signals that this function is being served. Thus, we know that some people watch television (Pearlin, 1959) or use alcohol (Pearlin and Radabaugh, 1976) for this purpose, but we know, too, that others engage in the same behaviors for very different reasons. Consequently, there is a vast array of responses that have the potentiality of being pressed into service for the management of stress but that may have other meanings as well.

Despite the variety, coping mechanisms of this type have in common their attempt to minimize the discomforts engendered by problems, but are not directed to the problems themselves. Of the 17 responses delineated in this study, four can be seen as functioning primarily for stress management. Two of them are in marriage: *emotional discharge vs. controlled reflectiveness,* where the former refers to the expressive ventilation of feelings as a way of handling marital problems; the other is *passive forebearance vs. self assertion,* the first pertaining to the containment of feelings and the avoidance of conflict, the second to a more open recognition of problems in moving toward conflict resolution. A third response of this type is represented in the parental *potency vs. helplessness resignation* factor, where resignation in effect proclaims the child as being beyond influence, thus possibly exempting the parent from a sense of failure and guilt. Finally, in the economic domain is *optimistic faith* in one's financial future, a rose-colored view of one's economic fate that perhaps helps to keep financial stress within manageable bounds. There are undoubtedly many more responses that stand side by side with these in people's repertoires, but the four included here touch on some of the principal themes and orientations underlying the management of stress.

Coping, in sum, is certainly not a unidimensional behavior. It functions at a number of levels and is attained by a plethora of behaviors, cognitions, and perceptions. It is useful, moreover, that coping responses be distinguished from what we have identified as psychological resources for coping, those personality characteristics that minimize threat to self. As important as psychological resources may be in confronting life-strains, we cannot completely understand coping without looking beyond the personality attributes of individuals to the specific responses to problems in different social roles. This will become evident in the evaluation of coping efficacy.

COPING EFFICACY

The fanciful ultimate in coping is where people deal so effectively with life-strains that they are permanently and completely eliminated, thus obviating the necessity of coping repertoires. Under these unlikely circumstances one would find neither problems nor coping responses to them. But, of course, people do not eliminate completely or permanently the conflicts, frustrations, and other life-strains engendered by societies. There may be periods of time when there are no active demands to cope, but even during these interludes coping patterns are ready to be mobilized when the need arises. The effectiveness of a coping behavior, therefore, cannot be judged solely on how well it purges problems and hardships from our lives. Instead, it must be judged on how well it prevents these hardships from resulting in emotional stress. Indeed, our criterion for weighting efficacy is simply the extent to which a coping response attenuates the relationship between the life-strains people experience and the emotional stress they feel. It is because of variations in coping efficacy that people exposed to similar life-strains may harbor quite different levels of stress.

Our criterion for evaluating coping efficacy rests on the examination of a full array of variables: the life-strains people experience in each of the four role areas: their psychological resources: the coping responses they call upon in dealing with the strains: and emotional stresses they feel. For the most part we shall rely on regression analyses, a technique appropriate to the multivariate nature of the issues with which we are concerned, and well-suited also to confirming the conceptual distinctions and independent effects of life-strains and the coping responses to them. The analyses will be organized around several queries concerning coping efficacy: (1) Are there some coping responses and coping resources that are appreciably more effective than others? (2) How does the effectiveness of specific coping responses compare with that of psychological resources? (3) Does the sheer scope and variety of a coping repertoire have any bearing on its effectiveness? Following the consideration of each of these issues, we shall be in a position to deal with a final question: What kinds of people employ what kinds of responses with what kinds of advantages?

What Coping Mechanisms Work Best?

The most fundamental question to which we can address

ourselves is whether coping merely creates within people the illusion that they are doing something of consequence or if, indeed, coping does help to avoid or manage stress. And if it does help, can we identify a particular mechanism or set of mechanisms that is especially efficacious. We shall observe first the efficacy of coping responses and then turn our attention to the coping resources.

Because coping is examined separately in each role, it is necessary to create four regression equations. Included among the independent variables are the strains within a particular role together with the different coping responses used in the role. The measures of strain are constructed by summing the scores that respondents have on the various strain factors within the role. This measure essentially represents the overall level of intensity with which people experience problems in the role area. Measures of coping are simply derived from respondents' scores on each of the various coping factors. It needs to be noted that in Table 6-I, which presents the results of these analyses, the coping variables are labeled so as to indicate that an increase in the named response is associated with the minimization of stress. The more one employs a particular response the more stress decreases, except in cases of selective ignoring, which in the marital and parental areas, is preceded by the word "low." This labeling is used to indicate that in these two areas the exercise of selective ignoring exacerbates stress, while in the economic and occupational domains "low" is not used, for in these areas the same response helps to contain stress.

To understand the presentation and meaning of the findings in Table 6-I, attention should first be directed at the vertical column showing the regressions of stress on strain. In marriage, for example, the standardized bivariate regression coefficient of stress on strain before taking account of copings is .62. One can then assess the effect that each of the six coping responses (X_1 to X_6) has by observing the reduction in the regression of stress on the role strain as the coping responses are added to the equation. It can be seen that at each step the relationship between marital strain and marital stress is reduced, the final coefficient being .30. These results indicate that whether or not the strains experienced by people in their marriages lead to emotional distress depends to a substantial extent on their coping responses to the strains. Coping has corresponding though smaller effects on the relationships between strain and emotional stress in parental and economic roles, but it makes no difference to this relationship in the occupational area. This resistance to coping efforts in occupation will appear throughout the analysis, suggesting that coping is least effective in areas of life, such as job, that are impersonally organized and in which the forces affecting people are beyond the kinds of personal coping controls that we have been examining. But within the three other roles, it is apparent that the things people do can make a difference in avoiding or minimizing the stressful impact of life-strains.

Are there specific responses that are especially outstanding in this regard? The answer to this question can best be found by examining

TABLE 6-I. STEPWISE REGRESSIONS OF STRESSES ON LIFE-STRAINS AND ON COPING RESPONSES IN DIFFERENT ROLE AREAS (STANDARDIZED)*

Role Area	Strains	Coping Responses						R²
		X_1	X_2	X_3	X_4	X_5	X_6	
Marriage								
Low Strain	.62							.38
Self-Reliance vs. Advice Seeking (X_1)	.58	.22						.43
Controlled Reflectiveness vs. Emotional Discharge (X_2)	.54	.23	.20					.47
Positive Comparisons (X_3)	.48	.24	.21	.12				.48
Negotiation (X_4)	.42	.25	.22	.14	.13	·		.50
Self-Assertion vs. Passive Forbearance (X_5)	.35	.27	.24	.17	.16	.15		.52
Low Selective Ignoring (X_6)	.30	.27	.25	.19	.17	.17	.14	.54
Parenting								
Low Strain	.48							.23
Positive Comparisons (X_1)	.40	.23						.28
Self-Reliance vs. Advice Seeking (X_2)	.37	.23	.14					.28
Low Selective Ignoring (X_3)	.36	.25	.15	.12				.31
Non-punitiveness vs. Reliance on Discipline (X_4)	.34	.25	.16	.13	.09			.31
Exercise of Potency vs. Helpless Resignation (X_5)	.33	.24	.16	.13	.09	.05†		.32
Household Economics								
Low Strain	.65							.43
Devaluation of Money (X_1)	.59	.17						.45
Selective Ignoring (X_2)	.58	.20	.15					.47
Positive Comparisons (X_3)	.54	.22	.15	.11				.48
Optimistic Faith (X_4)	.51	.25	.12	.12	.10			.49
Occupation								
Low Strain	.47							.22
Substitution of Rewards (X_1)	.47	.09						.23
Positive Comparisons (X_2)	.47	.09	.06					.23
Optimistic Actions (X_3)	.47	.09	.06	.05				.24
Selective Ignoring (X_4)	.47	.09	.06	.05†	.01†			.24

* All coefficients significant at the .05 level or better unless indicated by (†).

the bottom horizontal line of coefficients in each role, for it is here that direct comparisons of the relative independent efficacy of the different responses can be made. These coefficients are arranged, from left to right, in the order of the magnitude of their importance to stress. The first coefficient on the bottom row, in each of the four areas, shows the regression of stress on strain with the coping completely taken into account. The remainder of the coefficients along the bottom row reflect the independent relationships of each of the coping responses (X_1 through Xn) to stress after all the other responses are entered into the equation.

In the first three areas it is possible to discern that some responses are more effective than others, although differences among adjoining responses tend to be quite small. Again taking the marriage area as an illustration, and looking across the bottom line, .27 units of stress are dependent on one unit of the first coping variable (X_1, self-reliance vs. advice seeking), and .14 units of stress depend on the extent to which people eschew selective ignoring, the last and least important coping variable in the marital area (X_6). With regard to occupation, the comparison of the coefficients reveals that the amount of stress alleviated by any of the responses is considerably more limited than in the other areas. This, of course, is consistent with what we earlier observed of the general resistance of occupational problems to coping interventions.

Except in occupation, then, there are appreciable differences between the most effective and least effective responses. At the same time, the effect of any single coping mechanism is rather modest. Beyond these general observations, however, are some more specific patterns that should be pointed out. A somewhat surprising result is that self-reliance is more effective in reducing stress than the seeking of help and advice from others in the two areas in which it is possible to observe its effects, marriage and parenthood. This unexpected finding reminds us that help-seekers are not necessarily the same people as help-receivers, for the most effective copers may be those who have the capacity to gather support from others without having to solicit it. At any rate, it is evident that we do not yet know the conditions under which help from others can be effective.

Two additional observations can be made, one pertaining to the occupationl and economic areas, the other to marriage and parenthood. It is interesting that in economic and, to a modest extent, occupational roles, the most effective types of coping involve the manipulation of goals and values. In economics this entails the demeaning of the importance of monetary success, the devaluation of money. In limiting the importance of money, the deprivations that might ordinarily be felt as a result of having limited resources are buffered. In occupation, the corresponding response is the substitution of rewards, involving the devaluation of the intrinsic rewards of work and a valuation of extrinsic rewards, such as pay and fringe benefits. People seek to control stress in occupation, though without much success, by keeping work itself in a place secondary in importance.

But the manipulation of broad values and goals is far less psychologically wieldy in the close interpersonal relations of marriage and parenthood than it is in the household economics and occupational spheres. One cannot as easily demean the importance of a spouse or of a child as he can devalue his work or an unattainable life-style. On the contrary, the most effective responses in marriage and parenthood are those that involve the eschewal of avoidance and withdrawal. In marriage it is a reflective probing of problems, rather than the eruptive discharge of feelings created by the problems, that is among the more effective responses. Similarly, the most effective type of response to parental strains is not resigned helplessness, but the conviction that one can exert a potent influence over one's children. It appears that problems arising in the close interpersonal relations of family are least likely to result in stress when people remain committed to and involved in those relationships. The opposite is true in matters of money and work; here stress is less likely to result when people disengage themselves from involvement. It is important to understand that the observed stress-reducing efficacy of the various coping mechanisms is independent of the intensity of the role-strains. This independence is rooted in regression analysis itself, for the Beta weights reflect the changes produced by one variable after the effects of the others are controlled (Blalock, 1960).

Using the same procedures we employed in Table 6-I, we turn now from specific coping responses to a consideration of the relative effectiveness of the general psychological resources. For our present purpose we enter separately the three variables — self-denigration, self-esteem, and mastery — into a regression analysis, just as we did with the specific coping responses. Looking first in Table 6-II at the vertical columns showing the regressions of stress on role strains, it can be seen that these characteristics do help to reduce the relationships between strain and stress. In what is now a familiar pattern, the reduction is smallest in the occupational realm, but even there it is evident that the psychological resources embodied in self-attitudes can help blunt the emotional impact of persistent problems.

TABLE 6-II. STEPWISE REGRESSIONS OF STRESSES ON LIFE-STRAINS AND ON PSYCHOLOGICAL COPING RESOURCES (STANDARDIZED)*

Role Area	Regression Coefficients of Stresses on:				
		Psychological Resources			
	Strains	X_1	X_2	X_3	R^2
Marriage					.39
Low Strain	.62				.42
Low Self-denigration (X_1)	.57	.18			.43
Mastery (X_2)	.53	.20	.13		.44
Self-esteem (X_3)	.52	.20	.14	.07	
Parenting					.22
Low Strain	.47				.26
Low Self-denigration (X_1)	.43	.20			.29
Mastery (X_2)	.41	.20	.18		.30
Self-esteem (X_3)	.40	.20	.18	.09	
Household Economics					.43
Low Strain	.65				.46
Low Self-denigration (X_1)	.63	.19			.49
Mastery (X_2)	.57	.20	.17		.51
Self-esteem (X_3)	.55	.20	.19	.14	
Occupation					.22
Low Strain	.47				.27
Low Self-denigration (X_1)	.43	.22			.28
Self-esteem (X_2)	.43	.22	.10		.29
Mastery (X_3)	.42	.22	.11	.08	

* All coefficients significant at the .05 level or better.

With regard to the relative importance of the three resources, there is a clearer order than could be discerned among the responses in Table 6-I. In part this is because there are fewer variables involved, partly because the effects of the same dispositions are simply being re-observed in the different role areas, but mainly because there is considerable stability in the relative efficacy of the different resources from one role area to another. Thus, in all four role areas, stress depends more on self-denigration than on the other personality dimensions. And, with the exception of occupation, mastery is a close second in importance, positive self-esteem a third. There is, then, a fairly clear order in the efficacy of people's psychological resources in vitiating stress: freedom from negative attitudes toward self, the possession of a sense that one is in control of the forces impinging on one, and the presence of favorable attitudes toward one's self.

Which is More Efficacious: What People Do or What People Are?

According to Lazarus, Averill and Opton (1974), much of the research on coping has given greater emphasis to psychological dispostions that to situational specific responses to situational conditions. Traditionally, coping ability has been judged solely on the possession of personality characteristics that help people defend against external threats: having the "right" personality characteristics enables one to deal with life-problems effectively, whatever the nature of the problems or wherever they might spring up. According to this perspective, people develop modal styles of dealing with life-strains, styles that transcend role or situational boundaries. By contrast, we have been underscoring specificity, attempting to identify particular responses to life-strains in particular role areas. We need not debate which is more effective — the general psychological resources or the specific responses — for, within the limits of our data, we are in a position to observe the relative contributions of the two coping mechanisms.

To judge which is the more efficacious — personality characteristics indicative of the possession of psychological resources (self-denigration, mastery, and self-esteem) or specific responses to specific role strains — summary scores of the two types of coping were created. In the case of the specific responses, these scores were computed simply by adding respondents' scores on the separate coping factors within each role area. The same procedure was followed in forming a summary score for the three psychological resources; in this instance, however, there is but one measure that is being reobserved in the different role areas. The relative efficacy of coping responses and psychological resources could then be judged by placing the two summary measures in the same regression analysis, together with the role strain scores. This enables us to determine whether it is the responses or the resources that is more important in controlling the relationship between strains and stress. In Table 6-III strain is entered first in each of the equations, the other variables appearing in a stepwise fashion. Again the vertical columns show the changes in the relationship of stress and strain as the other variables are added to the equation. With the exception of occupation, where there is again little reduction in this relationship, it is clearly better to be armed both with a repertoire of responses and a reservoir of resources than to have either alone.

TABLE 6-III. REGRESSIONS OF STRESSES ON ROLE STRAINS, COPING RESPONSES AND COPING RESOURCES (STANDARDIZED)*

Role Areas	Regression Coefficients of Stresses on:			R^2
	Strains	Responses	Resources	
Marriage				
Strains	.62			.39
Coping Responses	.29	.50		.53
Coping Resources	.26	.46	.15	.54
Parenting				
Strains	.47			.22
Coping Responses	.36	.27		.29
Coping Resources	.32	.22	.21	.33
Household Economics				
Strains	.65			.22
Coping Resources	.55		.30	.36
Coping Responses	.46	.21	.26	.41
Occupation				
Strains	.46			.21
Coping Resources	.42		.22	.26
Coping Responses	.42	.05	.21	.26

* All coefficients significant at the .01 level or better.

More to the point of the present question, however, are the regression coefficients along the rows, for these show more directly the relative importance to stress of coping responses and psychological resources. In marriage, coping responses are considerably more important in blocking stress than are resources, this difference being reflected by the coefficients of .47 and .15, respectively. In the parental area, the advantage of coping responses almost disappears (.21 vs. .20). In dealing with problems of household finances, there is a turnabout, the regression of stress on resources now being somewhat greater (.26) than it is on responses (.21). In occupation, finally, stress hinges much more closely on psychological resources than on specific responses, although, as we earlier noted, neither has an appreciable part in buffering the stressful effects of job strains.

From these results it is again evident that the problems arising in the relatively impersonal milieu of occupation are less amenable to coping — either by the weight of one's personality or by the weight of his response patterns — than are problems occurring elsewhere. In the close interpersonal context of marriage, and to a lesser extent in parenting, it is the specific things that people do in dealing with life-strains that determine most closely whether or not they will experience emotional stress, while possessing the "right" personality characteristics is somewhat more effective in dealing with economic and job problems. In the light of these differences, it would be better to rephrase our question to ask not which is the more effective, response or resource, but where is one or the other likely to be the more effective. The evidence indicates that it is the psychological characteristics that are the more helpful in sustaining people facing strains arising out of conditions over which they may have little direct control — finances and job. But where one is dealing with problems residing in close interpersonal relations, it is the things one does that make the most difference.

Does a Varied Repertoire Help?

It is apparent from the foregoing analyses that the kinds of responses and resources people are able to bring to bear in coping with life-strains make a difference to their emotional well-being. And it is equally apparent that there is no single coping mechanism so outstandingly effective that its possession alone would insure our ability to fend off the stressful consequences of strains. The magical wand does not appear in our results, and this suggests that having a particular weapon in one's arsenal is less important than having a variety of weapons. The single coping response, regardless of its efficacy, may be less effective than bringing to bear a range of responses to life-strains. Perhaps, effective coping depends not only on what we do, but also on how much we do.

Probably the most direct way to assess the variety of one's coping repertoire is by simply counting the number of responses that one actively invokes among those being measured in the four role areas. We have done this by, on each of the seventeen coping factors, identifying respondents whose scores are above the mean or, in the case of coping responses that exacerbate stress, respondents whose scores are below the mean. We then assigned scores to each respondent based on the number of coping responses within a role on which the respondent fell into the active half. Because the number of responses being observed differs among the four roles, so does the maximum score. Thus, in marriage it ranges from 0 to 6, in parenting to 5, and in the economic and occupational areas the maximum score is 4. The important feature of this index to be kept in mind is that it disregards the substance of the responses and encompasses only the number of responses on which people actively call in coping with role strains.

To ascertain whether the variety of one's repertoire by itself is related to coping effectiveness, we have computed a series of zero-order correlations. Taking marriage to describe the meaning of these correlations, it can be seen in Table 6-IV that the correlation between strain and emotional stress in the role is .78 among people who actively use none of the coping responses being observed in this area. As the number of responses that people employ increases, stress becomes decreasingly likely to be associated with marital strains. Indeed, stress as a consequence of strain is virtually eliminated when people use as many as five or six of these responses. (Only four respondents are active users of all six responses, and they are combined with those using five.) In the parental area there is also a substantial difference between those with the most limited repertoire and those with the most varied, but between these extremes there is no clear linear relationship. Economic strains, however, like those in marriage, are decreasingly apt to result in stress as the number of coping responses people actively employ increases. And, consistent with what has now been observed with unbroken regularity, the variety of one's repertoire in dealing with occupational problems has no clear or consistent part in preventing stress from arising.

It can be noted in passing that the same kind of analysis of the psychological resources reveals a similar set of findings. In each of the four roles the relationship between strain and stress is greatest among respondents having scores that exceed the mean on none of the three resources and least among those who are above the mean on all of them. This decrease is not completely linear in the marital area, nor is it either linear or sizeable in occupation. Overall, however, these results, together with what we observed above, indicate that the sheer richness and variety of responses and resources that one can bring to bear in coping with life-strains may be more

TABLE 6-IV. CORRELATIONS OF ROLE STRAINS AND STRESSES AMONG PEOPLE WHOSE
COPING REPERTOIRES DIFFER IN SCOPE AND VARIETY

	Number of Coping Responses Actively Invoked					
	(Limited Repertoire)				(Extended Repertoire)	
Role Areas	0	1	2	3	4	5 and 6
Marriage	.78 (63)	.63 (207)	.49 (466)	.43 (514)	.33 (222)	.01 (24)
Parenting	.59 (40)	.29 (52)	.36 (126)	.47 (148)	.36 (102)	.15 (33)
Household Economics	.79 (112)	.71 (263)	.64 (817)	.51 (637)	.37 (332)	
Occupation	.60 (131)	.49 (309)	.44 (411)	.46 (277)	.51 (71)	

Note: The parenthetical N's represent the number of people on which each of the correlations is based.

important in shielding one's self from emotional stress than the nature and content of any single coping element. Of one thing we can be quite certain: except in occupation, using fewer coping responses and possessing fewer resources maximizes the probability that role strains will result in emotional stress, and being able to call on more of these mechanisms minimizes the chances.

Who Uses What Mechanisms With What Advantage?

As we emphasized at the outset, we are more interested in identifying coping responses and resources that are shared by collectivities than in clinical portraits of individuals' psychological defenses. Some idea of this sharing can be obtained by simply observing whether coping practices vary among people possessing different social characteristics. These kinds of variations would indicate whether different types of coping, like other behavior, are normative for different groups in the society. But perhaps more importantly, with what we have learned of coping efficacy it is now possible to ascertain if coping differences among groups may also signal coping inequalities. Variations in the use of coping mechanisms, in other words, may be inextricably intertwined with a corresponding inequality of coping efficacy. As we consider the question of "who uses what mechanisms?", we shall consequently be drawing upon the answers we now have to a kindred question: "with what efficacy?"

To look at all the coping measures in relationship to all the social background characteristics about which there is information would produce a vast web of data. Instead, we shall confine ourselves to the more outstanding of these relationships by considering only those

Family Stress, Coping, and Social Support

characteristics most frequently having close statistical associations with coping. There are four of these, two ascribed and two achieved: sex and age, education and income. In order to understand the direction and meaning of the correlations in Table 6-V, it needs to be recognized that, with regard to the coping variables, a high score always represents more of the named quality, while the scoring of the social characteristics is indicated in the column headings.

TABLE 6-V. CORRELATION COEFFICIENTS OF BACKGROUND CHARACTERISTICS WITH COPING RESOURCES AND COPING RESPONSES*

Coping Resources and Responses	Sex [a]	Age [b]	Education [c]	Income [d]
Psychological Resources				
Self-denigration	−.05	−.23	.06	−.05
Mastery	−.11	−.17	.28	.27
Self-esteem	−.05	.01†	.21	.15
Marriage Coping Responses				
Self-reliance vs. Advice Seeking	−.08	.17	−.08	.00†
Controlled reflectiveness vs.				
Emotional Discharge	−.16	.23	−.11	−.09
Positive Comparisons	.01†	.07	−.06	−.13
Negotiations	.04	−.06	.11	.05
Self-assertion vs. Passive				
Forbearance	.04	−.01†	.05	−.01†
Selective Ignoring	.12	.15	−.14	−.09
Parental Coping Responses				
Exercise of parental potency	−.05	−.19	.16	.12
Self-reliance vs. Advice Seeking	−.23	−.20	−.12	−.04†
Non-punitiveness vs. Reliance				
on Discipline	−.10	.09†	.05†	.03†
Positive Comparisons	.02†	.05†	.06	.03†
Selective Ignoring	.13	.03†	−.08	−.01†
Household Economic Coping Responses				
Devaluation of Money	.05	.29	.13	.21
Optimistic Faith	−.07	−.34	.18	.10
Positive Comparisons	−.11	−.05	.18	.53
Selective Ignoring	.05	−.24	.02†	−.03†
Occupational Coping Responses				
Substitution of rewards	−.01†	.15	−.36	−.22
Positive Comparisons	−.03†	−.24	.10	.05†
Optimistic Action	−.07	−.02†	.07	.11
Selective Ignoring	.22	.05	−.20	−.14

* All correlations significant at the .05 level or higher except where indicated by (†).
[a] Female=high score.
[b] Older=high score.
[c] More extensive=high score.
[d] Greater=high score.

We begin our overview of the relationships in Table 6-V with sex, where it is evident that there is a rather compelling pattern of differences. This pattern can be identified by pointing out, first, that there are 11 correlations of a magnitude greater than .05 associated with sex. Second, of the 11 correlations of this magnitude, three involve coping mechanisms found most commonly among women, the remainder being used more by men (a positive correlation indicates the mechanism is associated with women). Finally, of the three responses more often found in the repertoires of women, each entails selective ignoring, a response which in marriage and parenting, it will be recalled, actually exacerbates stress. Thus, there is a pronounced imbalance between the sexes in their possession and use of effective mechanisms. Men more often possess psychological attributes or employ responses that inhibit stressful outcomes of life-problems: and in two of the three instances where women more often employ a response it is likely to result not in less stress, but in more. Although these results cannot provide a complete picture of sex differences, they are sufficient to stimulate the question of whether the greater inclination of women to psychological disturbance, repeatedly established in research (Gove and Tudor, 1973; Pearlin, 1974; Radloff, 1975), is a consequence not only of their having to bear more severe hardships, but also of their being socialized in a way that less adequately equips them with effective coping patterns.

The imbalance that exists between the sexes in the distribution of efficacious coping is completely absent with regard to age. Thus, the younger are more likely than the older to be self-denigrating, but they are also more apt than the older to entertain a sense of mastery. In coping with marital problems, the older are more disposed to self-reliance (less often seeking advice) and more likely also to engage in a controlled reflection of marital problems, both of which help to limit stress: but the older, too, more often practice selective ignoring, which is counter productive in the marital and parental areas. As parents, breadwinner, and job-holders, the young and the old are each likely to employ mechanisms that support emotional well-being. Unlike the sharp differences observed between men and women, then, there seems to be a balance in the coping efficacy of younger and older people, each being about equally well-equipped with effective elements. These results certainly do not support views of aging as a process in which people inexorably become increasingly vulnerable, unable to cope effectively with life-strains. Although there are substantial relationships between age and coping, neither the younger nor the older appear to have any overall advantage in coping effectiveness.

Education and income are both indicators of socioeconomic status, of course, and for this reason there are similarities in their relationships to coping, with education having the closer overall association. Whereas sex and age represent ascribed statuses, these are achieved, and it is in the framework of this conceptual difference that some of the relationships are most interesting. Thus, we find that the self-attitudes of mastery and self-esteem are both closely associated with the achieved statuses. There are some substantial correlations in the marital and parental areas as well, but the most impressive associations are in economic and occupational roles. Understandably, for example, the better educated and the more affluent are able to rely on positive comparisons in dealing with money and job problems; they are able to maintain optimistic outlooks; and on the job they do not have to foresake intrinsic rewards. They have the further luxury of being able to attribute less value to monetary success. Some of these relationships raise the question of whether people have better access to the more effective coping techniques because of their privileged positions, as we have been implying, or if they were able to achieve the privileged position because of their coping effectiveness. There is some indication that it is the former, for when we substitute the occupational status of respondents' fathers for their own educational and economic achievements, essentially the same set of relationships appears.

The patterns of coping usage, then, suggest some concomitant patterns of differential coping advantage. Only with regard to age do the findings indicate a general equality. Between the sexes, men clearly appear to have an advantage, for the personality characteristics and response repertoires shown to have some potency in controlling stress are predominantly found among men. There is similarly no question where the coping advantages lie among people of different socio-economic status. There is some mix in the marital and parental areas, but elsewhere a resource or response that has been demonstrated to have some efficacy is likely to be in possession of the better placed. The less educated and the poorer are more exposed to hardships and, at the same time, less likely to have the means to fend off the stresses resulting from the hardships. Not only are life-problems distributed unequally among social groups and collectivities, but it is apparent that the ability to deal with the problems is similarly unequal.

SUMMARY AND DISCUSSION

In order to highlight what this paper may have succeeded in accomplishing, it is necessary to recognize what it could not do. Foremost in this regard is the abbreviated range of coping responses and psychological resources with which we deal, limitations imposed both by the state of our present knowledge and the constraining boundaries of a single study. A similar limitation concerns the range of sources of stress with which we deal. Our interests purposely centered on continuous and often undramatic strains built into daily roles. There are other sources of stress not included within this focus, such as the role and status transitions that occur in the normal life-cycle and the problems presented by unusual and unexpected crises. These kinds of events not only present people with problems different from those we considered, but they may also evoke different types of responses and produce a different outline of coping effectiveness. Our analysis, therefore, could only encompass a sample of coping responses and resources used in dealing with some commonly experienced life-strains; it is not an exhaustive treatment of either coping or stress-provoking conditions.

Another limiting problem concerns the criterion used to judge coping efficacy. Our evaluation of efficacy is based on the extent to which coping mechanisms reduce the relationship between role-strains and emotional stresses. By this criterion the effective coper is one who is under severe strains but feels no stress. The more efficient the coping, the more tenuous the statistical associations of strain and stress. As we noted in our discussion of coping function, however, some successful coping may reduce stress by first diminishing the role-strain itself, a mode of coping we were not able to capture. Such coping, curiously, would lead to a statistical underestimation of efficacy. If coping diminishes the strains, and this then leads to diminished stress, the net effect of the coping would be to create a closer rather than a weaker statistical relationship between role-strains and emotional stress. Within the framework we employed, therefore, such coping would appear to be ineffective. Thus, some of the coping mechanisms we have identified may provide a more formidable barrier to emotional stress than we were able to demonstrate.

The final caveat, related to the foregoing issue, concerns causation and the direction of influence. Throughout we have talked only of the impact of life-strains on emotional stress, and the ameliorating effects of coping elements. However, it is likely that emotional stress, once established, can in turn influence people's exposure to life-strains and the selective use of coping responses. A network of reciprocal effects undoubtedly exists, one whose exact nature would be best revealed in longitudinal studies.

However, although limited to cross-sectional data, we believe that we have been able to demonstrate that the style and content of coping do make a difference to the emotional well-being of people. Furthermore, the greater the scope and variety of the individual's coping repertoire, the more protection coping affords. But the complete story of coping efficacy must include not only an account of what people do, but where they do it as well, for the same kinds of coping mechanims are not equally effective in different role areas. With relatively impersonal strains, such as those stemming from economic or occupational experiences, the most effective forms of coping involve the manipulation of goals and values in a way which psychologically increases the distance of the individual from the problem. On the other hand, problems arising from the relatively close interpersonal relations of parental and marital roles are best handled by coping mechanisms in which the individual remains committed to and engaged with the relevant others.

Not only may the same individual have unequal coping success in different role areas, but different individuals have unequal success when dealing with the same life-problems. These differences make it imperative to know which groups and collectivities are most likely to utilize the more efficacious techniques and which the less. We find in this regard that social structural conditions not only discriminate in placing more strain on some groups of people than on others, but they seem as well to cause the very segments of society that are under the greatest strain to have less effective coping repertoires. The striking fact that groups most exposed to hardships are also least equipped to deal with it gives some urgency to understanding better the processes by which people are led toward or away from various coping responses and resources.

On the basis of the evidence brought together here we can assert that what people do or fail to do in dealing with their problems can make a difference to their well-being. At the same time, there are important human problems, such as those that we have seen in occupation, that are not responsive to individual coping responses. Coping with these may require interventions by collectivities rather than by individuals. Many of the problems stemming from arrangements deeply rooted in social and economic organization may exert a powerful effect on personal life but be impervious to personal efforts to change them. This perhaps is the reason that much of our coping functions only to help us endure that which we cannot avoid. Such coping at best provides but a thin cushion to absorb the impact of imperfect social organization. Coping failures, therefore, do not necessarily reflect the shortcomings of individuals; in a real sense they may represent the failure of social systems in which the individuals are enmeshed.

Chapter 7

THE STRESSORS AND COPING PATTERNS OF DUAL-CAREER FAMILIES

DENISE A. SKINNER

O NE of the more profound changes affecting American family living is the increasing incidence in employment of married women. During the 1970's, labor force participation by married women with husbands present increased 10 percent resulting in nearly half of all married women employed in 1979 (U.S. Department of Commerce, 1980). Although it is difficult to assess the percentage of married *career* women in the labor force, it is reasonable to assume that their numbers have grown concomitantly with the general increase in female labor force participation. As more and more women seek increased education and training, along with an increased demand for skilled labor and a greater awareness of sex role equality, the dual career life-style is likely to increase in prevalance and acceptability (Rapoport and Rapoport, 1976).

A significant feature of the dual-career life-style is that it produces considerable stress and strain. The often competing demands of the occupational structure and those of a rich family life present a number of challenges for dual-career family members. Much of the literature implies that the stress is inherent in a dual-career life-style. However, some of the constraints of the life-style might be explained by it being a relatively new and minority pattern. In coping with the pressures of this variant pattern, dual-career couples have been forced to come up with individual solutions, as no institutionalized supports exist (Holmstrom, 1973).

The research on dual-career families has been primarily descriptive in nature and has focused on women. Rapoport and Rapoport, who coined the term *dual-career family* in 1969, were pioneers in the study of the impact of career and family on each other. Their research was followed shortly thereafter by other definitive studies on the dual-career life-style (Epstein, 1971; Holmstrom, 1973;

Garland, 1972; Poloma, 1972). More recent dual-career research has focused heavily on the stresses of the life-style and on the management of the strains by the participants (Rapoport and Rapoport, 1978).

The purpose of this chapter is to delineate the sources of dual-career strain and to advance efforts aimed at systematically studying dual-career family coping repertoires. The *Dual-Employed Coping Scales* (DECS) is introduced as an instrument that attempts to identify and measure such coping behaviors and patterns. Hopefully, this summary will benefit family practitioners as they assist individuals in making adaptive life-style choices as well as aid dual-career participants in effective stress reduction and in developing coping strategies.

The Etiology of Dual-Career Stress

Rapoport and Rapoport (1978) in reviewing the 1960s studies of dual-career families have noted that the stresses of this pattern have been differently conceptualized by various researchers. "The concepts include *dilemmas* [such as] overload . . . , network, identity; *conflicts* between earlier and later norms . . . , *barriers* of domestic isolation, sex-role prejudices . . . , and *problems* such as the wife finding an appropriate job . . . " (p.5).

Although there is a considerable degree of variation in dual-career stress, there are also common patterns. In the review that follows, an adaptation of the Rapoports' (1971) delineation of strains confronting dual-career families will be used as an organizing framework in highlighting these common patterns reported in the literature. Although interactive and cyclical in nature, strains have been classified as primarily (a) internal: arising with the family or (b) external: the result of conflict of the dual-career family and other societal structures (Bebbington, 1973).

Internal Strain

Overload issues. The problem of work and role overload is a common source of strain for dual-career families (Epstein, 1971; Garland, 1972, Heckman, Bryson, and Bryson, 1977; Holmstrom, 1973; Poloma, 1972; Rapoport & Rapoport, 1976; St. John-

Parsons, 1978). When each individual is engaged in an active work role and active family roles, the total volume of activities is considerably increased over what a conventional family experiences (Portner, 1978). In dual-career families this can result in overload, with household tasks generally handled as overtime.

The feelings of overload and the degree of strain experienced varied for couples in the Rapoports' study (1976). The Rapoports suggested that overload was affected by four conditions, which were, in part, self-imposed: (a) the degree to which having children and a family life (as distinct from simply being married) was salient; (b) the degree to which the couple aspired to a high standard of domestic living; (c) the degree to which there was satisfactory reapportionment of tasks; and (d) the degree to which the social-psychological overload compounded the physical overloads (pp. 302-305). There was a positive relationship between the conditions in items (a), (b), and (d) above, and the degree of strain experienced. Satisfactory reapportionment of tasks was a coping strategy that helped alleviate strain.

Identity issues. The identity dilemma for dual-career participants is the result of discontinuity between early gender role socialization and current wishes or practices (Rapoport and Rapoport, 1976). The essence of masculinity in our culture is still centered on successful experiences in the work role, and femininity is still centered on the domestic scene (Heckman, Bryson, and Bryson, 1977; Holmstrom, 1973). The internalized "shoulds" regarding these traditional male and female roles conflict with the more androgynous roles attempted by many dual-career couples, resulting in tension and strain.

Bernard, (1974) focusing on professional women, observed that intra-personal integration of work and domestic roles and the personality characteristics associated with each, does *not* constitute the "psychological work" of the career mother. Rather, the major difficulty, according to Bernard, is that the woman *alone* is the one who must achieve this identity integration.

Role-cycling issues. The dilemma of role cycling, identified by Rapoport and Rapoport (1976), refers to attempts by the dual-career couple to mesh their different individual career cycles with the cycle of their family. Bebbington (1973) noted that role cycling, unlike other sources of strain, has a developmental pattern. Both employment and family careers have transition points at which there is a restructuring of roles, which become sources of "normative" stress.

Dual-career couples attempt to avoid additional strain by staggering the career and family cycles such that transition points are not occurring at the same time. Many couples establish themselves occupationally before having children for this reason (Bebbington, 1973; Holmstrom, 1973; Rapoport and Rapoport, 1976). Stress may also result when the developmental sequence of one spouse's career conflicts with that of the other (Bebbington, 1973). The structural and attitudinal barriers of the occupational world, yet to be discussed, further contribute to the difficulty in role cycling for many dual-career couples.

Family characteristics. Holmstrom (1973) identified the isolation of the modern nuclear family as a barrier to having two careers in one family. The difficulty of child rearing apart from relatives or other such extended support systems is a source of strain.

The presence or absence of children as well as the stage of the family life cycle seems to affect the complexity of the dual career lifestyle (Holmstrom, 1973, Rapoport and Rapoport, 1976). Heckman et al. (1977) found that it was the older professional couples and those who had not had children who saw the life-style as advantageous. The demands of child rearing, particularly the problems associated with finding satisfactory child care arrangements, are a source of strain for younger dual-career couples, especially for the women (Bryson, Bryson, and Johnson, 1978; Gove and Geerken, 1977; Rapoport and Rapoport, 1971; St. John-Parsons, 1978). In relation to this, a child-free life-style has been noted by Movius (1976) as a career-facilitating strategy for women.

External Strains

Normative issues. Despite changing social norms, the dual-career life-style runs counter to traditional family norms of our culture. Rapoport and Rapoport (1976) have explained that although intellectually the dual-career pattern is approved, internalized values from early socialization are still strong and produce tension, anxiety, and guilt. Pivotal points such as career transitions or the birth of a child can activate these normative dilemmas.

One of the more frequently cited problems by dual-career professionals is the expectation on the part of others that the dual-career husband and wife behave in traditional male/female roles (Heckman et al., 1977). This is consistent with the earlier findings of Epstein (1971) who indicated that dual-career individuals experienced guilt because they were not conforming to the socially approved work-family structure. Furthermore, the women often had to deal with the implied or overt social controls placed on them by their children according to Epstein's study.

Occupational structure. Holmstrom (1973, p. 517) has commented on the inflexibility of professions noting that "pressures for geographic mobility, the status inconsistencies of professional women because the professions are dominated by men, and the pressure for fulltime and continuous careers" are a source of strain for dual-career couples.

The demand for geographical mobility and its effect on dual-career couples noted earlier by Holmstrom (1973) was also examined by Duncan and Perrucci (1976). They found that the egalitarian orientation toward decision making promoted in dual-career living was not carried out in job moves with the wives experiencing more of the stress. However, Wallston, Foster, and Berger (1978) using simulated job-seeking situations, found many professional couples attempting egalitarian or nontraditional job-seeking patterns. These authors have suggested that institutional constraints are in part responsible for highly traditional actual job decisions.

Finally, the demands of particular professions for single-minded continuous commitment, for other family members' needs to be subordinated to the job, and for a "support person" (typically the wife) to be available for entertaining, etc., are a source of stress for dual-career couples. The "two-person career," (Papanek, 1973) which depends heavily on an auxiliary support partner, is incompatible with the dual-career orientation, according to Hunt and Hunt (1977). Handy (1978) in a study of executive men found that the dual-career relationship was infrequent and difficult when the husband was in such a "greedy occupation."

Social network dilemmas. Maintaining relationships outside the immediate family is a problem for dual-career members for a variety of reasons. The general dilemma exists because of the overload strain discussed earlier, which creates limitations on the availability of time to interact with friends and relatives (Portner, 1978).

Rapoport and Rapoport (1976) found that the dual-career couples whom they studied reported problems in sustaining the kinds of interaction that their more conventional relatives and friends wanted. Not only was there less time for socializing, but, also, kin were at times asked by the dual-career couples to help out, which sometimes produced tension. St. John-Parsons (1978) reported that kin relationships deteriorated when dual-career couples could not meet some of the expected social obligations. The husbands in his study experienced the greater loss as ties to their families of orientation lessened.

The study by St. John-Parsons (1978) revealed that none of the dual-career families maintained extensive social relationships. According to the author, "a salient reason for their social dilemma was their sense of responsibility for and devotion to their children" (p. 40).

Impact of Strain

The sources of strain delineated above suggest that dual-career families are vulnerable to a high degree of stress. However, family stress literature has indicated that the family's definition of the situation is an important component influencing the impact of various strains on the family (Burr, 1973). Bebbington (1973) has differentiated between the following two kinds of stress which can coexist or operate separately in a given life-style: "(a) that deriving from an unsatisfactory resolution of conflict as between ideals and behavior; and (b) that deriving from intrinsic properties of the lifestyle, though ideals and behaviors may be consistent" (p. 535). Bebbington has suggested that dual-career participants do not seem to find the principle of "stress minimization" operative with regard to the second type of stress, but rather, accept an orientation of "stress-optimization" in interpreting inherent life-style stresses. Dual-career couples have accepted a high degree of the second type of stress as their solution to the dilemma of avoiding the discontinuity stress of the first type, according to Bebbington. They come to view their problems as having both positive as well as negative components and of a more routine than unusual nature.

The cumulative effect of various strains arising from occupational and familial role transitions can be estimated as "transitional density" (Bain, 1978). Bain has hypothesized that the stress experienced and the coping ability of a family in a particular transition is proportional to the stress generated by the transitional density. Applied to dual-career families this idea is specifically related to the particular family characteristics and the multiple role cycling strains previously discussed. The degree of stress experienced from other sources of strain, e.g., overload, may be compounded for a given family by the strain of their family life cycle stage or the newness of the dual-career pattern for them.

Marital Relationship

A considerable portion of the dual-career literature focuses on the marital adjustment, happiness, or satisfaction of dual-career couples implying that the stress inherent in the life-style has an impact on the marital relationship. In Orden and Bradburn's (1969) study of working wives and marital happiness, they found that a woman's choice of employment (vs. full-time homemaking) strained the marriage only when there were preschool children in the family. They concluded that the woman's decision to work is associated with a high balance between satisfactions and strains for both partners.

Bailyn (1970) found that an all-consuming attitude toward career was associated with lowered marital satisfaction. Over involvement in one's career can result in strain on the marriage, according to Ridley (1973), who found marital adjustment highest when the husband was "medium" and the wife was "low" on job involvement. He concluded that tension in the marital relationship may occur when either partner becomes so highly involved in a job that family obligations are excluded. Occupational practices such as discriminatory sex role attitudes can also heighten the stress in the dual-career marital relationship (Holmstrom, 1973; Rosen, Jerdee, and Prestwich, 1975). Finally, Richardson (1979) examined the hypothesis that marital stress would be attendant if working wives had higher occupational prestige than their husbands. He found no support for this hypothesis and suggested that its "mythic content" may be sustained, in part, because it is congruent with conventional sex role orientations.

Rice (1979), focusing on personality patterns, noted the following psychological characteristics as typical of dual-career individuals: "A strong need for achievement, reliance on an extrinsic reward system (promotion, spouse recognition of efforts), hesitancy in making sustained interpersonal commitments, and vulnerability to self-esteem injury through dependency frustrations and fear of failure" (p. 47).

The adaptive aspects of high achievement, for instance, may facilitate career advancement for both partners and contribute positively to marital adjustment, or high achievement needs may contribute to competitiveness in the pair.

Sex Differences

An overwhelming proportion of the literature reports that the impact of dual-career stress is felt most by women. Bernard (1974) has noted that a man can combine a professional career and parenting more easily than a woman can because less is expected of the man with regard to familial responsibilities.

Overload strain is a significant issue for dual-career women. Heckman et al. (1977), in assessing problem areas for dual-career couples, found that the women reported more problems in more areas than did men and that many of the comments about problem areas by husbands were issues that had indirectly affected them because the issue had directly affected their wives. These researchers reported that several women in their study made significant concessions with regard to their careers because of family demands. They concluded that the continued existence of role conflict and overload strain are often at the expense of the woman's personal identity and career aspirations.

Occupationally, it has been the woman more often who takes the risks, sacrifices more, and compromises career ambitions in attempting to make the dual-career pattern operative (Epstein, 1971; Holmstrom, 1973; Poloma, 1972). Interestingly, however, some studies have reported that dual-career wives are more productive than other females in their respective professions (Bryson, Bryson, Licht, and Licht, 1976; Martin, Berry, and Jacobsen, 1975). One might conclude, as the Rapoports (1978) have done, that the wives were simultaneously exploited and facilitated.

Life for the dual-career male is not without its periods of stress, although the impact of various strains does not appear to be as significant as that reported for women. Garland (1972) reported that dual-career males felt strain in attempting to find free time, but overall, noted the advantages of the life-style. The findings of Burke and Weir (1976b) do not provide as positive a report for dual-career men, however. While working wives were found to be more satisfied with life, marriage, and job than nonworking wives, husbands of working wives were less satisfied and performed less effectively than husbands of nonworking wives. Burke and Weir indicated that the greater stress experienced by the dual-career husband may be due, in part, to him losing part of his "active support system" when the wife commits herself to a career outside the home and also to his assuming roles, e.g., housekeeping, which have not been valued as highly in our culture.

Using more sophisticated methodology, Booth (1977) replicated the Burke and Weir study and reported different conclusions. He found very little difference between working and nonworking wives, and reported that the wife's employment had little effect on the stress experienced by the husband. Furthermore, Booth concluded that the dual-career husband may be experiencing less stress than his conventional counterpart as the added income and personal fulfillment of the wife outweigh temporary problems in adjusting to the life-style.

Children

Dual-career couples may increase the degree of strain they themselves experience in an attempt to prevent the life-style from creating strain for their children. As was noted earlier in the study by St. John-Parsons (1978), some of the social strains the couples experienced were due to their sense of responsibility to their children. There is no evidence to suggest that the dual-career life-style, in and of itself, is stressful for children. What may be more significant for the children is the degree of stress experienced by the parents, which may indirectly affect the children. In her study of maternal employment Hoffman (1974) concluded that: "the working mother who obtains satisfaction from her work, who has adequate arrangements so that her dual role does not involve undue strain, and she does not feel so guilty that she overcompensates is likely to do quite well and, under certain conditions, better than the nonworking mother"

(p. 142).

Coping Strategies

Just as the type and degree of strain experienced varies for dual-career families, so do the strategies employed for managing the stress. As was mentioned earlier in this paper, Bebbington (1973) suggested that "stress optimization," the acknowledging of dual-career stress as inevitable and preferable to the stress of alternative life-styles available, is an orientation of many dual-career couples. Defining their situation as such may serve as a resource in successful adaptation to the stress. Dual-career couples also employ stress-mitigating strategies. These coping behaviors are aimed at maintaining or strengthening the family system and at securing support from sources external to the family.

Coping Behavior Within the Family System

Poloma (1972) outlined four tension-management techniques used by the dual-career women in her study. They reduced dissonance by defining their dual-career patterns as favorable or advantageous to them and their families when compared to other alternatives available. For instance, the career mother noted that she was a happier mother and wife because she worked outside the home than she would be if she were a full-time homemaker. Secondly, they established priorities among and within their roles. The salient roles are familial ones and if a conflict situation occurs between family and career demands, the family needs comes first. A third strategy employed was that of compartmentalizing work and family roles as much as possible. Leaving actual work and work-related problems at the office would be one way to segregate one's work and family roles. Finally, the women in Poloma's study managed strain by compromising career aspirations to meet other role demands.

Compromise is a common coping strategy noted in much of the dual-career literature as a way of reducing stress and making the life-style manageable. Women, in particular, compromise career goals if there are competing role demands (Bernard, 1974; Epstein, 1971; Heckman et al., 1977; Holmstrom, 1973). However, men in dual-careers make career sacrifices also, e.g., compromising advancement opportunities in an attempt to reduce role conflict.

Prioritizing and compromising are coping strategies employed not only to deal with conflicts between roles but also in resolving competing demands with roles. Domestic overload, for instance, may be managed by deliberately lowering standards. One compromises ideal household standards because of constraints on time and energy in achieving them. Structurally, the domestic overload dilemma can also be managed within the family system by reorganizing who does what, with the husband and children taking on more of what traditionally has been the woman's responsibility. In these instances dual-career families are *actively* employing coping behaviors within the family aimed at strengthening its functioning and, thus, reducing the family's vulnerability to stress (McCubbin, 1979).

Some dual-career individuals take a more reactive orientation toward stress, and cope by attempting to manage and improve their behavior to better satisfy all of the life-style's demands. Holmstrom (1973) reported that the couples in her study adhered to organized schedules and that the women, in particular, were very conscious of how they allocated their time and effort. Flexibility and control over one's schedule are highly valued by career persons in attempting to meet overload and time pressures.

Finally, the presence of what Burke and Weir (1976b) have labelled a helping component in the marital relationship can serve a stress-mitigating function within the dual-career family. Qualities such as open communication, empathy, emotional reassurance, support, and sensitivity to the other's feelings, characterize this therapeutic role; the presence of these qualities would serve to strengthen the relationship. Related to this, Rapoport and Rapoport (1978) reported that couples established "tension lines," "points beyond which individuals feel they cannot be pushed except at risk to themselves or the relationship" (p. 6). Couples organized their family lives with sensitivity to these tension lines.

Coping Behaviors Involving External Support Systems

Dual-career couples also employ coping strategies aimed at securing support outside the family to help reduce stress. Holmstrom (1973) reported that couples were quite willing to use money to help resolve overload strain. Hiring help, especially for child care, is a common expense in this life-style. Couples also buy time in various other ways, such as hiring outside help to do domestic work and purchasing labor — and time-saving devices.

Outside support in terms of friendships were also important to the couples in the Rapoports' study (1976). The dual-career couples formed friendships on a couple basis, associating with other career couples. "Friendships, while gratifying, are also demanding, and in many of the couples there was a relatively explicit emphasis on the mutual service aspects of the relationship as well as the recreational aspect" (Rapoport, p. 316). Thus, establishing friendships with couples like themselves helped to validate the life-style for these dual-career couples and provided a reciprocal support structure.

The literature suggests that dual-career couples are increasingly interested in negotiating work arrangements that will reduce or remove some of this life-style's stress. Flexible scheduling, job sharing, and split-location employment are used by some dual-career couples as coping mechanisms to reduce the family's vulnerability to overload stress.

Finally, most of the researchers noted that achieving a balance between the disadvantages and advantages of the life-style was the overriding concern of dual-career couples. Although noting the numerous strains associated with the life-style, dual-career couples were equally aware of the gains — things like personal fulfillment, increased standard of living, pride in each other's accomplishments, etc. The goal for most dual-career couples, then is to " . . . plan how to manage the meshing of their two lives so as to achieve an equitable balance of strains and gains" (Rapoport and Rapoport, 1976, p. 298).

Dual-Employed Coping Scales (DECS)

Building upon the findings of the previously mentioned dual-career studies as well as significant coping research, DECS (Skinner and McCubbin, 1981) has been developed in an attempt to more systematically study the coping behaviors and patterns of dual-career families. DECS consists of fifty-eight items, each of which addresses a specific coping behavior. Five coping *patterns* (combinations of the fifty-eight coping behaviors into various patterns) have been identified.

The first pattern — Coping Pattern I — focuses on behaviors that *maintain, strengthen, and restructure the family system*. Working out a "fair" schedule of household tasks for all family members and specifically planning family activities for all to do together are two examples of behaviors dual-career family members engage in to restructure and strengthen itself.

Coping Pattern II is composed of those behaviors that attempt to *modify conditions of the work/family interface*. This pattern of coping, which is aimed at accommodating family to work and work to family, is vitally important to the dual-career family as they strive to keep in balance these major roles.

Coping Pattern III involves a repertoire of behaviors that enables dual-career individuals to *manage psychological tensions and strains*. Coping behaviors that allow them to attend to personal needs, e.g., jogging, relaxation activities, and those that focus on reducing the demands of the present situation, e.g., lowering standards for "how well" household tasks must be done, are necessary and strengthening aspects of coping with dual-career stress.

Perceptually controlling the meaning of the life-style is Coping Pattern IV. Behaviors aimed at maintaining an optimistic definition of the situation and believing in the value of the life-style are important in strengthening the dual-career family. In focusing on the advantages of the life-style — things like personal fulfillment, increased standard of living, pride in each other's accomplishments, and providing desirable role models for their children — dual-career participants may be better able to accept some of the inherent stressors.

The final pattern — Coping Pattern V — is a mixture of behaviors aimed at *developing interpersonal relationships and procurement of support outside the family*. Having empathetic friends with similar values can be a real source of support for dual-career family members. Women, in particular, seem to see this support as very important. Likewise, being able to purchase goods and services, using modern equipment, e.g. microwave, and eating out frequently are just some of the ways dual-career couples "buy time" and, thus, reduce overload stress.

Management of the dual-career life-style seems to call for an orchestrated response utilizing the various coping patterns in a balanced manner. Adaptive dual-career coping, then, involves the ability to attend to family needs, promote family equity, and establish a healthy balance between work and family. It also calls for managing tensions, believing in the value of the lifestyle, and developing an outside support system of friends and services.

Implications for Practitioners

Increasingly, people are choosing dual-career living, a trend that will, no doubt, continue in the future. This has several implications for family life practitioners, particularly given the stress associated with the life-style. Certain changes seem necessary in facilitating dual-career living, but these changes must occur by concerted efforts at many levels (Rapoport and Rapoport, 1976).

Individuals opting for the dual-career life-style, or any other family form for that matter, would benefit from knowledge of the issues central to that life-style's functioning. Educators and counselors working with men and women in the occupational-planning stage of their life can assist them in exploring to what extent the dual-career life-style is for them. Those desiring a career, marriage (to a career person), and children could begin to plan taking all three goals into account.

Rapoport and Rapoport (1976) have suggested that ". . . the dissemination of a detailed knowledge of a range of life-styles like the dual-career families will increase the potential for satisfactory choice of options in future" (p. 21). Such an education would enlarge traditional conceptions about men's and women's occupational and familial roles, recognizing that different individuals would then have greater opportunities for making adaptive life-style choices.

Practitioners in marriage and family therapy may increasingly work with dual-career couples as their numbers increase and as the strains of the life-style remain. Rice (1979) has reported that competition, issues of power, and difficulty with the support structure are three common problem areas in dual-career marriages. He has suggested that "the guiding principle in therapy with dual-career couples is to help the partners achieve or restore a sense of equity in the marital relationship" (p. 103). Couples who are able to develop and use *all five* of the coping patterns delineated in the *Dual-Employed Coping Scales* are those most equipped to successfully manage the dual-career life-style. Therefore, another intervention strategy for therapists counseling dual-career couples is to help them examine the extent to which they are utilizing coping patterns in a balanced manner.

Group support sessions are suggested by Hopkins and White (1978) as a helpful therapeutic strategy with dual-career couples. Common-problem groups and groups of couples at differing life cycle stages can provide a supportive structure for mutual sharing of concerns and coping skills. The goal of both preventive and remedial approaches should be to help couples assess their needs, increase interpersonal competencies, and deal constructively with the stress they experience (Rapoport and Rapoport, 1976).

Each family life professional has the opportunity to serve as a spokesperson for societal and institutional changes that would positively affect the functioning of dual-career families. Societal changes that would increase the quantity and quality of all kinds of services (educational, domestic, child care, etc.) would strengthen the dual-career life-style. Institutional changes that would increase the flexibility of the occupational structure would also aid significantly in reducing or eliminating some of the stress associated with the life-style. Flexible scheduling, increased availability of part-time employment, on-site day-care facilities and maternity and paternity leaves are some of the occupational changes advocated to enable individuals to combine work and family roles with less strain. Assuming an advocacy role on behalf of the dual-career life-style involves initiating and supporting social policies that promote equity and pluralism (Rapoport and Rapoport, 1976). A society where these values prevail would enhance not only the dual-career life-style, but would serve to strengthen family life in general.

Chapter 8

PREVENTING FINANCIAL HARDSHIP: COPING STRATEGIES OF FAMILIES OF THE UNEMPLOYED

PHYLLIS MOEN

MOST families are supported by one or more jobs. When the major provider is laid off, the financial plight of the family can be devastating. But not all families of the unemployed suffer economically (Moen, 1980a) this paper examines some of the strategies family members use in cushioning the financial costs of unemployment. It is important to differentiate between *coping* behavior and *effectiveness* (Hill and Klein, 1979). *Coping* represents the actions taken to reduce the financial strain of unemployment. *Effectiveness* is a successful outcome of those actions.

Family stress theory underlines the importance of family resources in rendering families more or less vulnerable to stress (Burr, Chapter 1; Hansen and Hill, 1964; Hansen, 1965, Hansen and Johnson, 1979). Angell (1939) distinguishes between three types of family response to stress: invulnerability, readjustive invulnerability, and vulnerability. *Invulnerable* families are those able to resist the pressure of an event, such as job loss, without internal reorganization. In terms of unemployment, invulnerable families would be those whose breadwinner was able to become reemployed before serious impairment of the family financial situation occurred. Families with *readjustive invulnerability* are those who modify their activity in order to cope with the stress event. Families with an unemployed provider might adjust to this situation through the use of income transfer payments (unemployment compensation, AFDC) or the employment of other family members so as to prevent the crisis of economic hardship. Finally, there are the *vulnerable* families: those unable to prevent job loss from being a financial disaster.

There are two broad categories of resources available to families facing the reality of an unemployed breadwinner: family resources (in the form of the employability of the major provider and other family members) and community resources (in the form of income transfer payments). (Other supports, such as financial aid from kin or a possible financial reservoir of savings, will not be addressed in this research.)

FAMILY RESOURCES AND FINANCIAL HARDSHIP

Whether or not unemployment of the breadwinner results in a financial crisis for the family depends, in part, on the nature of that unemployment. A short-term spell of joblessness will be less disorganizing and do less financial damage than a long-term spell. Certain resources of the unemployed provider — age, education, work experience — shorten the duration of unemployment and thereby lesson the likelihood of a family financial crisis (Moen, 1979).

Another important family resource is the presence of secondary earners. As an adapting unit, families respond to changing economic pressures, when possible, with changing labor force participation. The form of this response depends on the nature of the resources at the family's disposal. A single-parent family, for example, is less likely to have potential secondary earners than is a two-parent family. The form of the response is also conditioned by cultural and institutional factors: the availability of alternative sources of income, employment opportunities for other family members, and the "costs" of employment. For women with preschool children, for example, the costs of going to work may outweigh the benefits.

The importance of additional earners on family economic well-being has been documented repeatedly with Current Population Survey data (Hayghe, 1976a, 1976b; Johnson and Hayghe, 1977). The fact that female headed families are less likely to have additional earners than are male headed families has been well substantiated (Hayghe, 1976a, 1976b). The significance of potential additional earners in the face of unemployment is underscored by the suggestion of Garfinkel and Haveman (1977) that an earnings capacity measure be developed. This would be an alternative indicator of economic status of the family, designed to measure the ability of a living unit to generate income relative to the human capital of all family members.

Another important resource is the breadwinner's "definition of the situation." Unemployed providers who are unsure of their family's financial future and uncertain as to their own sense of mastery are less likely to cope effectively with the financial realities accompanying joblessness.

SOCIAL SUPPORTS AND FINANCIAL HARDSHIP

It has been suggested that the presence of income transfer programs has removed the threat of financial hardships from families with an unemployed breadwinner (Feldstein, 1977). Income transfer in the form of AFDC cushions the effect of unemployment for the poor; income transfer in the form of unemployment compensation cushions the effect of unemployment for the middle class.

Welfare Transfers

The effects of these supports on the financial situation of families of the unemployed have not been adequately investigated, but there is some information on the effects of welfare and the distribution of that welfare across families. For example, in their analysis of data on the source and amount of income from the 1973 Population Survey, Palmer and Barth (1977) found that female household heads in the low income bracket relied more on welfare than did male family heads. One half of the female family heads depended upon earnings as a source of income, compared with 77 percent of the low income, male headed households.

Felicity Skidmore (1977) reports that the effects of transfer payments on the poverty status of families from 1965 to 1972 were predominantly directed toward female headed families. Prime-age male headed families are disproportionately more likely to suffer from the effects of a slack labor market because few welfare programs are directed toward male headed families in poverty. Robert Plotnick's (1977) analysis of the effects of cash transfers also underscores the differential distribution of transfer payments by family types: more female headed families are lifted out of poverty by income transfers than are male headed families, though the disparity is decreasing.

Unemployment Transfers

The rationale behind unemployment compensation is income replacement. Unemployment insurance is seen as insurance against catastrophe (Feldstein, 1977; Garfinkel, 1978). Many of the poor are excluded because they are in occupations, such as domestic work, that are not covered or they have exhausted their benefits.

Nevertheless, unemployment is an important income cushion for the unemployed. A record 75 percent of the jobless in 1975 are estimated to have received benefits (Bednarzik and St. Marie, 1977). Social insurance is estimated to replace, on the average, two-thirds or more of lost net income for those receiving it (Feldstein, 1977). However, the amount and extent of benefits varies considerably across the states. The "cushioning" effects of unemployment benefits for families of the unemployed have not been investigated.

FAMILY CHARACTERISTICS AND FINANCIAL HARDSHIP

Certain characteristics of families render them more or less "resourceful" in adjusting to unemployment. For example, single-parent families lack a partner to share the family responsibilities, which might prevent them from taking jobs that present problems of logistics and time scheduling. Single-parent families are less likely to have another adult earner to cushion the financial blow of joblessness.

Families headed by women also suffer additional barriers to economic well-being. A fundamental obstacle is the gross discrepancy between the earnings of men and women. In 1975, full-time year-around male workers earned a median income of $12,680. Full-time year-around women workers earned a median income of $7,990 (Young, 1977). Since the discrepancy between the income of men and women increases with age, it is likely that families headed by women are particularly susceptible to economic inadequacy during the later stages of the life cycle. A study of 6,831 recipients of extended unemployment benefits in fifteen states in 1975 found that the median hourly wage (prior to unemployment) for male recipients was $4.58; for females it was $3.07. This study also found that women recipients were less likely to be "job ready" than men. The unemployed women evidenced a greater need for testing, counseling, and training than men.

Another important family characteristic is life cycle stage. The timing of the event of unemployment in relation to the family situation may affect both its financial impact and duration. For example, families with young children are more vulnerable to a poverty level of living than are families with older children (Moen, 1980a, 1980b).

Family economic recovery in the face of unemployment of the breadwinner can be separated into two components: problem solving through coping (readjustive invulnerability) and problem resolution (invulnerability) (Hill and Klein, 1979). Coping behavior would be characterized by the use of community supports, such as unemployment insurance and AFDC, or the family support provided by an additional earner in order to fill the financial gap left through job loss. Problem resolution would require reintegration of the breadwinner into the work world. Hill's roller coaster profile (1958) suggests the need to consider the existing level of family organization in determining the adaptive abilities of families. Characteristics of the family, such as whether there are two parents or only one, and the stage of the family life cycle, also render families more or less effective in responding to the financial threats of joblessness.

FINANCIAL VULNERABILITY: OVERVIEW

Economic hardship can be characterized as a crisis on three levels: according to the view of an objective observer, according to the norms of the prevailing culture, and according to the subjective views of the family members themselves (Stryker, 1964). While the subjective definition of the situation is perhaps most important, there are nevertheless certain standards of economic well-being, the absence of which would be labeled a "crisis" both according to prevailing societal norms and in the perspective of an impartial observer. A substantial loss of family income or an income below that required for an adequate standard of living can both be considered "crisis" situations for families in the view of an objective observer as well as in terms of societal norms. Therefore, economic hardship is defined by two measures: economic *adequacy* (a measure of income over need) and economic *deprivation* (the loss of a substantial portion of previous income).

Economic adequacy can be operationalized as income over need, with need being measured by the number of dependents (Sweet, 1973; Duncan and Morgan, 1977). A more sensitive measure of the baseline of economic adequacy is the family budget equivalence measures. In these measures the income required for families at differing stages of the life cycle in order to experience equivalent standards of living is calculated (U.S. Department of HEW, 1976). The elements involved in this measure of economic adequacy are (a) family income, (b) family composition, and (c) stage of life cycle development.

A second measure of economic hardship involves major (30%) income loss. As Elder (1974) remarks, a crisis occurs not because of an event itself but because of the disparity between the claims of a family in a situation and its control of outcomes. Census data confirm the economic impact of unemployment on families. In 1975 the median income of all families whose head worked year round was $17,165, compared with $13,720 for all families who were unemployed or out of the labor force part of the year (U.S. Census, 1976).

This research uses data from the Michigan Panel Study of Income Dynamics (PSID) to examine the ways in which families of the unemployed dealt with the potential financial costs of job loss during the recession of 1975. The PSID is a nationwide sample of roughly 5,000 families. The subsample used in his analysis consists of all black and white families with children younger than eighteen present in the home (n = 2642). Nearly 17 percent of this subsample had their major earner unemployed at some time during the 1975 recession (n = 532). Forty percent of the families of the unemployed suffered a financial hardship. The question addressed here is the regenerative ability of these families. What are the characteristics of the families that manage to make ends meet in spite of joblessness?

In this sample of families of the unemployed, "effective" use of resources would mean that these families managed to prevent unemployment from resulting in financial hardship—either in the form of economic inadequacy (a poverty measure) or deprivation (severe loss of income). These "successful" or invulnerable families can be categorized according to whether or not they succeeded through the breadwinner's reemployment or by using various family and community supports to tide the family over in the face of a longer spell of unemployment. A study of the families' vulnerability to either economic inadequacy or economic deprivation reveals the following major findings: Nearly 60 percent of all families were not "vulnerable" according to the two measures of economic hardship used. More than 40 percent had breadwinners who were unemployed less than fifteen weeks during 1975 and were successful in preventing economic hardship.

Unemployed fathers were more likely to be successful at avoiding economic hardships than single-parent mothers; they were also more likely to be unemployed for a shorter period of time. Black families and those headed by single-parent mothers were more vulnerable to financial crisis and to a longer spell of unemployment than were white families or those where the father was the major provider. Looking at life cycle stage, it seems that vulnerability increases with each succeeding stage, such that more than half of the families with teenagers were susceptible to either low income or income loss, while only a little over a third of the families with preschoolers were similarly vulnerable. Just when the costs of children escalate and a family must consider financing post-high school education for their teenager, unemployment can have dire economic consequences. Moreover, family providers at this stage are more likely than at other stages to be unemployed for an extended period: two-thirds of the family heads at Stage 3 were either suffering a financial crisis and/or unemployed for fifteen weeks or more.

It is interesting to note that roughly the same proportion of husband/wife and female headed families as well as black and white families used coping strategies effectively: around 20 percent of all families managed to prevent economic hardship in spite of extended unemployment. Families with preschool children were more likely to be successful in coping with extended unemployment than were families with older children. Families with the greatest vulnerability appear to be female headed families, black families, and families with teenagers.

COPING MECHANISMS IN THE FACE OF UNEMPLOYMENT

Distribution of Coping Strategies

Coping strategies can involve either family or community

resources. From a policy perspective, it is important to note which family types are using community supports in the face of unemployment. For example, insurance in the form of unemployment compensation is designed to prevent unemployment from turning into a financial catastrophe for families. In this sample of families who had an unemployed breadwinner, more than half received unemployment benefits. Of those getting benefits, most received less than $2,000.

Almost half (49.2%) of the two-parent families with an unemployed bread-winner drew benefits; less than a third (25.2%) of the female headed families got benefits. Fathers who were high school graduates were more likely to get unemployment insurance than those who were high school dropouts. For mothers who headed families and were unemployed in 1975, those with less than a high school education were slightly more prone to receive benefits than high school graduates — but the difference was small.

Though single-parent mothers rarely received unemployment compensation, they may well have received income support in the form of AFDC welfare payments. Table 8-I gives the proportions of families of various types who received either unemployment and/or welfare (AFDC). While there are other forms of income supports — especially in-kind transfers, such as food stamps and medicaid — these are not usually counted as "income." Moreover it is highly unlikely that in-kind transfers alone would appreciably alter the family's economic position.

Nearly half (48.1%) of the families with an unemployed breadwinner in 1975 received *no* income supports in the form of *either* AFDC *or* unemployment benefits (*see* Table 8-I). Fewer than 1 percent of the sample families received both welfare and unemployment benefits. Nearly half (46.5%) got some unemployment compensation, but less than 5 percent received AFDC.

In terms of community supports, twice as many husband/wife families as female headed families received unemployment insurance, while AFDC was predominately given to single-parent mothers. Black families were more likely than white to be on AFDC but less likely to draw unemployment. *Both black families and families headed by women were more likely to be without either form of community resource.*

Turning to life cycle stage, families at Stage 2 — with school aged

Table 8-I

Community Supports as Coping Strategies for Target Families[1]
by Selected Characteristics

| | % Utilizing Community Support Strategies | | | |
	None	AFDC	Unemploy- ment Com- pensation	Both AFDC & Unemployment Compensation
All target families	48.1	4.5	46.5	.9
Family type				
husband-wife two parent families	47.5	2.5	49.2	.8
female-headed one parent families	52.4	20.3	25.2	2.1
Race of head				
white	46.3	3.4	49.6	.7
black	57.5	10.4	30.3	1.8
Life cycle stage (age of youngest child)				
stage 1 (under 6 years)	40.8	6.2	51.6	1.4
stage 2 (6-12 years)	62.5	2.4	34.7	.4
stage 3 (13-18 years)	49.2	1.8	49.0	.0

[1]Those families whose head was unemployed at some time during 1975. Subsample of black and white families with children under 18 from the 1975-76 waves of the Michigan Panel Study of Income Dynamics (% of weighted sample), N = 532.

children — were the least likely to have any form of income transfer. AFDC payments were most common for families with preschool children. Half the families with young children (Stage 1) and with teenagers (Stage 3) received unemployment insurance in 1975.

Relationships Among Coping Mechanisms

Community income supports are one strategy for coping with unemployment of the family breadwinner. Other mechanisms include reentry into the labor market of the laid off worker (short-term unemployment) and the employment of other family members, especially the wife. Another psychological form of coping is found in the way one defines (or redefines) one's financial expectations

(Gurin and Gurin, 1970).

To examine the relationships among community, family, and perceptual coping strategies, a log linear model was fit incorporating five strategies: (a) limiting the duration of unemployment, (b) employment of the wife, (c) receipt of AFDC, (d) receipt of unemployment compensation, and (e) financial expectations. Log linear analysis is a form of categorical analysis concerned with the patterning of relationships among variables (*see* Goodman, 1972a, 1972b, 1973; Fienberg, 1977). Log linear analysis can clarify the direct relationships among various coping strategies; it can also determine which variables are independent of others and which are conditionally independent.

The hypothesis testing process involved fitting a model of complete independence and one of two-way associations among the coping strategies of families faced with an unemployed breadwinner. The model with two-way associations fit the data. By excluding different two-way associations, it was possible to find the best fitting model. The most parsimonious model (LRX^2 = 43.46, d.f. = 33) that adequately estimated the relationships between the various coping strategies was used. The following relationships among coping strategies emerge: first, duration of unemployment is related to both receiving AFDC payments and unemployment insurance benefits; second, receiving unemployment compensation is related to other coping mechanisms — AFDC and the provider's expectations concerning the financial future of the family; finally, there is a relationship between AFDC and having a wife work.

Looking at the information provided by examining the parameters *not* included in the best fitting model proves interesting. For example, there is no relationship between employment of the wife and the head's expectations concerning the family's financial future. Controlling for unemployment insurance and expectations about the future, duration of unemployment, and being on AFDC are not related. Controlling for being on AFDC and duration of unemployment, unemployment compensation is not related to employment of the wife.

But what are the strongest relationships among these coping mechanisms? To understand more fully the relationships that do exist between the coping mechanisms requires turning to the effects and odds ratios of the best fitting model. The largest negative relationship is a common sensical one between receiving AFDC and the probability of a wife working. Since most AFDC recipients are female heads of households, one would naturally expect a negative relationship between these two coping strategies and the model supplies just that. The odds are high (1.76) that a person on AFDC will not have a wife who is working. The next most important relationship is between duration of unemployment and AFDC. The odds are nearly three to two (1.44) that an unemployed breadwinner on AFDC will be unemployed fifteen weeks or longer. AFDC recipients are not likely to be recipients of unemployment compensation. The odds are less than three to four (.71) that a family on AFDC will be receiving unemployment benefits.

There is also a slight positive relationship between receiving unemployment insurance benefits and the duration of unemployment. Families receiving unemployment compensation would be slightly more likely (1.14) to be unemployed fifteen weeks or more. The relationship between the breadwinner's financial expectancy and receiving unemployment compensation is an interesting one; family heads who expect things will get *worse* for the family financially are more likely than not to be receiving unemployment compensation.

What can one conclude about the distribution of coping resources among families of the unemployed? To some extent these findings show that the community support resources are working fairly well in that AFDC and unemployment insurance are complementary programs, and they are more active for those families whose breadwinners are unemployed for longer periods of time. But the fact that half of the families of the unemployed received no income transfers shows the uneven distributions of community supports.

EFFECTIVE AND INEFFECTIVE STRATEGIES

Resources and Vulnerability

The proceding analysis relates different coping resources to one another. But strategies should also be appraised according to their effectiveness: How well do they lessen the economic vulnerability of families stressed by unemployment? Families are *vulnerable* who experience economic inadequacy (income/needs ratio ≤ 1.23) or economic deprivation (30% or greater loss of income in one year). Looking at the association between this financial vulnerability and the use of community supports reveals a number of findings about the effectiveness of these supports.

1. *Most families (53.1%) whose heads were unemployed less than fifteen weeks and who were successful (invulnerable) did not use either welfare or unemployment compensation.*

Limiting the duration of the unemployment appears to be an important factor in preventing financial vulnerability for them. But 47 percent of these families did receive unemployment compensation; only 1.8 percent received AFDC payments.

2. *Unemployment benefits are an important coping strategy for families with a breadwinner unemployed for longer than fifteen weeks.*

Seventy-two point two percent (72.2%) of the successful (invulnerable) families facing longer term unemployment received at least some unemployment compensation.

3. *Most of the families (53.2%) facing economic crisis were without community supports.*

Nearly 11 percent of the vulnerable families — those with a high probability of either economic inadequacy or deprivation (or both) — were on AFDC. A third (34.8%) of this group received unemployment compensation.

Unemployment insurance, then, appears to be an important strategy in preventing economic crisis in families of the unemployed, as is limiting the duration of unemployment. AFDC payments, on the other hand, apparently do not prevent financial hardship (even though welfare is aimed at "lifting families out of poverty" (Skidmore, 1977).

Coping and Vulnerability to Economic Inadequacy

To estimate the relative importance of community income transfer programs and various family coping strategies on the financial vulnerability of families of the unemployed, two logit models were fit linking coping behaviors with economic inadequacy and economic deprivation as the criteria or dependent variables. (Logit models are similar to log linear estimates only with a particular dependent variable [Fienberg, 1977]).

A model of direct effects of coping mechanisms on economic inadequacy fits the data (LRX^2 = 100.83; d.f. = 122, p ^{3} .05). By eliminating each coping strategy from the model one at a time, it is possible to estimate their relative contributions to the probability of economic inadequacy. The following relationships emerged:

1. *Receiving AFDC is strongly related to economic inadequacy.* The odds are nearly three to one (2.82) that a breadwinner on AFDC will have an inadequate income. While it is true that the AFDC program is needs-tested, these data show that for families of the unemployed, welfare transfer payments do not bring family income up to an adequate level. Being on AFDC is a good "predictor" of economic inadequacy; it is not an effective strategy against impoverishment for families of the unemployed.

2. *Having a second earner in the family is strongly related to economic adequacy.* Families with an employed wife were half as susceptible to poverty (odds = .53) as families without an employed spouse (odds = 1.88). The cushion of an additional earner is the most effective coping strategy for preventing economic inadequacy.

3. *Limiting the duration of unemployment is also effective in preventing economic inadequacy.* Families whose breadwinners were employed less than fifteen weeks were far less prone to economic inadequacy (odds = .58) than those who were without a job more than fifteen weeks (odds = 1.73).

4. *Receiving unemployment compensation also cushions the economic impact of unemployment.* Families receiving benefits were less likely to experience economic inadequacy (odds = .75).

It is interesting that the two variables tested, which were *not* important in preventing economic inadequacy, are the attitudinal characteristics of the family head — financial expectations and feelings of mastery over one's life.

Coping and Vulnerability to Economic Deprivation

The second model examining the effectiveness of coping strategies links these strategies with major income loss — 30 percent or more loss in one year — which we have labeled economic deprivation. Model fitting coping strategies with economic deprivation followed the same procedure that was used in estimating economic *inadequacy*. The model of direct effects (separate relationships between each strategy and the likelihood of deprivation) fits the data. To assess the explanatory value of each variable, each was selectively dropped in a model fitting process. The following relationships emerged from this analysis.

1. *Lowering financial expectations is strongly related to experiencing major income loss.* Families whose breadwinners feel that things will be worse in the next few years have a two to one odds of experiencing ecomonic deprivation. This psychological strategy — acceptance or resignation — seems strongly linked to facing serious economic difficulties, while it was pointed out it was not related to less serious difficulty.

2. *Families whose breadwinners are unemployed fifteen weeks or more are more likely to face major income loss.* Those facing longer periods of unemployment face 1.5 to one odds that they will be economically deprived.

3. *Two other mechanisms reduce the changes that families will be economically deprived: Receiving unemployment compensation and having an employed spouse.*

SUMMARY

This research examined the strategies used by families of the unemployed to avoid economic deprivation in the recession of 1975. Some of these families were not exposed to economic hardship despite unemployment because the spell of joblessness was relatively short-lived (less than fifteen weeks). Other families managed to avoid a financial crisis — even in the face of prolonged unemployment — by using either family or community resources. However, a good number of these families (40.3%) were confronted with either major income loss or poverty level income along with the stress of unemployment.

Log linear analysis revealed the patterning of various coping strategies used by families of the unemployed. Various community supports and family resources were related. For example, receiving unemployment benefits was related negatively to the financial expectations of the breadwinner (a psychological resource) and positively to the duration of the spell of unemployment (a consequence of "human capital" resources). It is important to note which strategies were *not* related. For instance, receiving unemployment benefits was not related to whether or not a wife was working. Being on AFDC was not related to a breadwinner's expectations concerning the family's financial future.

Looking at the patterning of coping strategies tells us nothing about their *effectiveness*. To see the effects of community and family resources on the probability of economic hardship required examining the relationships between coping mechanisms and both economic inadequacy (a poverty measure) and economic *deprivation* (major income loss). One community support (AFDC) was positively related to economic inadequacy, which was not surprising since eligibility for welfare is based on a needs test. Families who were able to limit the duration of unemployment to less than fifteen weeks and/or who had a wife who was working were less likely to experience either poverty level income or major income loss. Community supports in the form of unemployment benefits were similarly important in warding off both forms of economic hardship. Psychological coping mechanisms, such as feelings of personal mastery and financial expectations for the future, were not important in predicting the economic inadequacy of the family, but financial expectations of the breadwinner did prove significant in estimating the likelihood of major income loss.

Two categories of resources had a tremendous impact on the economic situation of families of the unemployed: those which limited the extent of the spell of joblessness and those which provided additional sources of income. Two-thirds of the families who avoided a financial crisis had a breadwinner who became reemployed in less than fifteen weeks. The probability that a family faced with a short spell of joblessness would have a poverty level income or major income loss was less than 20 percent. This has obvious policy implications in the development of programs to reduce the duration of unemployment, if it cannot be prevented altogether.

Other sources of income were also important. The fact that families of the unemployed without an additional earner were more prone to financial crisis underlined the vulnerability of a particular category of families: those headed by a single parent. Unemployment insurance seemed to play a major role in warding off economic disaster; families who received benefits were less likely to have a financial crisis. Unemployment compensation was an especially important support for families faced with extended unemployment. More than 72 percent of the families whose breadwinner was unemployed fifteen weeks or more and who avoided an ecomic crisis received benefits. But the fact that half of the families of the unemployed received no unemployment compensation underscored the uneven distribution of this income cushion. For example, black families and female headed families were less likely to receive benefits than were white or husband/wife families.

AFDC was negatively related to economic well-being — payments were insufficient to push recipients to adequate income levels. The average monthly payment for an AFDC recipient in 1975 was $71.50 (U.S. Department of Commerce, 1977).

POLICY IMPLICATIONS

This study points to three factors that shield families of the unemployed from financial crisis: shortening the duration of unemployment, the availability of secondary earners, and receiving unemployment compensation. The family resource of a secondary earner is a real asset. The potentials of the two-earner families and the liabilities of single-parent families can be strengthened by hiring and wage policies that end discrimination against women. The two other factors, limiting the extent of unemployment and increasing the availability of unemployment compensation, will be discussed in detail.

Limiting the Duration of Unemployment

Strategies that shorten the spell of joblessness for breadwinners are obviously beneficial. Training programs, such as those embodied in the Comprehensive Employment and Training Act (CETA), are designed to that end.

But despite these programs, the fact remains that the "U.S. is far from having an active manpower policy of the Swedish variety in which training, employment, placement, and relocation programs have a major impact on the functioning of the labor market" (National Council on Employment Policy, 1977). Despite the implementation of emergency job creation programs, the 2.8 million first-time enrollments in 1975 represented only an eighth of persons experiencing unemployment during the year (National Council on Employment Policy, 1977). It is doubtful that present programs have made an effective dent on the employment and economic situation of American families.

Unemployment Insurance

A major and expanding form of community support in the face of unemployment is the unemployment insurance program. This form of social insurance is designed to be an "event-conditioned" transfer — paid to normally employed individuals who become unemployed (Feldstein, 1977; Garfinkel, 1978). Because unemployment benefits are tax free and because in some states they are quite generous, they are seen as mitigating the financial impacts of unemployment. Benefits are claimed to equal around two-thirds of the net income loss of families. When there are other earners present, unemployment compensation can in some cases represent a net *increase* in income (Feldstein, 1977).

However, because of its allegedly generous benefits, unemployment compensation is seen by some analysts as providing a disincentive to employment — increasing both the likelihood of temporary layoffs and duration of unemployment (Feldstein, 1977; Garfinkel, 1978; Marston, 1975). The data presented here on families with children question the adequacy of coverage of unemployment insurance. More than half the families in this sample who had an unemployed breadwinner in 1975 received no unemployment compensation. This program is not a general income transfer strategy. Benefits are paid only to those who are eligible, not to everyone without a job who wants to work (Feldstein, 1977). Moreover, there is a wide discrepancy in eligibility requirements and length of coverage across states. In this sample, for example, the benefits cushioned financial loss in only half the families of the unemployed.

Studies have shown that the duration of unemployment is affected by receipt of unemployment benefits; this relationship was confirmed in the data reported here. Looking at the various forms of coping strategies utilized by families of the unemployed, a relationship was found between receiving unemployment compensation and the duration of unemployment. Yet, family breadwinners have high motivation for work. They have traditionally had low unemployment rates. The provision of unemployment insurance probably does not dampen that desire for reemployment, but does offer support in the face of severe unemployment.

Conclusions

Two principal strategies have been followed in the United States in dealing with macroeconomic change. The first has been active fiscal and monetary policies to prevent or lessen a sluggish labor market. A healthy economy is assumed to provide the best job insurance for individual workers. But it is recognized that some persons are not reached through fiscal and monetary manipulations. Even in a "full employment" state 4 percent of the labor force are out of work. Moreover, there is lag between government action and economic response.

The second strategy — social supports in the form of job training, job creation, and unemployment insurance — has been devised to fill in the gaps left by macro policies. While these programs are expanding exponentially, the data from this research show that the financial hardships of unemployment are still very much a reality for a significant portion of American families.

Chapter 9

FAMILY COPING WITH CHRONIC ILLNESS: THE CASE OF CEREBRAL PALSY

HAMILTON I. McCUBBIN, ROBERT S. NEVIN,
A. ELIZABETH CAUBLE, ANDREA LARSEN, JOAN K. COMEAU,
AND JOAN M. PATTERSON

R ESEARCH on families with a handicapped or chronically ill child has had a long and meaningful history with social and behavioral scientists searching to understand the hardships and difficulties these families experience. More recently, we have witnessed a concerted effort among scientists to examine how families faced with the long-term care of these children are *able* to handle the financial, psychological, and interpersonal demands placed upon them. This interest in families represents a major shift in emphasis from the study of family *problems* and failures to the systematic assessment of how families cope with and adapt to a very difficult situation and at the same time promote the health, well-being, and development of children in the home. This study represents a continuation of this recent trend. It contributes to the ever increasing body of research on the care of chronically ill and handicapped children by underscoring the complementary relationship between the medical treatment of children with cerebral palsy and support of families responsible for these children over the life span. Although the family's role is difficult to assess, it is viewed as a vital part of the total medical program for children with cerebral palsy.

An estimated 25,000 children a year are newly afflicted with cerebral palsy (CP), and it is considered among the twelve major illnesses and diseases in the United States (Hatton, 1976). Cerebral palsy is a general diagnostic category used to specify a group of nonprogressive impairments of neuromuscular function (Chinn, 1979).

This research was supported by the Medical Education Research Association (MERA) of Gillette Children's Hospital, St. Paul, Minnesota, and by the Agricultural Experiment Station, University of Minnesota, St. Paul, Minnesota.

169

These impairments are usually exhibited by motor problems, which range from a slight and often unnoticeable difficulty with coordination to an extremely debilitating condition where the child needs specialized care. Further complications arising from this condition include: mental retardation, language and learning disorders, and sensory defects. Convulsive disorders are also evidenced in many cases. We have only begun to develop a comprehensive picture of the impact of a CP child upon the family unit. In reviewing the observations reported in case studies and research, we can summarize the hardships of family life into eight broad categories:

Altered relationships with friends and neighbors due to their reactions to the CP child along with parental and sibling embarrassment at how the CP child looks and acts leading to family social isolation.

Major changes in family activities, such as reduced options for family vacations, tightening parental work schedules, reduced flexibility in the use of leisure time, and shared family tasks and responsibilities.

Medical concerns related to side effects with medications, parents learning more specialized medical procedures, home treatment responsibilities, and problems with handling equipment for CP children.

Intra-family strains including overprotectiveness, rejection of child, denial of disabilities, ongoing worry about the CP child's safety and care, concerns about the extended parenthood, increase in the amount of time focused on the CP child at the possible expense of other family members, as well as discrepancies between children as a result of uneven physical, emotional, social, and intellectual development. Additional strains emerge from extended family members who may lack the understanding and appreciation of the concerns that parents and siblings of CP children have.

Medical expenses arising from the costs of specialized treatment and equipment.

Specialized child care needs and difficulties related to limited community resources, difficulties in finding the best care and services, and the extra costs of specialized care.

Time commitments that disrupt family routines, such as extra appointments to medical facilities, consultations associated with special education programs, and the predictable although disruptive situation of extra demands on family life due to the CP child's personal and emotional needs in the home setting.

Medical consultations, which call for repeated efforts to clarify and verify medical information, learning and implementing medical and treatment plans, and frustrations with the general quality of medical care, which does not match parent's expectations.

Families are called upon to attend to the ever changing needs of a developing CP child. Consequently, family responsibilities and tasks shift in response to both the CP child's changing medical condition *and* his or her developmental needs. When these developmental needs and demands on family life are viewed across time and family stages, we can begin to appreciate the emotional, financial, and interpersonal struggles for families with CP children.

However informative and instructive, systematic research on parental coping lags far behind our need to understand more fully how these families are able to do so well in the face of such difficulties. With the increasing emphasis on family counseling and the growing awareness of the critical role families play in the rehabilitative process, we can anticipate the need for more information about what coping behaviors parents employ and under what conditions. We need to examine more fully whether our interventions into family life are as effective when we deal with one parent, both parents, and/or significant others who play a major role in the care of a CP child in the home. We are at an important juncture in family research and would do well to build upon coping research conducted to date with a commitment to measurement and testing of the nature and impact of parental efforts to fulfill their responsibilities to the children and to themselves.

RESEARCH METHOD

This study emerged as a natural outcome of our prior research on families with chronically ill children and families coping with a range of stressful situations, such as father absence, corporate life, war, and a member held hostage in a foreign country.

On the basis of this prior research and our commitment to link social science research to research with medically related family hardships, this investigation had three fundamental objectives:

First, to document the medical and nonmedically related stressors and strains CP families experience; second, to document the family resources, coping behaviors, and strategies, which make a difference in how well families are able to maintain coherence and attend to the needs of the CP child and other members of the family unit; third, to develop a set of instruments to assess stress, resources, and coping, which would have respectable reliability and validity and which could be used in medical centers as a means of determining family "vulnerability" and as a tool to guide counselors in their work with "at risk" families.

The research design was guided by the Double ABCX family stress conceptual framework (McCubbin and Patterson, Chapter 2), which involves the study of family adaptation through the systematic assessment of the key independent variables of (a) family life events and strains, (b) family resources, and (c) parental coping behaviors and strategies and the dependent measure of family functioning.

The fundamental design for this part of the total project and the basis for the data presented in this report involved (a) the collection of questionnaire data from mothers and fathers; (b) the identification of high conflict and low conflict families; and (c) the analysis of research data to answer the basic questions stated for this study.

Subjects

Subjects were 217 families who had a child with cerebral palsy and who were seen at periodic intervals at Gillette Children's Hospital CP Clinic, St. Paul, Minnesota. The Gillette Clinic is a regional program involving rural and urban families in the treatment of patients from a five-state area: Minnesota, North Dakota, South Dakota, Wisconsin and Iowa. All families seen in the CP clinic who had at least one chronically ill child living at home were asked to participate.

Of the 577 families listed, seventy-five were never reached by phone or certified letter. An additional eighty-three families were determined to be inappropriate for the study. Thus, 397 families met the criteria for inclusion. Of these, 217 families agreed to participate and completed at least one phase of the study. The families who chose not to participate (180) were contacted to determine the reasons for their decisions.

Measures

Four measures were adopted for this investigation, three of which were developed and tested with families of chronically ill children — children with cystic fibrosis, myelomeningocele, and cerebral palsy.

Family stress: The Family Inventory of Life Events and Changes (FILE) (McCubbin, Patterson, and Wilson, 1981) is a seventy-one item self-report instrument,[1] which is designed to measure a family's level of stress by recording the normative and nonnormative life events and changes experienced by them during the past twelve months. Since families usually are dealing with several life changes or events simultaneously, FILE provides one index of a family's *vulnerability* as a result of this pile-up. All events experienced by *any* member of the family are recorded, since, from a family systems' perspective, what happens to any one member affects the other members of the family.

In this study, for two-parent families, the parents were asked to complete FILE together, and for single-parent families, the custodial parent completed FILE. Thus, there was one completed questionnaire for each family.

Family Resources: The Family Inventory of Resources for Management (FIRM) (McCubbin, Comeau, and Harkins, 1981) is a sixty-

---

[1] The seventy-one items of FILE are grouped into nine subscales:

1. *Intra-Family Strains* — 17 items relating to increased tension and strain between family members and particularly the hardships of parenting.
2. *Marital Strains* — Four items which reflect sources of tension in the marital role arising from sexual or separation issues.
3. *Pregnancy and Childbearing Strains* — Four items which relate to pregnancy difficulties or adding a new member to the family.
4. *Finance and Business Strains* — Twelve items reflecting strain on the family money supply due to increased expenditures or investments.
5. *Work-Family Transitions and Strains* — Ten items related to moving to a new location.
6. *Illness and Family Care Strains* — Eight items focusing on chronic illness or illness onset or dependency needs of children or grandparents.
7. *Losses* — Six items arising from the death of a member or friend or due to broken relationships.
8. *Transitions "In and Out"* — Five items which reflect a member's moving out or becoming involved outside the family or moving back home.
9. *Family Legal Violations* — Five items focusing on a member's breaking society's laws or mores.

nine item self-report instrument, which assess the family's social-psychological, community, and financial resources, the family system, and social support dimensions. FIRM's development along with initial tests of reliability and validity are reported elsewhere (McCubbin and Patterson, 1981). CP parents were asked to complete this questionnaire together (single parent individually) and to react to each "family statement," deciding to what degree each item describes their family situation on a four-point scale (from "not at all" to "very well"). Four of the five major scales of FIRM were used in this investigation:

Family Strengths I: Esteem and Communication Scale assesses social-psychological resources in six areas (a) family esteem (report from friends, relatives, co-workers, and among family members); (b) communication (sharing feelings, discussing decisions); (c) mutual assistance (helping each other and relatives); (d) optimism; (e) problem-solving ability; and (f) encouragement of autonomy of family members. The reliability (Chronbach's alpha) is .85.

Family Strengths II: Mastery and Health Scale assesses social-psychological resources along three dimensions: (a) sense of mastery over family events and outcomes (fate control, flexibility, managerial abilities); (b) family mutuality (emotional support, togetherness, cooperation), and (c) physical and emotional health. The reliability (Chronbach's alpha) is .85.

The Extended Family Social Support Scale contains items which show giving and receiving help from relatives in terms of physical and material help as well as through supportive communication (esteem, respect, appreciation). The reliability of this scale (Chronbach's alpha) is .62.

The Financial Well-Being Scale assesses the family's sense of well-being surrounding finances covering six areas: (a) ability to meet financial commitments; (b) adequacy of financial reserves; (c) ability to help others financially; (d) optimism about the family's financial future (adequacy of insurance, financial benefits from employment, retirement income, earning power, financial progress); and (e) effective financial management practices. The reliability of this scale (Chronbach's alpha) is .85.

Parental Coping: Coping Health Inventory for Parents (CHIP) (McCubbin, McCubbin Nevin and Cauble, 1979) is a forty-five item questionnaire checklist developed to provide information about how parents and individuals perceive their overall responses to the management of a chronically ill child and disturbances in family functioning. The coping behaviors, such as, "Believing that my child will get better," or "talking with the medical staff when we visit the medical center," are listed and parents are asked to record how helpful (on a three-point scale) the coping items were in managing the home-illness situation.

The psychometric details of the development of CHIP are presented elsewhere (McCubbin and Patterson, 1981). Briefly, three coping patterns were derived from factor analysis representing 71.1 percent of the variance of the original correlation matrix. Chronbach's alpha computed for the items on each coping pattern indicated respectable reliabilities of .79, .79, and .71, for the respective coping patterns to be described.

The first coping pattern is composed of nineteen items, which focus on the parent's outlook on life and the illness. It is labeled *Maintaining Family Integration, Cooperation, and an Optimistic Definition of the Situation.*

Coping Pattern II consists of eighteen behavioral items, which focus upon the parent's effort to maintain a sense of their own well-being through social relationships, involvement in activities which enhance self-esteem, and managing psychological tensions. It is labeled *Maintaining Social Support, Self-Esteem and Psychological Stability.*

Coping Pattern III focuses on eight behaviors dealing with the relationship with other parents with an ill child and with the medical staff. It includes things such as understanding the medical information needed to care for the child at home. This coping pattern is labeled *Understanding the Medical Situation through Communication with other Parents and Consultation with Medical Staff.*

Family Functioning: Parents were asked to complete the Family Environment Scale (FES) (Moos, 1974), which is composed of ninety items that evaluate the social climate of families. FES is composed of ten subscales that measure the interpersonal relationships among family members, the directions of personal growth, which are emphasized in the family, and its basic organization structure.

The eight subscales that focus on family functioning utilized in this study were:

Family Interpersonal Relationship Dimensions of (a) cohesion (how concerned, helpful, and supportive family members are to one another); (b) expressiveness (how much family members are encouraged to express feelings directly); and (c) conflict (how characteristic the open expression of anger and aggression is of the family).

Family Personal-Growth Dimensions of (d) independence (how much family members are encouraged to be assertive, self-sufficient, to make their own decisions, and to think things out for themselves); (e) active recreational orientation (how much the family participates actively in various kinds of sporting activities; and (f) moral-religious emphasis (how much the family actively discusses and emphasises ethical and religious issues and values).

System Maintenance dimensions of (g) organization (how important order and organization are in the family in terms of structuring of activities, roles and responsibilities, and financial planning); and (h) control (the extent to which the family is organized in an hierarchical manner, the rigidity of rules and procedures).

Criterion Measure of Family Functioning: The investigators selected the conflict measure from FES as the criterion measure of family functioning. The hardships and struggles families experience and must contend with when a member has a chronic illness requiring ongoing care are most likely to be manifest in intra-family communication difficulties, which characterize families under stress. The research and clinical literature on families faced with difficulties point to family conflict as one of the primary indices of family strains as well as family breakdown.

To determine the validity of this specific measure as an index of total family functioning, we separated the total sample of families into two groups. By using the median score as the cutoff point, families with scores *above the median* were placed in the "high conflict" group, and families with scores *below the median* were placed in the "low conflict" group. We then compared these two groups on additional measures of family functioning, that is cohesion, expressiveness, independence, active-recreation orientation, moral-religious orientation, organization, and control. The data reveal that the *high* conflict group is significantly *lower* on family cohesion ($F = 34.35$, $p = .0001$), family expressiveness ($F = 6.96$, $p = .005$), family independence ($F = 11.37$, $p = .0009$), and family organization ($F = 20.20$, $p = .0001$) and is significantly *higher* on family control ($F = 8.47$, $p = .0040$). These data indicate that our criterion — dependent measure of family conflict is a valid index of CP family functioning.

RESULTS

Profile of CP Families

Of the families participating in at least one phase of the study, 189 were two-parent families, (178 in first marriages, eleven reconstituted families) and twenty-eight were single-parent families. Eleven long-term foster families (who experience the strains of caring for a chronically ill child much as a child's biological family would) are included in this study.

The mean length of marriage was fifteen years, with a range from one to forty-eight years. The number of children per family ranged from one to fourteen with a mean of three. The average income for these families was $15,000 to $20,000 per year, with a range from less than $5,000 to $40,000 per year.

Families living within the metropolitan Minneapolis-St. Paul area accounted for 26 percent of the sample, with another 24 percent living in towns surrounding the Twin Cities area. Nearly half (44%) of the families lived in Minnesota towns outside the greater Metropolitan area. Only 6 percent of the families were from other states.

The mean age for parents in these families was 37 years for mothers, and 40.5 years for fathers. The mean number of years of education for mothers was 12.7, with 12.9 for fathers. The majority (62%) of mothers had a high school education. Nearly one third of the fathers (31%) had a high school education, with 19 percent having less than a high school diploma. Intermediate degrees/certificates were held by 17 percent of the mothers and 22 percent of the fathers. Less than one-tenth (9%) of the mothers had bachelor's degrees, and 2 percent had graduate degrees. The majority of the mothers (52%) were full-time homemakers and were not employed outside the family. The remaining mothers were either employed part-time (20%) or full-time (28%). For fathers, the vast majority were employed full-time or more. A small number of the fathers (3%) were employed part-time, with 6 percent unemployed or retired. The religious preference for these families was primarily Protestant (60%) or Catholic (35%). The majority of the families were White (90%), with the remainder being American Indian (9%) Black or Hispanic (1%).

Based on the age of the oldest child, these families represented several stages of the family life cycle: One percent were in the young children stage (birth to two years); 13 percent in the preschool stage (three to five years); 29 percent in the school age stage (six to twelve years); 28 percent in the adolescent stage (thirteen to twenty years) and 29 percent in the launching or launched staged (twenty-one years and over). None of the CP families had more than one cerebral palsied child. Of the 217 children, 49 percent were girls, 51 percent were boys. The mean age was thirteen years, with a range from two to twenty-three years.

Stress in CP Families

This study examined three aspects of stressful life events and strains in CP families: a. the most frequently occurring events and strains, b. the events and strains with the most persistent impacts, and c. the most stressful events and strains. The Family Inventory of Life Events and Strains (FILE) records two types of changes a family may experience in the past year: "events" and "strains," which are often the consequence of the family's response to an event, but become stressors in themselves.

Not surprisingly for families with a handicapped child, the two most frequently reported life events were child related— child changing to a new school (36%) and child becoming seriously ill (36%). In addition to a child's illness, parents and/or relatives (34%) became seriously ill in many of these families. These frequencies suggest that families with one disabled member frequently include other members who are experiencing health problems.

Deaths of extended family members or close friends (20%), employment-related stressors, such as promotion (19%), changing to a new job (21%) or stopping work for an extended period (14%) occurred frequently in these CP families. Indeed CP families do experience multiple life events simultaneously — the pile-up hypothesized in the Double ABCX model (McCubbin and Patterson, Chapter 2).

An analysis was made to determine which of the life events experienced most frequently had a persistent impact. The families appeared to adjust quite rapidly to a child's serious illness; only 6 percent reported continuing adjustment to this problem. This suggests the chronicity of a handicapping condition has enabled the families to develop and use coping strategies effectively. A normative event, like a child changing to a new school, results in more persistent effects, with 10 percent reporting that adjustment continues. The most persistent impacts are related to events involving family finances — taking out a loan, a major purchase, and stock market changes affecting investments (14% report that adjustment continues). The most difficult events for the CP families appear to be transitional occurrences, such as a member stopping work, a new person moving into the home, and the death of a close relative. The serious illness of a parent or close relative was perceived as more stressful than the illness of a child member.

The second type of change a family may experience are strains. The most frequent strain reported was increased expense for basic needs — food, clothing, etc., recorded by 83 percent of the CP families. Increased medical/dental expenses were reported as a source of strain by 50 percent of the families. With our current rate of inflation and the continual need for health care, neither finding is surprising. The frequency of increased involvement of their children in activities outside the family (27%) suggests that the child's social isolation or withdrawal from the community is *not* characteristic of many of these families. Predictably, increased difficulty managing a disabled or chronically ill member (16%) was among the frequent strains experienced. Given the pile-up of these sources of strains and particularly the ongoing reality of a handicapped member, it is not surprising that a frequently recorded strain was having a member with emotional problems (16%).

As was done for life events, persistent impact for strains was assessed. Most important is the greater persistence of life *strains* compared to life *events*. It would appear that events have a more discrete, manageable dimension, allowing the family to adjust and move on. Strains are more insidious. Their onset is more gradual, often reflecting management or relationship difficulties, which the family may need time to get into perspective. Examples are "increase in arguments between parents and children" (19%) and "increase in conflict among children in the family" (15%). These strains reflect intra-family tension and are very persistent.

Parental Coping in CP Families

Parental coping with the demands of family life and the CP child received careful attention in this investigation. The data from the Coping Health Inventory for Parents (CHIP) reveal that mothers and fathers share similar patterns of coping, but that they do differ in what specific behaviors they underscore as being most helpful to them. Mothers' helpful coping behaviors call attention to the importance of keeping the *family functioning together as a unit and stable*. Mothers emphasize the value of carrying on the routine of follow-up medical care for the CP child and the importance of taking care of themselves as individuals by keeping in shape, developing themselves as persons, and becoming more self-reliant and independent. They value the chance to talk with friends about their feelings. Predictably, mothers place a high value on carrying forth with the medical treatments for children in the home setting. To them, the *family linkage with the medical center* is of paramount importance.

Fathers present a similar profile. Fathers' helpful coping behaviors also emphasize the importance of attending to family needs and the *maintenance of family stability*. In contrast to mothers, CP fathers noted the importance of gaining support and understanding from their spouses by "talking over personal feeling and concerns with their spouses." Fathers also emphasized the value of keeping in shape and *investing in themselves as individuals*. However, they placed a greater emphasis on *investing time and energy on the job* and on *going out with their spouses on a regular basis*. Fathers also underscored the *importance of medical consultation* as a vital part of their coping repertoire, with particular commitment to ensuring that medical treatments were carried out in the home.

Low Conflict vs. High Conflict Families

Family Stressors — Pile-up: It was reasonable to hypothesize that families in the low and high conflict groups would differ on basic family characteristics, specifically in terms of length of marriage, stage of life cycle, mother's age, father's age, mother's education, father's education, and family income. In testing this hypothesis, we found that there were no significant difference between the two groups on any of these characteristics. Furthermore, we observed no significant differences on the age and sex of the children in both the low and high conflict families.

We hypothesized that families experiencing a pile-up of family life changes, i.e. high stress from events and strains, would have a family environment characterized by conflict. In comparing low with high conflict families on the nine subscales of family life changes and total family life changes recorded from FILE, only three scales were statistically significant. High conflict families have a greater number of life changes (events and strains) in the areas of (a) work-family transitions and strains, e.g. decrease in satisfaction with job/career, child changed to new school, or a member changed to new job/career, ($F = 4.35$, $p = .0381$); (b) intra-family strains (increase in conflict among children, increase in problems, and issues not resolved) ($F = 22.89$, $p = .00001$); and (c) total life events and strains ($f = 9.16$, $p = .0028$).

Family Resources: We hypothesized that families who had more social-psychological, community, and financial resources for managing their life situation would experience less internal conflict within their family environment than families with fewer resources. Of the four scales measuring family resources on FIRM, two were statistically significant in differentiating high conflict from low conflict families. The social-psychological resources of (a) esteem and communication (Family Strengths I) ($F = 17.20$, $p = .090$) and (b) mastery and health (Family Strengths II) ($F = 4.35$, $p = .0382$) were more characteristic of families who function with less conflict.

Families in the low conflict group indicate greater internal strengths in terms of (a) family esteem (respect from friends, relatives, co-workers, and among family members); (b) communication (sharing feelings, discussing decisions); (c) mutual assistance (helping each other and relatives); (d) optimism; (e) problem-solving abilities; and (f) encouragement of autonomy and independence in the family.

Additionally these families reveal a sense of control and mastery of their lives matched with a general sense of physical and emotional well-being. Specifically these families share (a) a sense of mastery over events and outcomes along with flexibility to adjust to demands; (b) family mutuality with a sense of interpersonal support, togetherness, and cooperation; and (c) physical and emotional health of family members.

In general, these low conflict families indicate a sense of internal stability, which appears to serve as a buffer against the hardships of caring for a CP child and the impact of predictable and unpredictable life events.

In comparing parental coping employed in low and high conflict CP families, a consistent set of differences was observed. Specifically, both mothers and fathers in the high conflict group score consistently higher on each of the three major coping patterns: family integration, social support, and medical consultation. Mothers' coping scores on all three scales presented in Table 9-I indicate that in high conflict families, mothers are called upon to employ a full range of coping behaviors designed to keep the family together, to develop support for themselves and the family, and to maintain contact with the medical staff. Fathers' coping scores presented in Table 9-II reveal the same pattern of higher scores in high conflict families.

Table 9–I

Mothers' Coping Patterns in Low Versus High
Conflict Cerebral Palsy Families

Coping Patterns	Low Conflict Families		High Conflict Families			
	Mean	SD	Mean	SD	F	P=
Mothers' and Family Integration	36.3	19.4	42.8	10.4	9.28	.0026
Mothers' and Social Support	24.0	14.4	30.9	8.4	18.01	.0001
Mothers' and Medical Consultation	13.7	8.0	15.8	5.1	5.15	.0242

Both Tables 9-I and 9-II reflecting mothers' and fathers' coping respectively suggest that coping is an active process responding to stressors and hardships in the family unit. As hypothesized, when studying families under stress or, in this case, "in conflict," we would expect coping behavior to be employed and therefore parental scores to be high. This finding and observation runs contrary to the

Table 9–II

Fathers' Coping Patterns in Low Versus High
Conflict Cerebral Palsy Families

Coping Patterns	Low Conflict Families		High Conflict Families			
	Mean	SD	Mean	SD	F	P=
Fathers' and Family Integration	30.5	21.7	36.1	17.2	4.4	.0037
Fathers' and Social Support	19.4	14.8	24.5	13.7	6.9	.0088
Fathers' and Medical Consultation	9.9	8.2	12.0	7.0	3.9	.0471

common-sense notion that coping automatically resolves problems. We appear to have captured the CP families in the process of attending to the intra-family strains and conflicts.

Critical Stressors, Resources and Coping Patterns

The families classified in the high conflict group present an interesting set of data, which suggests some conclusions about (a) what the major areas of family conflict are and (b) how parents cope with the difficulties they face and at the same time buffer themselves from total family dysfunction and breakdown.

The hardships and difficulties in families of CP children are not centered totally upon the medical and child care of a chronically ill member. The data clearly indicate that families also struggle with a host of events and strains, particularly intra-family and work strains, which are both causes and consequences of family conflict. The high conflict families face intra-family strains including parent-child, parent-parent, and child-child arguments. In general, these families were faced with child management responsibilities and strains, which ultimately affected members, including the CP child. Importantly these families also struggled with an increase in a parent's time away from the family as well as family concern for and about a member who appears to have emotional problems.

High conflict families also struggle with work-family transitions and strains. These families appear to face hardships associated with a child/adolescent member changing schools as well as difficulties experienced at work, which find their way into family life. The greatest frequency of work-family stressors involved a decrease in satisfaction with a job or career. A few family units faced major transitions at work such as losing or quitting a job and/or a member starting or returning to work.

Families characterized by conflict appear to be struggling with major family transitions and changes reflective of the ever-changing demands children place upon parents, who themselves are undergoing personal and interpersonal changes. Solutions to these intra-family, work-family, and illness stressors are not achieved quickly, nor are they gained without family communication, compromise, and the time needed to work things out.

A common-sense notion of coping led us to hypothesize the high scores on coping would be associated with low conflict families. However the data reveal that it is the high conflict families who score consistently higher on all coping scales. When these data are viewed in direct relationship with the stresses and strains of high conflict families, we can begin to appreciate the role of coping in parental management of stress. Several arguments may be made to clarify the meaning of the data: first, parental coping behaviors and patterns *emerge in response* to stressful situations; second, parental coping behaviors and patterns *will remain in operation* to deal with the hardships and strains in the family unit; third, parental coping behaviors and patterns are expected to be *most valued* and most apparent in stressful situations; fourth, parental coping behaviors and patterns will be *moderately helpful and only moderately apparent* in family situations which are *not* plagued by stressful life events and strains; and fifth, parental coping behaviors and patterns play a positive and supportive role in (a) managing stresses in the family and in (b) keeping the family unit in balance and stabilized in the face of stressors.

Therefore, in accordance with the perspective on coping, we would expect the high conflict families to score consistently higher on our indices of coping, particularly in light of the pile-up of life events and strains in these families. The findings also suggest that despite the high conflict status of these families, they are *not* to be viewed as dysfunctional or problem families. Their relatively high scores on mother's and fathers' coping suggest that high conflict families can best be described as families under stress in the process of struggling to manage the hardships they face.

One of the most striking and yet obvious findings of this investigation is the importance of (a) how *both parents* cope with the stressors and care of the CP child and (b) the three major coping patterns (family integration, social support, and medical consultation). Given the primary caretaking role mothers perform in the management of the home and the CP child, it comes as a confirmation of record data indicating the mothers' coping to keep the family together, to gain friendships and extended family social supports, and to consult with the medical team are all-important. It is, however, unique to record the same set of findings for fathers, which indicate the important role he plays in the stability of the family unit under stress and facilitating the care of the CP child. Both mothers' and fathers' coping appear to be major contributors to the well-being of the family under stress and ultimately to the well-being of the CP member. However obvious this may be, this investigation provides one of the most complete set of findings in support of this line of reasoning and the only quantitative data of the major role fathers play in the CP family unit.

These findings also suggest which families with a CP child would be the most vulnerable. We would suggest that the most vulnerable families are those who are experiencing a pile-up of life strains and events and where neither mother nor father have yet developed helpful coping behaviors to manage these stressors.

Families could be considered moderately vulnerable when (a) there is a pile-up of life changes, and it is only partially managed because only one parent is coping effectively. The other parent is low on coping or is absent from the family unit, or (b) there is a pile-up of stressors, and even with high scores on coping, the family system continues to be pushed to the point of exhaustion of breakdown, particularly if additional stressors were added on, or one or both parents "burn out" and can no longer sustain this active coping effort.

Finally, the least vulnerable families would be those without a pile-up and hence a relatively low level of stress, and, in addition, have either or both parents scoring high on coping. Also, families who indicate low level of stress and low scores on coping would be

considered in the low vulnerability group, although they could shift
to a more vulnerable group if they experienced more stress and did
not develop coping behaviors in response.

Families in the low conflict group appear to have developed a set
of internal resources, which serve them well in this particular situation. Specifically, these families have developed and maintained an
overall sense of stability characterized by a collective feeling of *esteem
and mutual support*. This dimension, of family strengths include the
sharing of feelings and decision making complemented by optimism
about the situation.

Despite the hardships and responsibilities associated with the
care of a handicapped member, low conflict families are able to
maintain a *sense of mastery* over life's hardships and demands. In other
words, these families appear to develop a sense of competence and
trust in their collective ability to manage whatever hardships and
problems they face. This sense of internal strength is not related to
family income or to parents' level of education, but rather to the
cohesive feeling among family members. This family characteristic
is complemented by the family's sense of emotional stability and a
positive assessment of the physical health of family members.

CONCLUSIONS

As we shift our attention from the statistics presented to the
potential implications of the findings outlined in this study, we can
begin to develop a set of basic conclusions and recommendations.

First, given the continued stressor of financial burdens on CP
families, it is important to acknowledge the value of the existing
medical-financial support programs available to these families.
However, the data clearly indicate the need for additional benefits in
terms of expanded coverage of insurance programs, prepaid medical
service, and financial counseling.

Second, the reported pile-up of family life events and strains,
particularly in the area of intra-family and work-family strains, suggests the need for additional family-oriented counseling. The findings also suggest that help for these families should not be limited to
the hardships surrounding the medical situation and the direct care
of the CP child. Other normative and nonnormative sources of
strain have an impact upon the family's ability to attend to the
specialized needs of the CP child and, equally important, to care for

other members and family itself.

The realistic limitations on staff time and energy, particularly that of the attending physicians, nurses, and physical therapists, would lead us to emphasize the importance of using behavioral scientists, such as social workers and psychologists, as part of the medical team working with CP families. Their training and expertise in the areas of psychological and interpersonal functioning might be given additional consideration as primary resources to strengthen CP families. This suggestion does not ignore the important role that these professionals already play in the clinic. Rather the recommendation underscores their importance and encourages an expansion of their role and increased application of their professional abilities.

Third, the instruments developed in this research project can help a clinic's staff in working with families with handicapped children. The research findings indicate that (a) the family screening and diagnostic instruments developed in this study may be employed in identifying vulnerable families, and (b) these same instruments may be used as a guide to assist counselors in identifying those critical areas of family life and parental coping deserving of immediate attention. Such a counseling strategy, which includes brief but reliable and valid instruments, may be helpful to family professionals whose access to CP families is limited. In situations where family contact is limited to clinic visits, a brief but accurate diagnostic profile would greatly enhance the counselor's efforts in crisis prevention and intervention.

Fourth, family counseling in the communities in which CP families live would be a helpful service to augment the support families get through the medical clinic. To encourage this kind of family counseling, we need to share the information from this and other research investigations and to make counseling tools — such as those developed in this study — more widely available to professionals.

Certainly, the research findings call attention to those important aspects of family life and coping, which merit professional consideration. As we shift our attention from family failures to family strengths, we can call upon the findings from this research to identify targets for family counseling and crisis intervention. The findings indicate the need to focus upon stressors and hardships, family strengths, and particularly upon how *both* mothers and fathers cope with the situation.

If there is any serious consideration and commitment to families with a cerebral palsy member, it is only reasonable to adopt the perspective that families are an intergral part of the rehabilitation team. Parental involvement and cooperation and particularly their commitment to follow through with the medical regimen in the home setting are absolutely essential to the long-term rehabilitation and development of the CP child.

Chapter 10

SOCIAL SUPPORT AND HEALTH THROUGH THE LIFE COURSE

SIDNEY COBB

ALL the world's great religions support the Golden Rule in one form or another. "Love thy neighbor as thyself," (Leviticus XIX:18) has been the advice of our spiritual leaders for many centuries. Only lately have those of us concerned with health come to realize the importance of this kind of prescription. We tend to call this social support and to fit it into a general notion of support systems. In this essay I shall attempt to do three things: explain what social support is and where it fits in a broader scheme of support systems, summarize the rather overwhelming literature relating this concept to various aspects of health, and discuss a possible theoretical explanation for the way in which social support acts to promote the health of individuals.

THE NATURE OF SOCIAL SUPPORT

There are four kinds of support. The first and most important is social support. It is sometimes called communicated caring. It is purely informational and it has three components: (1) Emotional support leading the recipient to believe that she is cared for and loved. (2) Esteem support leading the recipient to believe that she is esteemed and valued. (3) Network support leading the recipient to believe that she has a defined position in a network of communication and mutual obligation.

The second form of support is instrumental support or counseling. This involves guiding persons to better coping and/or adapta-

From Sidney Cobb, Social support and health through the life course, In Matilda White Riley (Ed.): *Aging from Birth to Death,* 1979. Copyright © 1979 by the American Association for the Advancement of Science. Reprinted by permission of the American Association for the Advancement of Science and Westview Press.

tion and to maximization of their participation and autonomy.

The third is active support or mothering. This is what mothers do for infants and nurses do for patients. When done unnecessarily it may lead to dependency.

The fourth is material support or goods and service. The provision of goods and technical services might be thought to include active support. The distinction can be made clear by the example of an overworked executive. On the one hand, if his boss comes and does part of the job for him, it comes under the rubric of active support and can fit into the sequence of mothering-smothering-spoiling. On the other hand, if the boss permits the executive to hire himself an assistant and/or buy a piece of equipment to expedite his work, it comes under material support.

It is important to note that instrumental support, active support, and material support may involve or imply social support. For example, taking the time to counsel a student may communicate that you care. In feeding a special meal to her grown son, a mother communicates love as well as providing nourishment. In giving a student a scholarship, one communicates esteem as well as providing money. Because of this confounding the focus of any support system will always appear to be on social support. This is important as a source of bias in research, but is probably entirely appropriate for it is my belief that social support is more important than all the others put together. (Cobb, 1976)

With this view of the position of social support, let us examine its components in more detail. Emotional support is information that one is cared for and loved or, as the Greeks might say, information about agapé. It is transmitted in intimate situations involving mutual trust. In a dyadic relationship this information meets Murray, Barrett, and Hamburger's (1938) need succorance for one person, need nurturance for the other, and need affiliation for both.

Information that one is valued and esteemed is most effectively proclaimed in public. It leads the individual to esteem himself and reaffirms his sense of personal worth, and above all it assures him of a personal and separate identity. It is called esteem support.

Information that one has a place in a network of communication and mutual obligation must be common and shared. It must be common in the sense that everyone in the network has the information and shared in the sense that each member is aware that every other member knows. The relevant information is of three kinds. The first is historical. A strong network has a history. The second pertains to goods and services that are available to any member on demand, and includes information about the accessibility of services that are only occasionally needed — e.g., equipment; specialized skills, technical information. The third contains information that is common and shared with respect to the dangers of life and the procedures for mutual defense. In this last sense the knowledge that a competently staffed hospital is available in case of need is socially supportive.

SOCIAL SUPPORT AND HEALTH

The effects of social support on health will be looked at in several categories: the effects during pregnancy, the effects on learning and early development, the effects on health at the time of various life crises, the relationship to various specific illnesses plus its effect on compliance with prescribed medical regimens, and its general life sparing effect.

During Pregnancy

With regard to the complications of pregnancy, Nuckolls, Cassel, and Kaplan (1972) have shown that there is an interaction between life change score and social support in the prediction of the proportion who will have one or another complication of pregnancy. My recalculation of her data shows that the interaction is significant and that 91 percent of those with a lot of life changes and low social support ended up with complications compared to 43 percent of the other three categories.

In addition to this there is some evidence that mothers with unwanted pregnancies are likely to have smaller babies than mothers who desired the pregnancy in the first place. The principal observation in this area comes from a study by Morris, Udry, and Chase in 1973. Curiously the findings are true both for blacks and whites, but only for those with at least a high school education. The findings were not confirmed by Hultin and Ottosson (1971) in Sweden but their analyses did not control for educational level of the mother. It is, of course, not reasonable to suppose that "wantedness" is information that is transmitted from mother to fetus and thus influences growth rate; rather it seems likely that a woman "rejects" her baby and functions less effectively as a mother because she is herself inadequately socially supported. The societal reaction to illegitimate pregnancy is a case in point. These two studies of birth weight did not look at concomitant environmental stresses, and one of them suffers from the disadvantage of being a retrospective inquiry.

In Early Development

The first real adaptive demand that is placed on the child is the achievement of sphincter control. Stein and Susser (1967) report that bladder control at night was significantly delayed for those children whose mothers went out to work while the children were in the second six months of life. This was not true if the mother went out to work earlier or later. Two studies of the children of mothers who requested abortion but had those abortions refused (reported by Forssman and Thuwe, 1966; Dytrych, Matejcek, Schuller, David and Friedman, 1975) both suggest, but neither really proves, that wanted children adapt to and/or cope with the stresses of growing up better than those who started out with parental request for abortion that was denied. The thrust of significant results of these two studies seems to be in the socialization area. Particularly striking was the lesser educational achievement of the unwanted children as compared to the controls. These studies, one done in Scandinavia and the other in Czechoslovakia, deserve to be replicated in this country now that abortions are more available.

In Life Transitions and Crises

The next area of concern is the transition to adult life. There are obvious stresses associated with the first job and with the beginning of marital and family responsibilities, but there seems to be little in the way of data about the effect of social support at the time of this transition. Research in this area is clearly indicated. Elsewhere (Cobb and Kasl, 1977) I have examined the effects of social support in moderating the consequences of job termination. The effects are striking with respect to most of the psychological variables, but with respect to the physiological variables examined the effects were only of border line significance. However, when it came to the disease category of arthritis, there was a tenfold increase in the frequency of joint swelling as one moved from the highest third of social support to the lowest.

Erikson (1976) has written eloquently of his observations in the case of the Buffalo Creek flood which destroyed so many homes. He makes it clear that from an observational standpoint at least, social support was an important variable. However, his most telling comments bear on the extent to which support networks were destroyed by the newly developed housing arrangements and the consequences of this loss of network support.

Weiss (1975) has noted the importance of social support for those going through a divorce, and many authors have noted the importance of social support under the stress of war (Mandelbaum, 1952; Reid, 1947; Rose, 1956; Swank, 1949; Titmuss, 1950). Menninger (1947), describing his World War II experiences, said, "We seemed to learn anew the importance of group ties in the maintenance of mental health."

As old age approaches, infirmity begins, and retirement takes place, further stresses occur. Much informal information has been published about the importance of social support at this time of life but there is relatively little hard evidence. Lowenthal and Haven (1968) present evidence that is at least suggestive that depression at this time of life is less frequent among those who are adequately socially supported. This, of course, is not a novel finding for, as will be seen in the next section, there is evidence that social support is protective with respect to depression throughout life.

When we come to bereavement the evidence is less strong than one might expect, for most of us act as though the bereavement period were a period requiring social support. Parkes (1972) and Burch (1972) present suggestive evidence. The data of Gerber, Wiener, Battin, and Arkin (1975) bear more directly on the subject but are disappointing in their presentation. They are at least suggestive of effects in the predicted direction. However, Raphael (1977) has presented striking evidence that those with little social support are more likely to report poor health thirteen months after bereavement than are those with more adequate support. Furthermore, he is able to demonstrate that supportive treatment for those with little social support leads to a return to the normal state of affairs at thirteen months. *See* Table 10-I.

Table 10–I

The Relationship of Perceived Social Support to
Health Status of Women 13 Months After the Death
of Their Husbands (Raphael, 1977)

Perceived Social Support	Reported Health at 13 Months			Percent Poor
	Good	Poor	Total	
1. Adequate	115	33	148	22
2. Inadequate	2	12	14	86
3. Inadequate — "Treated"	14	2	16	13

$$1 \text{ vs } 2 \; x^2 = 25.6, \; p \; 0.001$$

$$2 \text{ vs } 3 \; x^2 = 13.3, \; p \; 0.001$$

In Specific Illnesses

Having skimmed the life course and shown effects at almost every stage, it is time to turn to some specific diseases. The relationship to diseases is of two sorts. First, there are associations of lack of social support with onset of the disease: e.g. tuberculosis reviewed by Chen and Cobb (1960), depression (Brown, Bhrolchain, and Harris, 1975; Brown, Davidson, and Harris, 1977), arthritis (Cobb & Kasl, 1977), and coronary heart disease, noted by many authors in many ways (Caplan, 1971) but most notably by Parkes, Benjamin and Fitzgerald (1969) in their article entitled "The Broken Heart" in which they discuss the excess of coronary deaths among those men who have recently lost their wives. Second, there is evidence that recovery from cardiac failure (Chambers and Reiser, 1953), tuberculosis (Holmes, Joffe, and Ketcham, 1961), surgical operation (Egbert, Battit, Welch, and Bartlett, 1964), asthma (deAraujo, van Arsdel, Holmes, and Dudley, 1973), psychosomatic illness (Berle, Pinsky, Wolf and Wolf, 1952), and various psychiatric illnesses (Lambert, 1973; Caplan, 1974b; Hermalin, 1976; Brown, 1959) is accelerated or facilitated by high levels of social support.

In Compliance with Treatment

Part of this facilitation of recovery is mediated by improved compliance. It is an interesting and little known fact that the association of compliance and social support is one of the best documented relationships in all of medical sociology. Specifically, if a physician wants a patient to follow a complex routine for the maintenance of his health, as in hypertension, it is almost essential that he pay attention to the support systems in the patient's life. The literature in this area is summarized in two separate reviews (Baekeland and Lundwall, 1975; Haynes and Sackett, 1974). Of 41 articles, 34 support the association with compliance, 6 give insignificant results and 1 reports a negative finding. The association of lung cancer with cigarette smoking at the time of the Surgeon General's report was hardly stronger than that and yet this is an almost entirely neglected aspect of medical practice.

In Sparing Life

In the end one always gets involved with matters of life and death, and it is appropriate here to call attention to two important findings. The first has come to be known as the "Phillips effect." In a truly remarkable paper, Phillips and Feldman (1973) demonstrated in five separate studies that deaths are reduced in the six months preceding birthdays and increased in the succeeding six months. A summary of their data is presented in Figure 10-1. They went on to hypothesize that, if this were a social support effect, it should be more striking for the most distinguished people. They found this hypothesis to be dramatically confirmed.

The second important study was reported by Berkman at the last annual meeting of the American Public Health Association (1977). She provided data from the California Human Population Laboratory study of 7,000 residents of Alameda county which show that, over a ten year period, age adjusted mortality is reduced among those who have good network support. The support was measured in advance by 1) marriage, 2) contact with close friends and relatives, 3) church membership, 4) informal and formal group associations. There were successive decreases in age adjusted mortality rates for each of the four levels of social support for both males

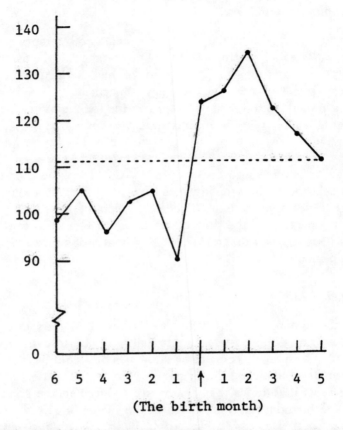

Figure 10-1. Number of deaths before, during, and after birth month. Redrawn from data of Phillips and Feldman, 1973. Reproduced with permission.

and females. The effect was independent of, and in addition to, the effect of positive health practices as reported by Belloc (1973). The risk of dying more than doubled from the highest to the lowest category of network support. We will all look forward with interest to the final publication of the detailed analyses of this important phenomenon.

INTERPRETATIONS AND IMPLICATIONS

Some of the effects of social support appear to be direct or main effects and others appear as interactions with stresses in the social environment. In my view it is not worth worrying about the distinction between main effects and interaction effects, for several reasons. The first is that few if any lives are entirely free of social and psychological stress so, when main effects appear, it may be that unmeasured stresses are producing an interaction effect that is large enough to appear also as a main effect. The second point is that it is quite reasonable to imagine that at very low levels of social support the deprivation would be strong enough to be a stress in itself, while at medium levels it would take some other environmental stress to highlight the deficit, and at the highest levels protection from strain might be very substantial. This notion is displayed graphically in Figure 10-2.

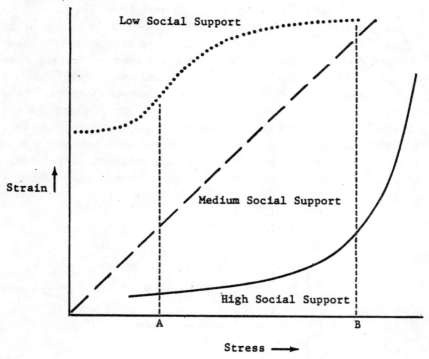

Figure 10-2. An hypothesis about the nature of the relationship of stress and strain in the face of varying levels of social support.

The implications of this theory are very interesting because they include the prediction that the interaction effect would look quite different for a dichotomy between high and medium than for the dichotomy between medium and low levels of social support. This would be especially true if the range of stress measured were limited, say from A to B in the diagram. If this formulation is correct, we should not be worried about main effects vs. interaction effects but should rather be concerned with mapping the three-dimensional relationship among the variables.

When it comes to thinking about the mechanism involved, it seems unlikely that social support could operate directly on so many indications of strain. It makes more sense to hypothesize that it operates to facilitate stress reduction by improving the fit between the person and the environment (French, Rodgers, and Cobb, 1974). The hypothesis is displayed in Figure 10-3. The three components of social support are located in the box in the middle of the figure. The arrows from Esteem Support and Emotional Support to Adaptation indicate the belief that those who are esteemed, therefore self-confident, and those who are emotionally supported, therefore comfortable, are more able to change themselves to fit into a changed environment. Similarly, those who are confident have a sense of autonomy and are more likely to engage in coping behavior, and so are more likely to take control of their environments and to manipulate these environments into a more acceptable shape. By the same token, Network Support and Esteem Support contribute to a

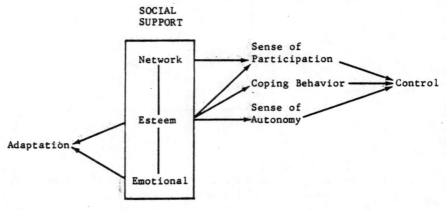

Figure 10-3. An hypothesis about the mechanism through which social support might operate to improve an individual relationship with the environment, thereby reducing psychosocial stress and thus relieving strain.

sense of participation in decision making, which likewise contributes to environmental control, or at least to the "illusion of control" which Perlmuter and Monty (1977) have shown may be as important as actual control.

In summary, social support, defined as the sum of emotional support, esteem support, and network support, has beneficial effects on a wide variety of health variables throughout the life course from conception to just before death, and on the bereaved who are left behind after a death. There are many faults in the various studies, but the repetitive nature of the effects using varied techniques is impressive. The pervasiveness of these social support effects suggests that we are dealing with a very general phenomenon and a really fundamental variable. One cannot escape the conclusion that the world would be a healthier place if training in supportive behavior were built into the routines of our homes and schools, and support worker roles were institutionalized.

Chapter 11

THE FAMILY AS A SUPPORT SYSTEM

GERALD CAPLAN

THE SUPPORT SYSTEMS MODEL

IN a recent book (Caplan, 1974) I proposed a conceptual model that focused on the health-promoting and ego-fortifying effects on individuals of what I called "support systems." I defined these as "continuing social aggregates (namely, continuing interactions with another individual, a network, a group, or an organization) that provide individuals with opportunities for feedback about themselves and for validation of their expectations about others, which may offset deficiencies in these communications within the larger community context." I linked this definition with the epidemiologic and ethological researches of Cassel (1974) who has demonstrated that subpopulations influenced by such aggregates have a lower incidence of mental and physical disease than their neighbors, especially under conditions of acute and chronic stress associated with rapid physical and social change.

I postulated that "the characteristic attribute of these social aggregates that act as a buffer against disease is that in such relationships the person is dealt with as a unique individual. The other people are interested in him in a personalized way. They speak his language. They tell him what is expected of him and guide him in what to do. They watch what he does and they judge his performance. They let him know how well he has done. They reward him for success and punish or support and comfort him if he fails. Above all, they are sensitive to his personal needs, which they deem worthy of respect and satisfaction.

"Such support may be of a continuing nature or intermittent and short-term and may be utilized from time to time by the individual

From Gerald Caplan, The family as a support System, In Gerald Caplan and Marie Killileu (Eds): *Support Systems and Mutual Help,* 1976. Reprinted by permission of Grune & Stratton, Inc. and the author.

in the event of an acute need or crisis. Both enduring and short-term supports are likely to consist of three elements: (a) the significant others help the individual mobilize his psychological resources and master his emotional burdens; (b) they share his tasks; and (c) they provide him with extra supplies of money, materials, tools, skills, and cognitive guidance to improve his handling of his situation" (Caplan, 1974).

In my recent book, I discussed how support systems seem to operate in our current social life through kith and kin groups and networks, via the informal operations of individual nonprofessional caregivers, and through such organizations as religious denominations, fraternal associations, and mutual assistance and self-help groups. I used this discussion as a basis for proposing some innovations in mental health and human services practice which stimulate the development of nonprofessional support systems to augment on a community-wide scale the capacity of individuals to master their environment in mentally healthy ways, particularly individuals made vulnerable because they are involved in acute crises, life transitions, or chronic privations. My main thesis was that we professionals must learn to appreciate the fortifying potential of the natural person-to-person supports in the population and to find ways of working with them through some form of partnership that fosters and strengthens nonprofessional groups and organizations. I wish now to focus on one segment of this field by examining how the concept of support systems illuminates a particular aspect of the functioning of family life and to use this in developing some preliminary guidelines for helpful community action.

TODAY'S FAMILY AS A SOCIAL UNIT

Until recently, I, like many other caregiving professionals, maintained three beliefs about the modern American urban family. First, I believed that, in contrast to the extended family of traditional rural America, the modern urban family is mainly a small, nuclear unit of two parents with one to three children, relatively cut off from grandparents and other close relatives. A corollary of this was my second belief that most older people lived isolated lives, effectively separated from their children and grandchildren. Third, I believed that a large proportion of people over the age of 65-70 are chronically sick, dependent, and ineffectual, which I linked with their having been extruded from the labor force and separated from their children so that they have neither public nor private roles that satisfy them. Since advances in public health and clinical medicine have led to an increase in the proportion of our growing population who are over 65 (Claven and Vatter, 1972a) I felt that the two-pronged problem of isolation of family units and of the older generation would lead to the need to provide specialized public care-giving services to both on a large and increasing scale.

I now realize that all three of my fundamental beliefs are false. A series of empirical researches — particularly those of (Sussman 1959; Sussman and Burchinal, 1962) — has demonstrated that the modal family of present-day urban America is still an extended family in which grandparents and often great-grandparents, although they may live in separate households, remain active participants in the primary kin network. Ethel Shanas (1973) has shown that not only in the cities of the United States but also in England, Denmark, Yugoslavia, Poland, and Israel, the majority of older persons live either in the same household or within 10 minutes of one of their children. From 70 to 80 percent of the elderly persons studied by Shanas and her collaborators and personal contact with at least one of their children within the previous week.

And, finally, my third belief — that most people over 65 are sick, ineffective, and dependent — is as false as the others. Two of our recent Harvard studies on different populations have revealed that 80 to 85 percent of men and women over 65 are, and feel themselves to be, active and in good health, irrespective of current age (Ryser and Sheldon, 1969) — findings that are consonant with those of several other researchers. In other words, the elderly are about as healthy and potentially as active as younger people. Their life expectancy is, of course, shorter; but until they fall ill and die, they remain capable of playing an active role in public and family affairs.

The findings of such studies reveal that the modern American family, far from being a small, isolated, nuclear unit of parents and their children, is in the majority of cases an interdependent network involving parents and their siblings, children, grandparents, and increasingly great-grandparents living under one roof or in nearby households.

I will now examine the average family's operation as a support system, with the understanding that there are many deviations from the ideal-type pictured, which will entail supplementation of social policies and service programs that we plan on the basis of the modal patterns.

SUPPORT SYSTEM FUNCTIONS OF THE FAMILY

The Family as a Collector and Disseminator of Information About the World

This is a fundamental support system function. Traditionally, most people have thought of it mainly in connection with the socialization of children, and surely it is important that parents share their store of information about the outside world with their children so that the latter are not forced to collect all this knowledge themselves, even though there is a limit to what a person can learn vicariously from the experience of others. In a multigenerational family, information from grandparents helps their adult children learn the parental roles, and grandparent-child interaction provides a situation where the giving and acceptance of information may often be easier because the usual tensions produced by the reality-based obligations of the parent-child relationship are absent or reduced.

It is important to realize that a multigenerational family also provides a vehicle for information to flow in the reverse direction, so that the younger members, from their own unique age-linked experiences of the current world, tell their elders what is actually happening "out there." This is particularly significant at the present time when the speed of change is such that knowledge about the world quickly gets outdated.

The Family as a Feedback Guidance System

The researches of Cassel alert us to the crucial importance for physical and mental health of the capacity of individuals to make valid assessments of feedback cues in their environment, especially in new and therefore potentially bewildering situations. In animal population experiments, this is shown by the increase in morbidity and mortality produced, apparently by nervous and hormonal depletion, when the size and density of the population are increased so that animals are not able to differentiate friends from foes and are therefore forced continually to be on guard to fend off possible attacks. An analog in humans is the personality disorganization resulting from culture shock. A family provides a continuing training ground for members to learn how to adjust to immediate feedback about what other people feel regarding their behavior, because signals in the family are usually obtrusive and easily understandable. It also provides a receptive group where members can relatively undefensively report what they have done and how people have reacted to their actions, so that the rest of the family can help them understand what went on.

From this we can see the significance of what occurs in most families where, shortly after members come home, they give detailed reports on their behavior at school, work, or in social situations, together with how others reacted to them, especially if these reactions were upsetting, surprising, or incomprehensible. In some families, such discussions take place regularly at mealtimes and have almost a ceremonial aspect. During these discussions, the other members of the group help the person evaluate not only his own reported behavior in the light of the family value system but also the meaning of the reactions of the people with whom he was involved.

The Family as a Source of Ideology

The family group is a major source of the belief systems, value systems, and codes of behavior that determine an individual's understanding of the nature and meaning of the universe, of his place in it, and of the paths he should strive to travel in his life. Together with the stream of cumulative information about the concrete nature of the real world, these systems of belief and values provide the individual with a map of his universe, and with a set of goals and missions, as well as a compass in finding his way. Part of this information comes from explicit teaching, part comes from introjection of assumptions and meanings that characterize family culture with its traditions, memories, and myths, and part comes from conscious copying, or unconscious identification, with family role models and with relationships among family members and between them and outsiders.

These processes are buttressed by the expectations of the social milieu that individuals will naturally conform to the dominant views, beliefs, motivations, and practices of their family. This is well illustrated by the usual reciprocal reinforcement of family units and religious denominations. Most denominations recruit their members from family units. Religious rituals focus on developmental incidents and transitions of family life, from dealing with which the denomination derives much of its potency as a power for social integration, while at the same time it strengthens the family as a social unit. Religious denominations are the leading social institution that deals with the entire family as a unit throughout its developmental history. Conversely, families inculcate and foster among their members the value and belief systems and code of ethics of their religious denomination and strive to recruit the marital partners of their children to the same beliefs, as well as to ensure that grandchildren follow a similar path.

The strengthening power of these internalized systems of beliefs and values as well as the abstract and concrete maps of the world, and the prescriptions for wise conduct that go with them, can be seen in operation whenever a family member, even in geographical isolation, is faced with an acute crisis. At such times, the individual is faced by novel problems that he is not able to solve quickly with his usual problem-solving and coping mechanisms, and he is inevitably frustrated and confused because he is not able to predict the outcome of the predicament — he cannot, as it were, see round the corner. At such times, it is very hard for him to choose what path to take, and he usually feels weak and helpless. That is just the time when he may derive particular benefit from the traditions of his family. They may tell him, for instance, to stay with the problem and to keep struggling to find its solution by trial and error, with the expectation that eventually something constructive will emerge, rather than to quickly admit defeat and give up the struggle, as he may naturally be inclined to do. If, in addition, his family code is part of a larger religious tradition, he will feel a deeper faith that he is moving in a wise direction by continuing the struggle, and he will feel buttressed by the multitudes of his coreligionists. Moreover, by relying on the accumulated wisdom of his family and of the previous generations of members of his religion, whose trials and errors in the past have led to the traditional action prescription, he is likely, in reality, to be acting more wisely than if he has to choose his path based only on his own individual wisdom, particularly during the confusion of crisis.

Years of crisis research have given me many illustrations of the advantage of individuals who conform to family and religious traditions over the nonconformists, the rebels, and the irreligious — except, of course, for "rebels with a cause" who are strengthened by the ideology of their social or political movement, even though it may be explicitly antifamilial and antireligious. This was brought home once again to me when I was in Israel during the Yom Kippur War, helping to organize services for the relatives of casualties. I was much impressed by the steadfastness of those with a strong family, religious, or other ideological identification compared with those who lacked these internalized supports, even though the nature of the situation was such that it evoked for all of the sufferers an outpouring of living concern and concrete help from the entire population. Time after time I heard from religious and social leaders when they returned to report to me on their visit of condolence to a bereaved family, "We came to offer them our consolation in the name of the community, and instead they consoled and comforted us, telling us how much they appreciated the good work we were doing and reassuring us that our efforts were worthwhile and that we were earning God's blessing." Such bereaved families were invariably either deeply religious or members of the ideological elite, the heroic Israelis who had a long family tradition of national service and sacrifice. In contrast, the irreligious and those without a strong family culture or Zionist ideological commitment were expectedly distraught and dispirited — they had less of an internalized structure to hold them together, and their poise had to come from their constitutional ego-strength plus the active support and help of their families and neighbors. When any of these factors was deficient, they tended to collapse, at least for a while.

The Family as Guide and Mediator in Problem Solving

In addition to the incorporation within individuals of cognitive maps and codes of conduct derived from their participation over many years in family patterns of organized behavior, members benefit from here-and-now guidance when they become involved in crisis or long-term burdens. Most families encourage members to communicate freely about their personal difficulties, many of which are likely to involve some or all of the other members of the group. In either case, the family shares the problem, and other members offer advice and guidance either as an organized group or as individuals, in accordance with family tradition and the respective talents and roles of its members.

An important element in a family's helping a member with a problem is not only telling him how to find external sources of care and assistance, such as health and welfare agencies, but actually helping to make the arrangements for the relevant caregivers to take action. This may mean calling them in or actually going with the person in distress to the community institution. Most families over the years accumulate a list of dependable community professional and nonprofessional caregivers and agencies and build up a network of relationships with key individuals in the health and welfare field to whom they can turn when a family member is in need.

The problems and challenges of life emerge not only from acute mishaps and long-term disabilities but also from the necessity to alter attitudes, skills, and perceptual patterns with the changing roles demanded by a changing social and physical world. What characterizes our era historically is the quantum leap in the rapidity of social change linked with our technological accomplishments that have revolutionized communication, transportation, and energy control. The adaptive challenge for most individuals in our times demands a flexibility, readiness, and speed in giving up old roles and acquiring new roles that may be historically unique. The multigenerational family unit provides its members with important help in this matter.

Boulding, (Boulding, 1972, pp. 186-191) in a recent paper, expressed this very well:

> The family as a unit is continually in transition from one stage of the family cycle to the next, so that it can never be in a static condition. Family life is a swiftly moving series of identity crises as members of various ages are socialized into new roles . . . In addition to the identity crises that stem from aging and individual pathologies, there are externally-triggered crises that may result in unemployment, separation, injury, and death of family members . . .
>
> Fortunately, the identity-crises that people go through do not make them unrecognizable to each other. There are constants as well as variables, and the group culture created by every family unit that lives together through time . . . provide[s] some security and stability for in-

dividual members . . . we can see the family as a workshop in social change.

Since people are undergoing similar role changes in the non-family settings in which they perform daily, the fact of individual growth and change is not a unique property of the family. What is unique about the family is that only in this setting are people intimately confronting role changes in other people who are much older or much younger. Thus the family setting continually prods individuals into a better understanding of themselves.

I would add that, in addition to its long-term training in the skills of role changing, living in a family setting necessarily inculcates the expectation and acceptance by individuals of a series of inevitable personal role changes; and the family group actively assists members in dealing with their cognitive and emotional difficulties during periods of role transition.

Leadership inside many family groups in alerting individual members to the need for adjustment and adaptation to social change is not fixed but varies in relation to the presenting problem. In particular, younger members who are actively in touch with specific changes in the outer world and whose perceptions may be less distorted than those of their elders by preconceptions, may sound the alert and suggest novel paths for exploration, as symbolized by the story of "The Emperor's New Clothes." But in our society that so downgrades the effectiveness and wisdom of the old, I feel it is worth emphasizing that grandparents and great-grandparents often have a very special contribution to make in the area of encouraging readiness and flexibility in the altering of roles to conform to social and physical environmental change. Meierowitz (1974) has recently pointed out that, contrary to our usual stereotypes, many older people are likely to be better prepared than young people to change their attitudes and acquire new skills in adjusting to new conditions. Youth and early adulthood is often a period of dogmatism and rigidity because limited experience causes the individual to oversimplify and to cling uncritically to a newly learned system of ideas and skills. After putting in so much time and effort in learning these, it is hard for the young person to give them up or even to accept their limitations, especially as he has been promised that they will assure him continuing rewards, and he still has not learned about possible alternatives. Old people, on the other hand, have discovered the hard way that their learned ideas and skills do not in fact lead to the wonderful results promised by their teachers; and they have also been forced to learn how to compensate for waning personal capacities in one area by developing in others — for instance, the old tennis player who wins his points by outwitting his opponent rather than by his strength, speed, and agility of the past. Eventually, of course, the old man may become too frail to play tennis at all; but, as I mentioned previously, most old people are not in fact as weak as we used to believe, and until that eventual stage is reached, many of them can not only play well themselves, but, of special importance in the present context, they can coach others in the flexibility and adaptive skills that their own personal development has forced them to master.

The Family as a Source of Practical Service and Concrete Aid

Until recently, few studies dealt with the practical assistance given by the family group to its members as long-term contributions or in responding to acute need. In the past 15 years, however, there has been a rapidly growing research literature dealing with this topic. (Sussman and Burchinal, 1962, pp. 231-240) have written a comprehensive review of empirical studies. They showed that most families studied, irrespective of social class, reported giving aid to relatives and receiving aid from them. Assistance included continuing and intermitent financial aid, sometimes disguised as gifts of money or valuable goods at times of marriage, birth of children, birthdays, Christmas, or to help with hospital or funeral expenses. It included help with shopping and care of children, physical care of old people, performing household tasks, and practical assistance at times of crisis, such as hospitalizations because of illness or accident, or during transition ceremonies such as weddings and funerals.

A particular significance of these contributions of resources and services is that during crises and periods of transition an individual is usually preoccupied with his current predicament and not only pays scant attention to the demands of ordinary life tasks but also has little personal energy available to deal with them. Either the household runs down or he must exert special effort to maintain it — and this is at the expense of energy and attention needed to deal with his predicament.

During the Yom Kippur War, I was impressed by the acute need of many families of wounded or fallen soldiers for help in shopping, doing household chores, getting lifts to a distant hospital, and taking care of young children or elderly relatives. The timely mobilization of the family network to accomplish these tasks enabled those most centrally affected to devote all their energies to visiting the wounded or mourning the dead. I felt that in addition to the benefit of the concrete help, the fact that it was immediately available as needed, usually without having to be asked for, was a source of great strength at a time when people felt particularly weakened by their sense of vulnerability and increased dependency. When a person knows that he is receiving what he needs as his right and not at the price of having to ask or beg for it, his pride in his own autonomy and his self-respect are likely to be maintained even though he is actually a dependent recipient.

The other thing that impressed me over and over again was the specially strengthening effect of giving material help in maintaining the household, doing the shopping and cooking, and caring for children and aged parents and grandparents. These actions seemed to convey more powerfully than any words of consolation and solidarity the message that the helper was an effective and involved participant in the tragedy and was automatically sharing its burdens.

The Family as a Haven for Rest and Recuperation

In most healthy families, every member knows all the other members very well and feels himself equally known and understood. Within the boundary of privacy that surrounds this group, he usually feels free to relax and "be himself." As a lifelong member of the family group from which he knows he will not be extruded except for some enormous transgression, he can feel confidence in revealing aspects of himself that he would hide even from his friends. This is probably linked with the fact that the fate of all members of the family group are to a considerable degree connected, so that inescapably one member's problems must to some extent be shared by the others and vice versa. If we add to this that every family member is being continually observed at first hand from many points of view over a very long period — in the case of children from their earliest beginnings — we realize that the family group is without equal as a reservoir of developmental personality data about each member.

All this adds up to the family being a group in which each member has the possibility of being understood and dealt with as his own unique self, and in which his idiosyncratic needs are recognized, respected, and satisfied to the degree that this is possible within the limits of available resources.

It is these aspects of family life that make the family a sanctuary or haven, namely a place where it is safe to relax and be oneself, where despite continual changes, the other people are well known, where one can speak one's own language and be readily understood, and, most important, where one can set aside the burdens and demands of the outside world for as long as both the person and the family consider appropriate. Since we now know that what is particularly hazardous about prolonged strain is the possibility that it will have an unremitting character that leads to an inexorable buildup of toxic metabolites which have no discharge routes, so that they rise above the capacity of the organism to bear them, with resultant disorganization and disintegration, this haven function of the family can be understood to be most significant in protecting its members from morbidity.

Another relevant function is the operation of the family group as a monitor of fatigue when a member is grappling with crises. The confusion and frustration of crisis, together with the pressure of prolonged emotional arousal and of efforts to master these emotions as well as to cope with the crisis tasks, lead inevitably to fatigue. When this rises above a certain threshold, the individual's efficiency and effectiveness, begin to fall. A vicious circle may be produced as the individual mobilizes more and more effort to overcome his fatigue and only becomes more tired and ineffective. At such times the family may play an essential role by telling the individual that he is tired and that he should rest, advice which they make possible for him to accept by temporarily taking over certain essential aspects of his crisis tasks, such as caring for a sick child or parent. When they feel that he is sufficiently rested, they call him back to continue his struggle. Of particular significance in this sequence is the legitimation by the family of the need for a rest period, since many people in crisis feel that the crisis tasks are so essential and urgent that if they put them aside even for an instant it must be because they are lazy or selfish and unwilling to put up with the personal burden. Left to themselves this guilt might drive them to wear themselves out.

The Family as a Reference and Control Group

Because an individual's fate is so bound up with his family and because he realizes that they know him so well, he is likely to be quite sensitive to their opinions about his attitudes and behavior, and especially to their judgment of how well he adheres to the family code. This is likely to be consolidated by his trust that they have his best interests at heart, since such trust, which is hard to build in a relationship with a nonkin counselor or therapist, comes naturally inside the circle of a family, where the reputations and interests of all members are inextricably intertwined.

In an era when the dominant philosophy of clinicians is nonjudgmental it may be well to emphasize that a nonjudgemental approach inside the family in our culture is not necessarily of value. The essential element of an effective reference group is that it does judge; and if it is also to control and mold the behavior of its members, it must also reward success and punish failure in adhering to its code. Types of reward and punishment vary from family to family in accordance with social class and subculture, but even punishments that might seem savage to outsiders are usually well tolerated within a family because members are used to them and feel that, unless they have committed an offense so terrible that they will be expelled, whatever punishment they incur is designed to foster their acceptance by the group — they are being punished for what they did — but regardless of this they will continue to be accepted for what they are, namely lifelong members of the family.

The Family as Source and Validator of Identity

The clarity and security of a person's self-image and his confidence in the stability of his own identity are a major source of his fortitude in grappling with life's problems. In particular, they provide the foundation upon which he bases his courage in facing the complexities of the unknown and his tolerance of frustration during periods of struggling with the temporarily insurmountable problems of crisis, or in coming to terms with the long-term privations of loss. It is, therefore, an irony of fate that there is a natural tendency of individuals during crisis and role transition to become vague and confused about their identity, just when they are most in need of clarity and confidence in this area. Another characteristic of persons in crisis is that they usually become more open and more susceptible to the influence of other people, particularly significant figures in their social milieu. The result is that a person in crisis or in a period of life transition normally relies in large measure on the messages he receives from his social environment in appreciating his own identity. This is one of the major features of his increased dependency at such times.

His family, which in any case is a primary source of the ingredients that molded the individual's identity in the first place, therefore often has a crucial role to play in buttressing it during the confusion and uncertainty of crisis and transition by reminding him of those elements, particularly his abilities and strengths, about which he is temporarily in doubt or which he has entirely forgotten. In other words, during the frustration and confusion of struggling with an at-present insurmountable problem, most individuals feel weak and impotent and tend to forget their continuing strengths. At such times, their family reminds them of their past achievements and validates their precrisis self-image of competence and ability to stand firm.

The Family's Contribution to Emotional Mastery

This topic is so well known that I need only make brief mention of some of the main issues:

1. Short-term crises and long-term challenges and privations inevitably evoke a complex of negative emotions — anxiety, depression, anger, shame, guilt, and the like. Not only are these painful in themselves but they also reduce effectiveness in grappling with the problems of external physical and social reality because of the energy needed to control and contain them and because they distract attention. A major contribution of the family is to augment the efforts made by the individual on the basis of his ego capacities to master and control these emotions.

2. I have repeatedly referred to the feelings of frustration that characterize crises and periods of life transition. In addition to

the pain they engender, these feelings press the individual toward premature closure in his adaptation work, and this is one of the main causes of failure. The family can add to a member's ego-derived capacity to tolerate such frustration by expressing solidarity and by offering love, affection and comfort.

3. Families can help individuals accomplish their "worry-work" and "grief-work" during crises and the much longer periods involved in adjusting to loss and deprivation. They do this not only by offering guidance on the basis of past experience of family members but also by counteracting despair and feelings of helplessness through their continuing presence and expressions of love, and through maintaining hope in an eventual triumph.

4. A person who loses a love object by death or desertion, his bodily integrity by illness or crippling, or his major role by unemployment often feels a debilitating loss of personal worth. His family can counteract this and help him see his loss in realistic perspective by continuing to treat him with love and respect and by providing him with transitional objects or roles in the family circle until such time as he can rebuild his life once more. Sometimes, the family may provide him with a permanent replacement for the objects or roles lost in the outer world or with a permanent source of alternative emotional satisfaction.

LIMITING FACTORS

Most of these support system functions depend on a significant level of intactness, stability, and integration in the family. Of particular importance is a common language and free communication among family members, especially between the generations. During a period of rapid sociocultural change, such as we are currently experiencing, the generation gap is a major factor that impedes essential aspects of this communication — many young people today speak a quite different language from their parents, let alone their grandparents. Among immigrants and in upwardly mobile families, this will be exaggerated because of the greater gap between their sociocultural world of today and that of their past.

Another element that is clearly a precondition of most of the supports I have discussed is that the interpersonal relationships in the family should be healthy; namely, that individuals should be dealt with in their own right and not as symbolic manifestations of other objects or personality attributes. Since disordered relationships, based on unconsciously linking another family member with the actors in some past psychological conflict, are so commonly found in the families of psychiatric patients, we clinicians are often prone to see families in general as potentially pathogenic rather than as supportive, especially in dealing with family members with emotional burdens who are so much in need of the kind of support I have been discussing. I have no empirical research on which to base this statement, but it is my impression that unhealthy relationships of the type commonly encountered in clinical practice do not occur in more than about 10 to 15 percent of families in the general population. We clinicians should therefore not exaggerate the prevalence of this factor.

A third factor that is possibly of greater frequency is related to the fact that a family is likely to be optimally supportive only if its members accept its ideology and code of behavior, including the obligations of mutual concern for each other, as well as the social mission of the family in monitoring and controlling individual behavior. This, in turn, depends on consonance, or lack of dissonance, between the culture of the family and that of the ethnic, religious, and community systems of which it is a part. Whenever these outer cultural circles become disorganized, or where for a variety of reasons the family culture gets out of line with them, certain members are likely to be partially or totally unlinked from the family group, and what they gain by their freedom to move easily in the outside would may be offset by loss of the personalized benefits of the internal family support system.

IMPLICATIONS FOR PLANNING AND SERVICE

Social Policy

Social planning should promote the intactness, integration and mutuality of extended families:

1. Income maintenance programs should direct funds into family coffers; and the family as a group should be responsible for their disbursement to individuals.
2. Housing programs should provide residential accommodations

so that old people and their families can choose to live in the same household or in the immediate vicinity. Housing for the aged should be distributed throughout the community and not be segregated far away; the same applies to housing designed for young married couples.

3. Priority of installation of telephones and special low rates should encourage all old people to acquire and use telephones to communicate regularly with children and grandchildren. Similarly, public transportation should be free or very cheap for old people so they can visit their families easily.

4. The Census Bureau should alter its definition of a family from kin living in the same residential household to kin who interact frequently and are bound together by positive concern. This will provide us with readily available demographic data about families as a valid basis for planning and evaluating social policy and services, which we do not have at present.

Health and Welfare Services and Community Institutions

1. Services should avoid, wherever possible, segregating and isolating family members. For instance, old people who are sick should be cared for at home or in day hospitals; full hospitalization should be avoided with them, just as we have learned to do with children. If hospitalization is unavoidable, it should be as short as possible; we should encourage visiting by the entire family group and the family should be actively involved in plans for convalescence and rehabilitation. Also, diagnosis and therapy of individuals should actively involve the personal participation of the total multigenerational family group — once upon a time in child guidance clinics we treated the child in isolation, then we included the mother, and eventually also the father; we should henceforward regularly include the rest of the family, including grandparents. I am not here advocating specific family therapy, useful as this certainly is at times, but I am suggesting that we actively promote family cohesion in relating to a member with difficulties.

2. We should involve the total family unit in all crisis intervention. Professional and nonprofessional caregivers should exploit every opportunity for convening family groups and facilitating the

organization of family action projects. Crises, which naturally excite human interest and mobilize energy and motivation to help others, provide us with an excellent opportunity to promote family support systems. Not only can the caregiver make use of the family supports to help the individual in crisis but also, perhaps more important, by an educational and communication bridge-building approach the caregiver can use this as an opportunity to train the family group to improve its problem-solving and mutual help skills.

3. Community recreational and religious institutions should modify their facilities and patterns of organization to cater to total family groups, as was done years ago at the Peckham Health Center in London and as is done in some community centers and settlement houses today.

Development of Programs to Bridge the Generation Gap

What is involved is bringing the older and younger generations together in situations where each can learn to respect the other, can learn each other's language, and can discover and appreciate the other's capacities and potential helpfulness. Examples include the Foxfire Project (Wigginton, 1972; Wigginton, 1973) in rural Georgia where a group of high school students went into the countryside with tape recorders and cameras and recorded for subsequent publication the personal accounts of old people of their traditional crafts and country lore, such as hog dressing, log cabin building, spinning and weaving, wagon making and other affairs of plain living. As Pete Seeger says in the book that emerged, the project "proves that old folks and kids can be great allies. May it show young people in thousands of other communities how they too can link up with the oldest and youngest generations and be proud of our country, not for its power and production, but for its many different ways of living, and how to make do with what we have" (Wigginton, 1972; Wigginton, 1973).

Other examples include numerous volunteer programs in which retired persons are brought into school systems to act as counselors and to tutor children with learning difficulties; "foster grandparent" projects in which old people act as friendly helpers in institutions for retarded or emotionally disturbed children or in community programs for delinquent youth; and work-study and volunteer programs in colleges in which students volunteer to help in institutions and community services for the aged (Freund, 1971, pp. 205-208; Lebel and Lebel, 1972).

Development of Educational Programs that Promote Ethnic Pluralism

These go beyond such projects as Foxfire. What is intended here is to break from the tradition of the American "melting pot" and to replace it by building knowledge and respect among young and old for the rich traditions and folk wisdom of their ethnic group sub-culture, as well as an appreciation, tolerance, and respect for the different heritage of other ethnic and religious groups in our pluralistic society (Bede, 1970; Giordano, 1973; Olds, 1973, p. 26; Sherman, Brittan, and Friedelson, 1970). Such programs not only promote intergeneration identification and communication but also contribute to reducing dissonance between second and third generation immigrant families and the culture of the large heterogeneous general American society by locating within the latter a subculture with which the family can meaningfully articulate and from which it can draw external support, guidance, and sanction for its own ways of life.

Development of Neighborhood Educational Programs

Neighborhood programs should be developed to emphasize the importance of family life, to provide detailed information on the ways families can help individuals deal with short-term and long-term challanges and burdens, and to promote the idea of volunteerism and mutual support. We should produce manuals and audiovisual aids to help in this public education campaign, and we should also experiment with short-term residential institutes where family units can be trained by being involved on action projects.

Use of Retired Persons

We should train and utilize retired men and women to act as family educators and we should use them also as counselors to offer guidance to families that are currently trying to support their members during a life crisis or in adjusting to a permanent burden or disability. These elders should also be used as liaisons between the professional caregivers and the families of the population. They will thus help keep the focus of the professionals on the total family unit and prevent a return to the old individual focus.

Use of Family Units

We should experiment with innovative methods for training and utilizing family units as corporate caregivers, not only for their own members but also for other families. I am advocating a family-to-family mutual help approach. This is being tried at present both in Boston and in Israel in poverty-stricken populations where families who, despite their poverty, are living a rewarding life are linked as groups of volunteer counselors and role models to families that are failing. In Israel, a similar pattern has also been suggested among new immigrants, using families that have successfully worked through their adjustment phase to help those who have just arrived and are still floundering.

Development of a Multigenerational Family Structure

We should find ways of rebuilding a multigenerational structure for those families that are incomplete in this regard. A most promising example has been described by Claven and Vatter (Claven and Vatter, 1972a, pp. 407-412; 1972b, pp. 499-504). They describe a pattern that they call the Affiliative Family, which they have discovered to be a rapidly developing phenomenon in a number of communities. They define an affiliative family as "any combination of husband/father, wife/mother, and their children, plus one or more older persons, recognized as part of the kin network and called by a designated kin term. They may or may not be a part of the residential household. Monetary remuneration may or may not be involved. Voluntary commitment to responsibility for one another within the unit is the single basic criterion." What is involved is an analog of the foster family or adoptive family in the case of childless parents and parentless children. In affiliative families, we are dealing with old persons who currently lack children and grandchildren, and nuclear or one-parent family units without grandparents nearby. The two incomplete units team up to produce a multigenerational unit of adopted kin, which then develops a role pattern that takes better care of household tasks and operates as an integrated support system to produce reciprocal rewards for all concerned.

Chapter 12

HUSBAND-WIFE HELPING RELATIONSHIPS AS MODERATORS OF EXPERIENCED STRESS:

THE "MENTAL HYGIENE" FUNCTION IN MARRIAGE

RONALD J. BURKE AND TAMARA WEIR

IN their day-to-day living individuals meet with a variety of problems and difficulties and experience tension and strain as a result. Our own personal experiences, discussions with other individuals, and research findings (Gurin, Veroff, and Feld, 1960; Burke & Weir, 1976a; McCubbin, Dahl, Lester, Benson and Robertson, 1976) lead us to conclude that people are frequently motivated to seek out informal helpers when they are troubled. Characteristically, such helpers emerge from one's immediate sphere of social contacts and are usually individuals who share some aspect of one's daily life.

Previous investigations (Blood and Wolfe, 1960) have highlighted the actual or potential importance of the marital relationship as a source of help to individuals in times of stress. As one of our studies showed (Burke and Weir, 1975), out of all their possible social contacts both men and women selected the spouse as the person they would most likely turn to for help with their problems and anxieties. This finding is not surprising since there are very few dyadic relationships in our society that provide individuals with the degree of proximity, accessibility, commitment, interdependence, and opportunity for intimacy that marriage does.

Blood and Wolfe (1960) used the phrase "mental hygiene" func-

Preparation of this chapter was supported by the Associates' Workshop, School of Business Administration, University of Western Ontario and by Imperial Oil Limited. We would like to acknowledge the tremendous cooperation of the respondents in making the studies possible and the assistance of Richard DuWors in the data analysis and Veronica Libby in the preparation of the manuscript.

tion of marriage to refer to the latent contribution one spouse made (or could make) to the mental health of the other. Mental hygiene was termed a latent function of marriage because individuals were seldom aware of it even though it existed, and although they did not consciously perform it, it occurred nevertheless.

Other research studies have shown that husbands and wives do provide emotional support to each other, as well as undertaking specific activities designed to offer relief to the partner (Mann, unpublished manuscript; Burke, 1971; Burke and Weir, 1975, 1976). What remains to be determined are (1) What functions are served by these husband-wife helping relationships? (2) What kinds of help do husbands and wives give each other? Is the main ingredient understanding, as proposed by Blood and Wolfe? Or do specific acts to assist one's partner have value as well? (3) Are there empirical findings indicating a tangible benefit to the recipients of helping from their spouses? (4) What constitutes effective helping to one's spouse? (5) And finally, what demographic characteristics are associated with elements of the husband-wife helping relationship?

Based on recent findings and theoretical work (Pinneau, 1976; Cobb, 1976; Gore, 1973, 1978; Pearlin & Schooler, Chapter 6; Lin, Simeone, Ensel & Kuo, 1979) helping relationships were proposed to have three effects. The first, a *preventative* effect, was to reduce experienced life stresses. The second, a *therapeutic* effect, was to directly enhance measures of satisfaction and well-being. The third effect of spouse helping relationships was a *buffering* effect on the stress-well-being relationship itself.

The remainder of the chapter summarized the results of a prior investigation (Burke and Weir, 1977) and described a second, which replicates and extends the results of the first.

FIRST INVESTIGATION

Subjects

The respondents were 189 married husband-wife pairs. The husbands were employed full-time and were members of one of three professional associations: professional engineers, industrial accountants, or chartered accountants. Approximately 28 percent of the wives were employed full- or part-time (n = 54) and about half of the couples had children (n = 89).

Measures

The process of giving and receiving help was investigated by nine Likert-type questionnaire items, identical for husbands and wives. There were a number of standard demographic items determined, such as age, education, income, length of time married, number of children, and wife's employment status. Figure 12-1, a model showing the framework underlying this study, indicates specific variables that were examined to assess potential benefits of spouse's helping (Burke and Weir, 1977).

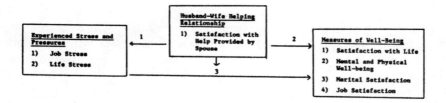

1. **Preventative Effects of Spouse Helping**
2. **Therapeutic Effects of Spouse Helping**
3. **Moderating or Buffering Effects of Spouse Helping**

Figure 12-1. Hypothesized effects of spouse helping variable.

Results and Discussion[1]

Satisfaction with spouse's help and well-being. Husbands and wives (and pairs) who were more satisfied with the amount and kind of informal help provided by their spouse were also more satisfied with their jobs, their lives, and their marriages and reported fewer psychosomatic complaints. These findings support the existence of the therapeutic effects of spouse helping.

Stress and well-being. Individuals reporting greater life and job stress were also less satisfied with their life and job situations and their marriages and reported more psychosomatic symptoms.

Stress and satisfaction with spouse's help. Individuals who reported

---

[1]The actual data are reported in detail in Burke and Weir (1977).

greater satisfaction with their spouse's help also experienced less stress. These findings support the existence of the preventative effects of spouse helping. These data also suggested that the relationships between satisfaction with spouse's help and the measures of well-being might be a function of the fact that those individuals who were satisfied with their spouse's help *also* experienced less stress.

Benefits of spouse's help under high and low experienced stress. The relationship between spouses' help and well-being, partialling out the effects of levels of experienced stress, was then determined.

Husband-wife helping. A number of significant sex differences emerged from the comparison of data for husbands and wives on the helping relationship variables. The indications were that wives were generally more active in initiating the helping process in their marital relationships: being more willing to disclose and discuss their problems with their spouses than were the husbands with their wives (Burke and Weir, 1976a). Wives were more likely to select and turn to their husbands as helpers of choice than were husbands to select their wives.

Furthermore, not only were wives more active in roles of helpee but they were also more active as helpers as well. They had a greater awareness of concrete helping behaviors, which they could employ to help their husbands deal with their tension, and were more active in the performance of these. Wives also perceived themselves as more helpful resources to their husbands than husbands did to their wives.

These findings suggest that wives generally set the stage for the discussion, the alleviation, and the resolution of anxieties and tensions arising for either partner of the marital pair. Perhaps the different socialization of the sexes in our culture, which allows women a freer rein with their emotions and is more accepting of their dependence, makes it easier for the wives to admit when they are under stress and to seek help as required. Data from Rosenthal and his colleagues (1974) offer convincing evidence that females are better able to respond to nonverbal communication cues than males. Perhaps it is this sensitivity that permits wives to recognize more easily the emotional states of their spouses and to respond more readily as helpers to their spouses than husbands can to their wives.

It is also evident that marital pairs differed from one another in the extent to which they expressed satisfaction with the helping process in their marriage. Those pairs who were more satisfied with their mutual helping are characterized by a number of behavioral and attitudinal features. The six significant relationships found suggest that greater self-disclosure, trust, mutual reliance, awareness and performance of concrete helping activities, and greater confidence in the ability to be helpful to one's spouse are important features associated with higher satisfaction with the marital helping transaction.

Correlates of Marital Helping

A number of the factors conceptualized as correlates were shown to be significantly related to the quality of the helping interactions found in marriage. The couples who were older and married longer showed a diminished level of helping activity occurring between them, a decrease in communication about problems and tensions, and a greater criticalness of each other's functioning as a helper. Older wives in particular indicated that their first preference would be to go to someone other than their husbands with their difficulties. With the passing of time, husbands and wives moved in the direction of withdrawing their interest, motivation, and efforts to be helpful to one another. There is room for conjecture as to why older couples seemed much more alienated from and unresponsive to one another's needs. Perhaps the older individuals in the sample belong to a generation that placed an emphasis on the material or situational aspects of marriage as opposed to relational concerns. Or, it may be that as individuals progress through stages of the life cycle, they inevitably confront numerous situations that demand heavy expenditures of their time, energy, and commitment. In the face of these events, the relational aspects of marriage may be easily relegated to a position of low priority and show a gradual deterioration over time.

The introduction of children into the family unit offered diminishing returns to the husband-wife helping relationship. Although spouses with children were more reliant on one another, they reported receiving less help from their spouses and gave less in return. It is not difficult to imagine that children would be a competing force for the energies and attention of the parents so whatever stresses accrue to them remain unnoticed or unattended.

Working wives presented some potential problems for the marital helping relationship as well. Husbands of working wives indicated that they were less likely to reveal their problems and tensions to their wives and tended to be less satisfied with their wives as confidantes. Working wives, on the other hand, indicated that they wanted their husbands to be more active in helping them deal with their problems. With the wife taking on the increased responsibilities of a job, her own needs for help appear to be greater and at the same time, her availability to her husband may be decreased. Apparently then, the wife's work status might cause ripples of discontent within the pair with regard to their helping interaction.

In looking at the data in the area of job stress, an interesting family dynamic emerged. The greater the husbands' job stress, the more likely they were to disclose their problems and tensions to their wives but the less satisfied they appeared to be with their wives' help and the greater their expressed need to have other close relationships to rely on for help. The greater the wives' job stress, the more likely they were to describe their husbands as more active helpers. However, they perceived themselves as not being very helpful to their husbands.

Irrespective of whether it was the husband or wife who was experiencing the severe stresses, it was the wife's helping role that was called into question. A number of possible explanations suggest themselves. It may be that wives found it difficult to relate to the stresses their husbands experience at work. They may have felt less confident in their ability to be helpful in these areas and hesitated to interact with their husbands around such issues. In addition, wives who were involved in demanding jobs as well as filling the traditional housewife's role may very well have found their resources depleted and be less able to respond to their husbands' needs for help. In either case, the wife's usefulness as a helper appeared diminished.

In contrast with the above, severe life stresses made both husbands and wives feel less effectual as helpers to their spouses. Thus the greater the life stresses for the pairs, the less satisfied they were with one another's helping, the less helpful they perceived themselves being to one another, the less likely they were to depend on one another for help, and the more likely they were to express a need for closer relationships with others who could act as helpers.

The findings lead one to believe that serious problems arising for a couple in areas of mutual concern can have a debilitating effect on both individuals and reduce their motivation to support or encourage one another through the adversities.

Inherent in the concept of marital helping is the belief that to be helpful to one's spouse, one must first understand him/her. One significant way of reaching this understanding is through verbal communication. It was not surprising, therefore, to discover that the communication measures employed here were positively related to the helping-relationship items. Couples who showed a higher agreement on the importance of communication about a variety of specific issues and indicated they actually talked about these with their spouses were more likely to disclose their problems and anxieties to one another, to feel more satisfied with one another as confidantes, to view themselves as being more helpful to one another, and to express greater satisfaction with one another's helping endeavours. It appears then that couples who have established good channels of communication around broad areas relevant to their life together can better meet the challenge of helping one another under conditions of stress and strain.

Consequences of Marital Helping

A consideration of the findings in the area of outcome measures suggests that the husband-wife helping process is an important factor contributing to the marital, job and life satisfaction of the pair and their mental and physical well-being as well. There were a number of features of this process that distinguished the pairs who expressed greater satisfaction with their marriage. These couples were better confidantes to one another; they were more open and communicative about their problems and concerns; they were more cognizant of their partners' helping needs and exerted themselves more actively to meet them; they were less critical and more satisfied with the quality and quantity of the help they received, and in turn were more confident in their own helpfulness to one another. The mutuality established by these pairs seemed to mitigate the need for people outside the marriage to serve as helpers.

Those pairs who expressed a greater satisfaction with life in general shared many of the same features. They too had attained a more satisfactory helping relationship with one another. In addition, they had a higher level of trust in one another as confidantes, a greater estimation of their helpfulness to one another, and a lesser need for individuals outside the marital unit to depend on for help.

The couples who, according to our measures, were in better mental and physical health showed the following characteristics. They selected one another as first choice of helper under situations of stress, they viewed themselves as being good helpers to their spouses, and they expressed greater satisfaction with the helping interaction established between them.

Although pairs' values of the relationship between job satisfaction and the helping variables were not obtained, the findings from husbands and wives individually indicated certain similarities. Both males and females who reported greater satisfaction with their job situations described their spouses as more satisfactory helpers and more satisfactory confidantes.

The overall findings were distilled to focus attention on the variable satisfaction with spouse's help, our proxy measure of effectiveness of marital helping. This particular factor was significantly and positively associated with all the outcome measures of satisfaction, i.e. job, marital, and life, and with the emotional and physical well-being measure as well.

SECOND INVESTIGATION

The purpose of this research was to replicate and extend the conclusions of the first investigation. In order to accomplish these objectives, as well as to further our understanding of husband-wife helping relationships, it was imperative that a more detailed and descriptive measure of the husband-wife helping relationship be developed. In addition, it was desirable to include a greater number of sources of experienced stress and well-being. Finally, our intention was to undertake a more sophisticated set of analyses, particularly of the hypothesized moderating or buffering effects of spouse helping.

Subjects

The husband-wife pairs consisted of correctional administrators and their spouses living in a single Canadian province. This province maintained fifty correctional institutions. Each institution was managed by senior correctional administrators in three positions: superintendents, deputy superintendents, and assistant superintendents. All 150 of these job incumbents were invited to participate in the research. A total of 127 volunteered (almost 85%). Each job incumbent completed a questionnaire in small groups of between five and ten at a university location.

Job incumbents who were married (N = 101) were asked to have their spouses complete a questionnaire at home. This questionnaire was to be completed separately and anonymously and mailed back to a university address. Responses were received from eighty-five spouses (about 85%), all females. Thus three samples were available: 1. 127 job incumbents (122 male, five female); 2. 85 spouses, all females; 3. eighty-five husband-wife pairs.

Although the data will not be presented here, a wide range of response was present on demographic variables. Ages ranged from under twenty-five to older than sixty; educational levels ranged from less than ninth grade to beyond the master's degree; years married ranged from less than one to more than thirty; number of children ranged from none to more than eight; and almost half of the spouses were working for pay outside the home on either a full-time or part-time basis.

Measures

Husband-wife helping relationship. A thirteen-item scale measuring both psychological and emotional help as well as concrete assistance from one's spouse was created. Some items were adapted from earlier work by Gore (1973) and Caplan, Cobb, French, Harrison, and Pinneau (1975); others were written specifically for this investigation. Examples included: I talk about my work concerns and difficulties to my wife; my wife goes out of her way to be helpful to me when my work gets me down; my wife is willing to listen to my personal problems; and my relationship with my wife is pretty superficial. The same items, with minor changes in wording were used for both husbands and wives. Internal consistency reliabilities of the husband-wife helping relationship scale were .91 for both husbands and wives.

Experienced stress: Job incumbents. Three areas of experienced stress were considered: (1) life worries (2) concrete stressful life events

(Holmes and Rahe, 1967); and (3) various occupational demands (Caplan et al., 1975).

Experienced stress: Spouses. Two areas of experienced stress were examined (1) life worries and (2) concrete stressful life events (Holmes and Rahe, 1967).

Well-being: Job incumbents. Six areas of well-being of job incumbents were examined. These were: (1) negative affective states (Cobb, Brooks, Kasl and Connelly, 1966); (2) life satisfaction (Quinn and Shepard, 1974); (3) psychosomatic symptoms (Gurin, Veroff and Feld, 1960); (4) marital satisfaction (Orden and Bradburn, 1968); (5) impact of job demands on personal, home, and family life (Burke, Weir and DuWors, 1979); and (6) job satisfaction (Quinn and Shepard, 1974).

Well-being: Spouses. Six areas of well-being of spouses were examined. These included the first five dimensions used for the husbands and a self-esteem measure (Rosenberg, 1965).

Results

Husband-wife helping relationship measures. The correlation (N = 85) between husbands' and wives' assessments of the quality of helping provided by their spouses was .28 (p = .05). Husbands experiencing a higher quality of helping from their wives were paired with wives who also reported a higher quality of helping from their husbands.

Demographic variables and quality of spouse helping. Of the range of demographic variables examined for wives, e.g., age, years of formal schooling, years married, number of children, regularity of church attendance, etc., only one was significantly related to the quality of helping reported from spouses. Older wives reported significantly less helping from their spouses than did younger wives.

Three significant relationships were observed for husbands. These involved: age, income, and number of children. Husbands who were younger were earning less income and had fewer children reported a higher quality of helping from their spouses. These three variables were, themselves, significantly intercorrelated.

Spouse helping and experienced stress (preventative effects). Table 12-I presents the correlations between the spouse helping measures and various sources of experienced stress. Data from the wives (top half of the table) provides strong support for the preventative function of

Table 12-I

Spouse Helping and Experienced Stress

Measures of Experienced Stress

Wives	Help from Husband
Life Worries	.48*
Number of Stressful Life Events	.21***
Upsettingness of Life Events	.17

Husbands	Help from Wife
Life Worries	.18***
Number of Stressful Life Events	.08
Upsettingness of Life Events	.12
Number of Work Life Events	−.08
Upsettingness of Work Life Events	.05
Number of NonWork Life Events	.16***
Upsettingness of NonWork Events	.21**

* (P = .001)

** (P = .01)

*** (P = .05)

spouse helping. Wives reporting higher quality of spouse helping also reported experiencing fewer life worries and fewer concrete stressful life events in the year prior to the study. Data from husbands (bottom half of the table) provides weaker support for this line of reasoning. That is, quality of spouse helping was found to have the predicted preventative function only for severity of life worries and number and upsettingness of nonwork stressful life events. Quality of spouse helping had almost no relationship to experienced occupational demands.

Spouse helping and individual well-being (therapeutic effects). Table 12-II shows the correlations of the quality of spouse-helping measure and various aspects of individual satisfaction and well-being. The data for wives (top half of table) provides modest support for the link between quality of spouse helping and positive well-being and

Table 12-II

Spouse Helping and Well-Being

Measures of Well-Being

Wives	Help from Husband	Help from Husband[a]
Self-Esteem	.12	-.08
Negative Affective States	-.39*	-.06
Life Satisfaction	-.36*	-.13
Psychosomatic Symptoms	-.24***	.08
Marital Satisfaction	-.51*	-.47*
Impact of Job on Home and Family	-.51*	-.34**

Husbands	Help from Wife	Help from Wife[a]
Negative Affective States	-.37*	-.25**
Life Satisfaction	-.22***	-.16***
Psychosomatic Symptoms	-.14	-.04
Marital Satisfaction	-.14	-.07
Impact of Job on Home and Family	-.11	.00
Job Satisfaction	-.07	.00

[a]Partial correlations between spouse helping measure and measures of well-being controlling for levels of experienced stress.

* (P = .001)

** (P = .01)

*** (P = .05)

satisfaction. Two of these relationships remained when experienced stress was controlled. Thus, for wives, quality of helping from spouse remained significantly related to important satisfaction and health measures when effects of experienced stress were controlled.

The data from husbands (lower half of table) indicates modest support for the hypothesized link of quality of spouse helping and well-being. Only two of the six relationships reached statistical significance.

Spouse helping and the stress-well-being relationship (moderating effects). Table 12-III shows correlations between two sources of experienced

Table 12–III

Spouse Helping and the Stress–Well–Being Relationship

Husbands	Help from Wife*		
	Most Helped	Intermediately Helped	Least Helped
Life Worries with:			
Negative Affective States	$-.38^{ab}$	$-.57^{a}$	$-.61^{ab}$
Life Satisfaction	$-.11^{c}$	$-.29$	$-.42^{c}$
Psychosomatic Symptoms	$-.43^{d}$	$-.34^{e}$	$-.70^{de}$
Marital Satisfaction	$-.05^{f}$	$-.52^{fg}$	$-.21^{g}$
Impact of Job on Home and Family	$-.35^{hi}$	$-.55^{h}$	$-.71^{i}$
Job Satisfaction	$-.30$	$-.26$	$-.42$
Number of Stressful Life Events with:			
Negative Affective States	$-.08^{jk}$	$-.28^{j}$	$-.50^{k}$
Life Satisfaction	$.11^{lm}$	$-.28^{ln}$	$-.50^{mn}$
Psychosomatic Symptoms	$-.08^{op}$	$-.32^{o}$	$-.33^{p}$
Marital Satisfaction	$-.29$	$-.31$	$-.21$
Impact of Job on Home and Family	$-.22^{qr}$	$-.44^{q}$	$-.60^{r}$
Job Satisfaction	$.15^{st}$	$-.33^{s}$	$-.32^{t}$
Lack of Influence with:			
Negative Affective States	$-.16^{uv}$	$.42^{u}$	$.30^{v}$
Life Satisfaction	$.08^{w}$	$.26$	$.30^{w}$
Psychosomatic Symptoms	$-.15^{xy}$	$.22^{xz}$	$.47^{yz}$
Marital Satisfaction	$-.29^{ab}$	$.29^{a}$	$.30^{b}$
Impact of Job on Home and Family	$-.22^{c}$	$.03^{d}$	$.53^{cd}$
Job Satisfaction	$.42^{e}$	$.00^{ef}$	$.37^{f}$

*Correlation with same superscript are significantly different ($p < .05$).

life stress and one source of job stress and six aspects of satisfaction and well-being for husbands reporting varying levels of quality of spouse helping. Spouse helping would have a moderating or buffering effect on the stress-well-being relationship if different magnitudes of correlation appeared between husbands reporting varying levels of spouse helping. More specifically, correlations should be lowest between measures of experienced stress and measures of satisfaction and well-being for husbands having greatest spouse helping. The data in this table provides clear support for this proposition. Relationships between stress and satisfaction and well-being are almost always lower for husbands reporting the highest quality of spouse helping, and in many cases the difference in magnitude of the correlations obtained in the most helped and least helped groups reach statistical significance.

Table 12-IV presents comparable data for wives. The pattern of correlations differs considerably from the data obtained from the husbands (Table 12-III) and offers little support for the buffering or moderating effect of the spouse helping variable. More correlations between experienced stress and measures of satisfaction and well-being are *higher* for the most helped group than the least helped group, contrary to the hypothesis.

Table 12-IV

Spouse Helping and the Stress-Well-Being Relationship

| | Help from Husband* | | |
Wives	Most Helped	Intermediately Helped	Least Helped
Life Worries with:			
Life Satisfaction	$-.26^a$	$-.44$	$-.55^a$
Negative Affective States	$-.50$	$-.40$	$-.40$
Psychosomatic Symptoms	$-.34^b$	$-.48$	$-.58^b$
Marital Satisfaction	$.24^c$	$.00^{cd}$	$-.21^d$
Impact of Job on Home and Family	$-.48$	$-.34^e$	$-.60^e$
Self-Esteem	$.40^f$	$.55^g$	$.07^{fg}$
Number of Stress Life Events with:			
Life Satisfaction	$.01$	$.04$	$.04$
Negative Affective States	$-.66^h$	$-.46^i$	$-.11^{hi}$
Psychosomatic Symptoms	$-.66^j$	$-.56^k$	$-.00^{jk}$
Marital Satisfaction	$.04^{lm}$	$-.18^l$	$-.19^m$
Impact of Job on Home and Family	$-.43^{no}$	$-.20^n$	$-.12^o$
Self-Esteem	$.58^p$	$.61^q$	$-.32^{pq}$

*Correlation with same superscript are significantly different ($p < .05$).

Discussion

The measure of spouse helping created for this investigation was found to have both internal consistency and construct validity. Reliability estimates for both husbands and wives exceeded .90. In addition, a higher quality of helping from spouse was associated with a greater sense of belonging to a supportive relational network as well as a diminished preference for keeping one's problems to oneself. Other evidence of the construct validity of the spouse helping measure resides in the significantly higher quality of helping present from spouses than from individuals outside the marital relationship.

The latter findings, consistent with the central role accorded to spouses in earlier research (Burke and Weir, 1975), once again highlighted the central role of spouse helping in one's supportive network. Interestingly, the availability of spouse helping bore no relationship to the availability of help from specific sources outside the marital pair.

Husbands and wives generally reported similar levels of spouse helping in their descriptions and the pattern of intercorrelation of the spouse helping variable with other variables was nearly identical for husbands and wives.

Based on the findings of the first study we expected to find differences in husbands' and wives' perceptions of their spouses' help. This was not the case, however. Perhaps the fact that a different measurement approach was used, that the husbands were more attuned to helping because of their profession, or that the wives had lower expectations of the prospects of help from their spouses because of their excessive job demands could all account for this finding.

Let us now focus on the various effects attributed to the spouse helping variable. Three effects were considered: (1) preventive (*see* Table 12-I); (2) therapeutic (*see* Table 12-II); and (3) buffering or moderating (*see* Tables 12-III and 12-IV). The data in Tables 12-I and 12-II provided modest support for the hypothesized preventative and therapeutic effects of spouse helping. The preventative effect, in particular, was problematic. But when one considers that many stressful life events are, in fact, beyond one's control, the latter finding should not be surprising. On this basis, one might expect preventative effects on the upsettingness of those stressful life events that are encountered. This expectation was partially supported. Stronger therapeutic effects were observed (Table 12-II), but some of these vanished when the direct effects of experienced stress on well-being were partialled out.

Interestingly, the strongest effects were present when spouse helping was treated as a moderator variable (Table 12-III and 12-IV). This was particularly true for husbands. Taken together, the results of the two studies are encouraging in indicating tangible emotional health benefits to recipients of high quality spouse helping.

These effects, i.e., moderating, were equally striking when the stress was discrete, i.e., a specific event, as well as when the stress was more general and amorphous, i.e., life worries. Cobb (1976) has reviewed several studies of benefits of social support and concluded that over a variety of *transitions* in the life cycle, social support was protective. Our data indicated benefits when stresses are both global or specific. However, we would expect that the effects of spouse helping might be negligible on the impact of chronic stress, such as that experienced by air traffic controllers, and greater for nonwork sources of stress than for work sources of stress.

Conclusions and Implications

The following rationale is offered as a possible explanation for the positive findings in the two studies.

It is common knowledge that living in a state of heightened and prolonged tensions can negatively affect an individual's perceptions of himself and his world. It can also cause his emotional and behavioral responding to become increasingly dysfunctional in relation to his external environment. The marital helping interaction by giving explicit recognition to the personal distress of one or other spouse sets the process in motion of dealing with stressful events as they arise and interrupts the building up of tensions. It can provide for the comfort, support, and validation of the distressed spouse through selected environmental manipulations and/or through personal attention and understanding. It can offer the individual short-term relief by giving him an opportunity to ventilate his feelings in an atmosphere of concern and caring. It can holdout the promise of long-term relief by providing the occasion for him to clarify his perceptions of the problem areas and to consider appropriate behavioral strategies for resolving these. Thus, the marital helping process by minimizing and resolving the stressful experiences of husbands and wives can increase the likelihood that their perceptions of their life's experiences will be more positive and reduce the potential that accumulated tensions will be translated into pathology.

On the basis of the above findings, the husband-wife helping relationship emerges as a significant factor influencing the quality of life of the marital partners. Unfortunately it is an aspect of marriage that often remains undeveloped or at best is left to evolve haphazardly. The nature of the conclusions obtained in this study suggest that continued examination along similar lines can yield useful information regarding the characteristics of individuals and processes that contribute to effective helping interactions in marriage (McCubbin, Hunter, and Dahl, 1975; McCubbin, Dahl, Lester and Boss, 1975). Such information is essential for informing, educating, and counselling individuals on the potential but often unrealized "mental hygiene" function of marriage. To paraphrase Blood and Wolfe (1960), where better than in the marriage relationship, based on mutual affection, commitment, and accessibility, should one find lifetime help as needed?

Future research needs. We hope the present volume serves as a stimulus to other researchers to undertake studies of family stress and the potential therapeutic benefits to individuals from sources of help existing in their social milieu. A series of reports has recently examined the help of parents and peers to adolescents (Burke and Weir, 1978, 1979). We observed that a measure of combined satisfaction with help of parents and peers had preventative, therapeutic, and moderating effects in this sample.

We believe that future research must focus specifically on the spouse helping concept itself. What constitutes spouse helping? Is it more than emotional and psychological support? How does spouse helping operate in order to yield whatever beneficial effects it is found to have? Greater effort must be devoted to the conceptual level. Following this, more attention must then be turned to the measurement of spouse helping. That is, better measures of spouse helping must be created, and this is a time-consuming and painstaking process. Finally, greater attention should be devoted to the identification of particular sources of life stress to be assessed. Ideally, measures of concrete life transitions as well as more general feelings of stress should both be assessed. Then, an examination of the presence as well as the absence of relationships with spouse helping measures would increase our knowledge of conditions associated with beneficial effects of spouse helping.

It is important to realize that not all spouse relationships are helpful (Handy, 1978), and this obviously applies as well to relationships outside the marital pair. In addition, it is important to appreciate the fact that not all "problems" that are experienced by individuals in their day-to-day activities can be solved by help from another individual. That is, in some cases the problems individuals are attempting to deal with are structurally rooted. Thus the limitations of spouse helping should be recognized, too (McCubbin, Dahl and Hunter, 1976).

But the fact that some life events that result in strain are extremely unmanipulatable and are sometimes impossible to reverse by external forces, e.g. termination at work, complications during pregnancy, death of a loved one, may place an increased emphasis on informal helping, from spouse or others, which can be manipulated and enhanced. Particularly if further research continues to show tangible benefits to the recipients of spouse helping.

Chapter 13

LEVELS OF STRESS AND FAMILY SUPPORT IN BLACK FAMILIES

HARRIETTE P. McADOO

THE stress experienced by those in a devalued minority group and their means of coping with stress are two areas with very little empirical data. This study was conducted in order to explore the presence of stress in one group of blacks — those who moved up to middle-class status. A secondary purpose of this research effort was to determine if certain cultural patterns were maintained after mobility had occurred into middle-class status. This particular group was selected for focus because it was possible to control for the established negative effects of unemployment, poverty, and poor living conditions. It also allowed us to explore whether black families, not adversely impacted by precarious economics, would be able to escape the pressures of discrimination as they moved into suburbia and stable urban areas.

An underlying thesis of this research was that black families, through a blending of Afro-American, African, and Euro-American cultures over generations, had developed life-styles and family patterns that were similar to, but different in many subtle ways, from nonblack families. Those differences have formed the core of black culture. This cultural content or ethnicity has now been recognized in many diverse ethnic, religious, and nationality groups as the soul-satisfying component of contemporary family life (Mindel and Habenstein, 1977; Levine & Giordano, 1978). These cultural patterns, found in most black families at all income levels, have been documented as: strong reliance on the family (Billingsley, 1968; Hill, 1971; Stack, 1975; McAdoo, 1978); a strong sense of movement and religiosity (Nobles, 1978); an active involvement of both parents in child rearing and decision making (Staples, 1971; Mack, 1974); and the continual defense against discrimination.

The most oppressive source of stress for blacks has continued to

239

be the omnipresence of racism, discrimination, and economic isolation. These, coupled with the lack of majority appreciation of their culture and the denigration of their ethnic group, may not be as overt as in the past, but are covertly present and do not appear to be decreasing. Economic and historical stresses have resulted in some differential life-style patterns that have produced lower incomes for blacks at all social levels, regardless of education and occupation; surpluses of marriage-aged females; and a higher proportion of one-parent homes. The impact of low income on family structure is shown by the fact that in black families with an annual income of less than $4,000, only 20 percent are two-parent families compared with 37 percent for white families. But for black families earning $15,000 or more annually, 86 percent have two parents, a pattern similar to nonblack families at the same income level (U.S. Census, 1979). These figures indicate that black families under economic restrictions have to endure greater stresses. Public policies have contributed to the patterns found at lower income levels.

Although families with more limited physical or economic resources generally have greater problems, this should not be viewed as a measure of the functionality of the famiy. Certain cultural patterns have evolved to help the black family cope with limited economic resources. The extended family-help system, the "elasticity" of family boundaries, the high level of informal adoption, and the important supportive role of the black church have augmented existing internal family supports used to cope with stress. However, these means of managing stress are more than simple survival tactics or coping strategies. These family patterns have become components of the Afro-American cultural heritage now found in black families of all social classes.

METHODOLOGY

Sample Selection

To evaluate the level of stress, black families of school-age children with middle-income parents were selected. Half of the sample was urban and the other half was suburban, both from the middle-Atlantic area of the United States. The suburban families were randomly selected from a list of black families generated from the black churches, social and professional groups, and public and private schools in the area. Using education and income, a comparable urban sample was selected from a city located fifteen miles away.

All of the parents had to meet the following criteria: (a) black; (b) a middle-income status (minimum income of $10,000 for one-parent families and $14,000 for two-parent families); (c) school age children living in the home under the age of eighteen years; and (d) one parent older than twenty-five years. The parental age cutoff was used because the period before age twenty-five is the time during which the prerequisites of socioeconomic status usually are developed, i.e. education, occupation, and income level.

Procedure

Interviewing. In each family, the father was interviewed by a black male interviewer, and the mother was interviewed separately by a black female interviewer. Each parent was then asked to fill in a personal data sheet (which took approximately forty-five minutes) that provided background demographic information and data for three separate scales.

In one-parent homes, the head of the household was asked to fill out a background data sheet on the absent parent. While there was some missing information on the nonresident or deceased parent, we were able to obtain some mobility data for both parents of all our families. Analyses were made on both the paternal and maternal lines in an effort to understand the family's mobility over three generations. While data were obtained from or about both parents in the home, the family as a whole was the unit of analysis.

Interview protocol. The instruments used gathered data on (a) basic background information, (b) educational and occupational mobility over three generations, (c) levels of stress, (d) satisfaction with life, and (e) preference for and utilization of support systems.

The Holmes and Rahe schedule of life events (1967) was used to measure levels of stress. This instrument measures both fortunate and unfortunate changes that have occurred in the past two years. The instrument also provides a measure of the amount of change that a given event requires of an individual or family through the use of standardized weights. Different events have been weighted by hundreds of people from different populations across the country on a scale that gives a higher score for major changes, e.g. divorce, 73; death of a child, 63; and a lower score for less traumatic events, e.g. vacation, 13. The Holmes and Rahe scale uses two years as the time interval during which change is measured. For this study, a two-step time dimension was added to the scale to get an additional breakdown of significant change events that occurred within the past six months. Subjects were asked to indicate events that had happened within the past six months and those that occurred seven months to two years previously.

The Standard Happiness Scale (Bradburn and Caplovitz, 1965), used widely in nationwide surveys, was adopted for this study as a measure of satisfaction with life. This scale measures global constructs such as marital happiness and life satisfaction (Gurin, Veroff, and Feld, 1960; Bradburn, 1963; Bradburn and Caplovitz, 1965; and Hill, 1971). Families were asked in general about their level of happiness and their satisfaction with their present family situation.

Sample Description

Three hundred and five parents were included, 174 mothers and 131 fathers, representing 178 family units. The same proportion of one-parent (28%) to two-parent (72%) families were found in each site. Almost all families were nuclear, composed of one or two parents, while 6 percent were extended families.

This was a geographically stable sample since 42 percent had never moved from the middle-Atlantic area and 43 percent had moved only once. The subjects were, for the most part, the children of migrants from the South who had moved to the metropolitan Baltimore-Washington area, whose children and grandchildren had remained in close proximity to them. Generally speaking, these families had not been as mobile as has been reported for white middle-class families, probably because of more limited occupational opportunities than those available for the white families.

The mean age of the urban fathers was 40.7 years and 37.5 years for the mothers. The suburban ages were 37.5 for fathers and 37.0 for the mothers. Of the subjects 423 children, 51 percent were boys and 49 percent were girls in both sites, with an average of 2.37 children per family.

The average income was $19,749 for men and $11,247 for women. The combined family income which was similar in both settings, was $32,730 urban and $33,000 suburban (1976 dollars). Eighty five percent of mothers in both sites worked. Single parents (both mothers and fathers) had lower incomes in both sites.

Most of these families were at least of middle-class status, using the standard Hollingshead-Redlich scale (upper-class — 43%; middle class — 47%; and lower class 8%). We also used a modified version that gave more weight to subjects' education levels, than to occupational status (allowing for occupational discrimination against blacks) and found more (57%) moved to the upper-class status level. More suburban than urban families were in the upper class SES group. Parents rated their own class status lower than objective measures did. (For more demographic information on this sample, *see* McAdoo, 1979.)

RESULTS AND DISCUSSION

Changes in economic status have been found to be one of the factors that cause stress within the family and threaten family stability. In light of the social mobility and improvement in economic status of these families, the parents' level of satisfaction with life and their levels of stress were examined.

Level of Satisfaction with Life

No differences were found between the urban and suburban samples on satisfaction with their life in general or with their family situations. Fifty-two percent felt basically satisfied with life and 40 percent said they were very happy. Only 8 percent reported that overall they were unhappy. These results are consistent with nationwide surveys indicating general life satisfaction for adults in higher status.

These families appeared to be even more satisfied with their family life than they were with life in general. A very high number responded (81%) that they were satisfied with family life. Separately we asked them to tell us what the most positive things were about their family. They felt that the love and concern for each other and the willingness to work were the most positive aspects (38%). The next most important aspect was the sense of togetherness and respect for openness felt for each other (33%).

Furthermore, it is important to note that mothers from both sites felt their present neighborhood was better than where they lived before.

Level of Stress

The stress measurement indicated a high and continuing level of stress for these families. The majority of the families had experienced significant life changes within the past two years. Holmes and Rahe (1974) using clinical follow-up, grouped the stress scores into three categories: mild stress (150-199 life change units), moderate stress (200-299 life change units), and major stress (300 + life change units). The families in this study had stressful life changes that were in the moderate range. Their mean score over two years was 247.93. Holmes and Masuda (1974) found that 51 percent of the individuals in their study within this score range developed a major illness associated with this moderate continuing level of stress. If this amount of stress were prorated for each six-month interval over the two years, there would be an average of fifty to seventy-four life change units for each six-month period. The parents in this sample, reporting life events for the most recent six months, obtained a much higher mean score of 103.65. This increased level of stress for the most recent six months was associated with the occurrence of more stressful life events. They reported that they had experienced a mean of 10.96 such events over two years and 4.98 of them in the past six months.

One-parent homes had experienced more significant life events than two-parent homes. Families that moved into a suburban setting had not experienced more significant life changes than urban families. While the move to suburbia had been made within the past few years, the often related stress of moving and resettling the family did not appear to have resulted in higher stress scores than those found in the city. No significant demographic differences were found between sites over the past two years (t (159) = − .589, n.s.) or within the past six months (t (159) = 1.33, n.s.). Stress appeared to have occurred equally in both sites.

A comparison of stress levels was made on the basis of present

SES status. No differences in levels of stress were found for families who were rated as upper class compared to those who were rated middle-class. It was anticipated that stress would be greater for families who were newly mobile than for those who had been at this status for several generations, but this was not supported. In fact, the newly mobile often had lower stress scores than those with long-term middle-class status and the lowest scores were found in upwardly mobile families for each generation.

An unexpected reversal was found for stress scores based on life changes occurring within the past six months. Those who had been in the middle class for three generations had a significantly higher stress score than the newly mobile ($F(3,106) = 2.65$, $p < .05$). Their stress score ($M = 133.24$) for the most recent six months was almost equivalent to the mild stress range (150-199) based on the total two years. The next highest stressed group was the newly mobile ($M = 90.46$), followed with much lower stress in those upwardly mobile for two generations ($M = 58.86$) and those whose parents (but not themselves) had been upwardly mobile ($M = 59.12$).

It would appear that the socioeconomic status of the father is related to stress. The group with the lowest stress also had the highest average income, highest occupational status, highest education, and also the *lowest* level of maternal employment (76%) outside of the home. In contrast, the group with the highest stress scores had the lowest status in income, occupation, and education. The highly stressed group also had the highest level of maternal employment (89%).

The resultant picture presented is that those families with the greatest resources faced fewer stressful changes. The higher economic level plus the greater availability of the mother as a full-time homemaker appeared to be associated with less stress. It is impossible to determine any definitive causal factors or direction of effects. Did having fewer resources mean that stressful change could not be prevented? Or did stressful changes result in underemployment of the father, requiring mother to work at a greater level, thus making them less prepared to cope with additional changes?

Families were divided into high and low stress groups based on the mean of the total stress score and reexamined on the major variables. There were no income differences between either fathers or mothers in the two groups. There also were no occupational status or present SES differences between the high and low stress groups. Over the past three generations no differences were found in occupation or SES in the fathers' line.

We found that more of the maternal grandmothers of the low stress group (75%) had worked than the maternal grandmothers of the high stress group (63%). When employed, the maternal grandmothers of low stress families were in significantly higher status managerial jobs (29% for low stress families versus 17% for high stress families) and skilled level jobs (14% for low stress families versus 3% for high stress families) $(X^2(6) = 12.35, p < .02)$. We also found that mothers in both groups had similar levels of employment in full and part-time jobs. Mothers of the present generation who did not grow up in homes with a role model of maternal employment may experience greater stress as they learn a new role necessitated by economic conditions that require them to seek employment.

Stress related to race. The Holmes and Rahe scale does not include a dimension for stress associated with racism and discrimination. It seems likely that an addition of this dimension would have brought these families well into the major stress range, for many of the parents reported that they felt under extra stress because they were black. For example, they reported that in the work environment, insidious and sometimes overt discrimination interfered with their career development. They also reported that they continually were forced to act as a buffer between their children and their teachers, persons, and community institutions. They related small events, such as being treated harshly by a storeclerk, which singly were not serious but when they reoccurred in many settings, led to feelings of rage: "We have had to live under a great deal of stress and uncertainty and poverty. We have been forced to play the role of second-class citizens for so long."

Because the association between stress, illness, and reduced life span has been well documented, we asked the parents to respond to the statistic that, on the average, blacks die ten years earlier than nonblacks. Only 3 percent disagreed with the statement, and 4 percent had no opinion. The balance of them agreed and gave several reasons that they felt accounted for this difference in life span. The largest response was that the psychological and social pressures of racism in their everyday environment was the greatest contributor to black stress (38%).

No significant differences were found between urban and suburban responses regarding race and stress, although suburban parents tended to be more concerned with discrimination (25%) than those in the city (17%). Perhaps, suburban families, living in a more integrated environment, interact to a greater extent with nonblacks, exposing them to more abrasive attitudes and behavioral cues that could be perceived as discriminatory. The lack of stress and degree of comfort felt within all black settings is one of the reasons given for preferences for all black social interactions.

They appeared to feel that forces beyond their control in their environment were the main cause of blacks experiencing more stress and a shorter life expectancy. There often was a sense of powerlessness on the racial issue as expressed by this parent:

> Cut off expectations. I mean no matter how good you are, you will always be a nigger. Hey, that puts strain on people. I mean you can be smart, have a lot of bread, but you know that you will not be able to give your children or yourself an equal chance and this takes its toll. A lot of really good blacks, that have a lot on the ball, end up on dope, alcohol, or one thing or another. I mean everyone that I know has one of these problems because of this racist society. Let me tell you, I do not have any hope for the future.

Support Systems

Stress and kin help exchange. These families were undergoing significant changes in their lives that, when added to the everpresent strain provided by racism, required that a continuing level of internal and external support be provided for them. The strains faced by these families led to the continued cultural pattern of involvement with the kin help system. It would, therefore, follow that parents undergoing greater stress would be more involved in the kin help system than those who were under less stress. We found that parents at all levels of stress gave help to and received help from kin. In all cases, the kin provided more help than friends or community agencies.

However, the families under stress appeared to be more dependent on the kin network and interacted more frequently with kin. While high and low stress families lived similar distances from their relatives, the frequency of contact was much higher ($X^2(5) = 12.12$, $p < .03$) for high stress families. Of the mothers under high stress, 42 percent saw kin about twice a week, while only 29 percent of those under low stress interacted that much. Low stressed families tended to see kin about twice a month. Fathers from high stress families also indicated greater contact with family members.

High stressed families received help in many more areas $(X^2(2) = 7.64, p < .02)$ than low stressed families. Fifty-four percent of the low stressed received no help compared to 26 percent for the high stressed. The real difference in help received by the high stressed families was for child care. While both groups had equal maternal employment $(X^2(6) = 10.01, p < .03)$, a difference in the ages of their children was found. Low stress families had more children who were old enough to be in school all day (32% versus 24% for high stress), and therefore may have needed less child care. One-third of each stress group used paid babysitters. Those of low stress (18%) made greater use of day care and nursery centers than did those of high stress (7%). The high stress families (20%) used relatives more than low stress families (11%). For social occasions, no differences in child care were found, only during employment. Kin also assisted more in child care when parents faced significant life changes. The stress of the families may be increased when children are younger and more dependent, requiring more primary care. The reliance on kin did not appear related to financial need, since both groups had similar income, but rather was related to the need for help with care of children. The level of stress for these parents was related to the intensity of involvement with kin, further supporting the concept of a cultural pattern of preference for reliance on kin rather than institutions when in need. While families at both stress levels felt some reciprocal obligation to their kin for help received, mothers under high stress (62%) felt more obligated than low stress mothers (39%) to help other members of the wider family who were not as fortunate as they were $(X^2(2) = 10.16, p < .01)$. Because their interactions had been more intense and they had received greater assistance in many areas, they felt obligations to help those in need were probably greater.

The relationship between stress levels and help exchange with friends was also examined. Both stress groups gave similar amounts and kinds of help to friends and received similar help from friends. However, when asked to evaluate the contact they had with their friends, high stress families (81%) felt their contact was "just right," while 39 percent of the low stress group felt their contact was "too little" ($X^2(2) = 6.61$, $p < .04$). While attitudes about obligations towards friends for help received were similar for mothers of both groups, fathers of high stress families felt a greater obligation to friends for help received ($X^2(2) = 7.11$, $p < .02$). The greater frequency of contact with friends in the high stress group may indicate a greater dependency on friends when undergoing changes.

Support needs of black families. The ecology of the black family predisposes continuing stress with little chance of changing, creating an ongoing need for internal cultural supports for these families. Because the black families' kin are also in vulnerable situations and may not always be able to provide the needed support, external programs may be needed by these families. For this reason, the parents' utilization of and attitudes toward existing programs were explored, along with the kind of support they would like to have in light of their families present situation and the stress they have faced in the immediate past.

In light of the high rate of mobility, change, and stressful events these families had experienced in the past few years, we asked them to consider how they had handled problems in the past and what external support they needed from outside agencies. We asked them to think about the crises they had faced in the past few years and tell us how they were met. When crises occurred, the majority of the families went first to their family and discussed it, and then they made a decision (62%). The second most frequent response was to "think about it myself, stay calm, and do what was needed" (23%). Five percent indicated that they would get outside help. Only one family indicated that they were unable to cope, and one said they went to nobody outside of the family. Nine percent indicated that their family had not had a crisis.

Both suburban and urban families had similar reactions in going to the family first for help. More of the suburban families (30%) worked out their problems by themselves, as compared to the urban ones (18%). More urban (7%) got outside help than suburban (2%). The suburban families, all of whom had lived in suburbia only a few years, had faced crises, but 15 percent of the urban families, who had been established for nine or more years, had not faced a crisis.

Our main finding on family needs was that black families preferred not to seek outside help for cultural reasons and because they felt community agencies were unsympathetic to their unique stresses. External support from existing community agencies appeared to be requested only after no internal solution could be found. The parents indicated that ideally, external family support systems would involve an extensive counseling program for personal, marital, and financial matters. Concerns existed about their children and the need for job placement for male and female heads of household. The needs of the families differed depending on urban and suburban residence. Urban families needed more help in meeting their family's basic needs of health, education, recreation, and child care but were comfortable in a predominantly black environment. Suburban families had more of these resources available but were under financial strain. They also appeared to be reacting to their minority status by seeking greater involvement with the social cultural community and were more sensitive to the race of the provider of these services. Policymakers and program planners need to be sensitive to demographic differences. The external support network for families requires the coordination of many agencies. They need to augment rather than replace the help exchange, to allow families to provide for their own supportive needs.

CONCLUSION

These families were high achievers who valued education, were under a continuing moderate degree of stress, and were acutely aware of the impact of racism on their lives and on their children. The families who had been upwardly mobile in each of the generations had parents with the highest educational and occupational status, the lowest maternal employment, and the highest level of satisfaction with their lives. They apparently had more human and financial resources available to their domestic unit.

The coping strategies used to protect the unit in a hostile ecological setting (kin help exchange, shared parenting, decision making, and maternal employment) evolved into cultural patterns that were not eliminated when the black family moved into a different social class situation. The extended kin exchange patterns continued, with more help being provided to those in poorer situations. Most felt positive about these relationships, and only the most recently mobile felt pressured to provide aid to family members.

Parents struggle with the dilemma of providing conflicting messages to their children in relation to the American dream, i.e. "If you do well in school and work hard, doors will open for you. However since you are black, some doors will be opened only reluctantly and you may never be able to fully enter, regardless of your ability." These parents tend to be protective of their children and attempt to act as a buffer against such conflicts, while helping each child to develop to his/her highest potential. These parents also feel that the black culture (their family's history and information on the saga of blacks in the African and American continent) needs to be preserved and passed on to their children. They feel that this element of their culture is often ignored by school and the media and that it is too important an element to allow to disappear. Lower stressed parents were more active in all-black activities. The parents appear to be attempting to maintain a balance between their aspirations of upward mobility and economic stability, while not electing the option of total assimilation into the dominant culture. They have developed a positive sense of the value of their diverse African-American experiences that *in toto* form the American black culture.

In spite of their stress and the frequency of changes in their lives, they exhibited an overall level of satisfaction with their life situations and were very pleased with their family situations. They were aware of the limits placed on them personally by discrimination and had no expectation that this situation would change in the next few generations, if ever. They felt that they had accomplished something important against great odds, and therefore, felt a degree of satisfaction with their lot, especially in relation to their reference group of the wider black community.

Although the family support system provided physical and emotional support as the families were mobile and was the preferred source of help, they faced strains for which external supports were needed. The personal and financial strains they were under led them to desire several forms of personal and financial counseling that were not perceived as being present in their communities. They wanted competent services, sensitive to the unique strains brought by omnipresent racism and had a strong preference for services being provided by persons from similar cultural backgrounds. However, while many such services were available, these families were hesitant to use them. Service agencies and their staff need to be sensitive to these issues and to work to minimize conflicts between the black cultural patterns and agency policies and practices.

REFERENCES

Alexander, J. F., and Barton, C.: Behavioral systems therapy for families. In D. H. Olson (Ed.): *Treating Relationships.* Lake Mills, Iowa, Graphic Publishing, 1976.

Allport, G. W.: The open system in personality theory. *Journal of Abnormal and Social Psychology, 61:*301-310, 1960.

Angell, R. C.: *The Family Encounters the Depression.* New York, Charles Scribner's Sons, 1936.

Baekeland F., and Lundwall, L.: Dropping out of treatment: A critical review. *Psychological Bulletin, 82:*738-783, 1975.

Bailyn, L.: Career and family orientations of husbands and wives in relation to marital happiness. *Human Relations, 23:*97-113, 1970.

Bain, A.: The capacity of families to cope with transitions: A theoretical essay. *Human Relations, 31:*675-688, 1978.

Baldwin, W. H.: Adolescent pregnancy and childbearing: Growing concerns for Americans. *Population Bulletin, 31(2):*1-34, 1976.

Bebbington, A. C.: The function of stress in the establishment of the dual-career family. *Journal of Marriage and the Family, 35:*530-537, 1973.

Bede, H. H.: *Lecture to the National Association of Welfare Workers,* Chicago, February 9, 1970.

Bednarzik, R. W., and St. Marie, S. M.: Employment and Unemployment in 1976. *Monthly Labor Review, 100(2):*3-13, 1977.

Bell, N. W., and Vogel, E. F.: *The Family.* Glencoe, Illinois, Free Press, 1960.

Belloc, N.: Relationship of health practices in mortality. *Preventative Medicine, 2:* 67-81, 1973.

Belloc, N. B., and Breslow, L.: Relationship of physical health status and health practices. *Preventative Medicine, 1:*409-421, 1972.

Benedek, T.: *Psychosexual Functions in Women.* New York, Ronald Press, 1952.

Benedict, R.: Continuities and discontinuities in cultural conditioning. *Psychiatry, 2:*161-170, 1938.

Berkman, L. F.: *Psychosocial Resources, Health Behavior and Mortality: A Nine Year Follow-up Study.* Paper presented at the American Public Health Association Meeting, October, 1977.

Berle, B. B., Pinsky, R. H., Wolf, S., and Wolf, H. G.: Berle index: A clinical guide to prognosis in stress disease. *Journal of American Medical Association, 149:*1624-1628, 1952.

Bernard, J.: *The Future of Motherhood.* New York, Penguin Books, Inc., 1974.

Billingsley, A.: *Black Families in White America.* Englewood Cliffs, New Jersey, Prentice-Hall, Inc., 1968.

Bird, C.: *The Two-paycheck Marriage.* New York, Rawson Wade, 1979.

Blalock, H. M.: *Social Statistics.* New York, McGraw-Hill Book Co., 1960.

Blood, R. O., Jr., and Wolfe, D. M.: *Husbands and Wives: The Dynamics of Married Living.* Glencoe, Illinois, Free Press, 1960.

Booth, A.: A wife's employment and husband's stress: A replication and refutation. *Journal of Marriage and the Family, 39:*645-650, 1977.

Boss, P.: A clarification of the concept of psychological father presence in families experiencing ambiguity of boundary. *Journal of Marriage and the Family, 39:*141-151, 1977.

Boss, P., McCubbin, H. I., and Lester, G.: The corporate executive wife's coping patterns in response to routine husband-father absence. *Family Process, 18:*79-86, 1979.

Boulding, E.: The family as an agent of social change. *The Futurist, 6(5):*186-191, 1972.

Bowen, M.: The family as a unit of study and treatment. *American Journal of Orthopsychiatry, 30:*346, 1961.

Bradburn, N. M.: *In Pursuit of Happiness.* Chicago, National Opinion Research Center, 1963.

Bradburn, N., and Caplovitz, D.: *Report on Happiness: A Pilot Study of Behavior Related to Mental Health.* NORC Monograph in Social Research No. 3. Chicago, Aldine Publishing Co., 1965.

Broderick, C. B., Williams, P., and Krager, H.: Family process and child outcomes. In W. Burr, R. Hill, I. Nye and I. Reiss (Eds.): *Contemporary Theories About the Family,* Vol. I. New York, Free Press, 1979.

Brown, G. W.: Social factors influencing length of hospital stay of schizophrenic patients. *British Medical Journal, 2:*1300-1302, 1959.

Brown, G. W., Bhrolchain, M. N., and Harris, T.: Social class and psychiatric disturbance among women in an urban population. *Sociology, 9:*225-254, 1975.

Brown, G. W., Davidson, S., Harris, T., Pollock, S., and Prudo, R.: Psychiatric disorder in London and North Ulst. *Social Science & Medicine, 11:*367-377, 1977.

Bryson, R., Bryson, J. B., and Johnson, M. F.: Family size, satisfaction, and productivity in dual-career couples. In J. B. Bryson and R. Bryson (Eds.): *Dual-Career Couples.* New York, Human Sciences Press, 1978.

Bryson, R., Bryson, J., Licht, M., and Licht, B.: The professional pair: Husband and wife psychologists. *American Psychologist, 31(1):*10-16, 1976.

Buckley, W.: *Sociology and Modern Systems Theory.* Englewood Cliffs, New Jersey, Prentice-Hall, Inc., 1967.

Burch, J.: Recent bereavement in relation to suicide. *Journal of Psychosomatic Research, 16:*361-366, 1972.

Burke, R. J.: Are you fed up with work? *Personnel Administration, 34:*27-32, 1971.

Burke, R. J., and Weir, T.: Giving and receiving help with work and non-work related problems. *Journal of Business Administration, 6:*59-78, 1975.

— — — Disclosure of problems and tensions experienced by marital partners. *Psychological Reports, 38:*531-542, 1976a.

— — — Relationship of wives' employment status to husband, wife and pair satisfaction and performance. *Journal of Marriage and the Family, 38:*279-287, 1976b.

— — —Marital helping relationships: The moderator between stress and well-being. *Journal of Psychology, 95:*121-130, 1977.

— — —Benefits to adolescents of informal helping relationships with their parents and peers. *Psychological Reports, 42:*1175-1184, 1978.

— — —Helping responses of parents and peers and adolescent well-being. *Journal of Psychology, 102(1):*49-63, 1979.

Burke, R. J., Weir, T., and DuWors, R. E., Jr.: Type A behavior of administrators and wives' reports of marital satisfaction and well-being. *Journal of Applied Psychology, 64:*57-65, 1979.

Burr, W. R.: *Theory Construction and the Sociology of the Family.* New York, John Wiley & sons, 1973.

— — —*Successful Marriage: A Principles Approach.* Homewood, Illinois, The Dorsey Press, 1976.

Caplan, G.: *Principles of Preventative Psychiatry.* New York, Basic Books, Inc., 1964.

— — —*Support Systems and Community Mental Health.* New York, Behavioral Publications, 1974.

Caplan, R. D.: *Organizational Stress and Individual Strain.* Unpublished doctoral dissertation, University of Michigan, 1971.

Caplan, R. D., Bobb, S., French, J. R. P., Harrison, R. V. and Pinneau, S. R.: *Job demands and worker health.* (Department of Health, Education, and Welfare Publication No. [NIOSH] 75-160). Washington, D. C., U.S. Government Printing Office, 1975.

Cassel, J. C.: Psychiatric epidemiology. In G. Caplan (Ed.): *American Handbook of Psychiatry,* Vol. II. New York, Basic Books, Inc., 1974.

Cavan, R. S., and K. H. Ranck: *The Family and the Depression.* Chicago, University of Chicago Press, 1938.

Chambers, W. N., and Reiser, M. F.: Emotional stress in the precipitation of congestive heart failure. *Psychosomatic Medicine, 15:*38-60, 1953.

Chen, E., and Cobb, S.: Family structure in relation to health and disease: A review of the literature. *Journal of Chronic Diseases, 12:*544-567, 1960.

Chinn, P. L.: *Child Health Maintenance.* St. Louis, C. V. Mosby Co., 1979.

Clavan, S., and Vatter, E.: The affiliated family: A device for integrating old and young. *Gerontologist, 12:*407-412, 1972a.

— — —The affiliated family: A continued analysis. *The Family Coordinator, 21(4):* 499-504, 1972b.

Cobb, S.: Social support as a moderator of life stress. *Psychosomatic Medicine, 38:* 300-314, 1976.

Cobb, S., Brooks, G. W., Kasl, S. V., and Connelly, W. E.: The health of people changing jobs: A description of a longitudinal study. *American Journal of Public Health, 59:*1476-1481, 1966.

Cobb, S., and Kasl, S. V.: *Termination: The consequences of job loss.* (NIOSH, Publication Number 77-224, USDHEW). Washington, D.C., U.S. Government Printing Office, 1977.

Coelho, G., Hamburg, D., Adams, J.: *Coping and Adaptation.* New York, Basic Books, Inc., 1974.

Craddock, A. E.: *Social influence and conflict within the marital dyad.* Unpublished doctoral dissertation, University of Sydney, Australia, 1977.

— — —*Marital problem solving as a function of couple's marital power expectations and marital value system.* Unpublished manuscript, 1978.

deAraujo, G., van Arsdel, P. P., Holmes, T. H., and Dudley, D. L.: Life change, coping ability and chronic intrinsic asthma. *Journal of Psychosomatic Research, 17:*359-363, 1973.

Deutscher, I.: Socialization for post-parental life. In A. M. Rose (Ed.): *Human Behavior and Social Processes.* Boston, Houghton Mifflin Co., 1962.

Dohrenwend, B. S., and Dohrenwend, B. P., (Eds.): *Stressful Life Events: Their Nature and Effects.* New York, John Wiley & Sons, Inc., 1974.

Dohrenwend, B. S., Krasnoff, L., Askenasy, A. R., and Dohrenwend, B. P.: Exemplification of a method for scaling life events: The PERI life event scale. *Journal of Health and Social Behavior, 19(2):*205-229, 1978.

Dubos, R.: *Mirage of Health.* Garden City, New York, Doubleday & Co., Inc., 1959.

Duncan, D.: Family stress and the initiation of adolescent drug abuse: A retrospective study. *Corrective and Social Psychiary, 24(3):*111-114, 1978.

Duncan, G. J., and Morgan, J. N.: *Five Thousand American Families. Patterns of Economic Progress,* Vol. 5. Ann Arbor, Michigan, University of Michigan, Institute for Social Research, 1977.

Duncan, R. P., and Penrucci, C.: Dual occupation families and migration. *American Sociological Review, 41:*252-261, 1976.

Duvall, E. M.: Loneliness and the serviceman's wife. *Marriage and Family Living, 4:* 77-82, 1945.

— — —*Family Development* (4th ed.) Philadelphia, J. B. Lippincott Co., 1971.

Dyer, D.: Parenthood as crisis: A re-study. *Marriage and Family Living, 25:*196-201, 1963.

Dytrych, Z., Matejcek, Z., Schuller, V., David, H. P., and Friedman, H. L.: Children born to women denied abortion. *Family Planning Perspective, 7:*165-171, 1975.

Egbert, L. D., Battit, G. E., Welch, C. E., and Bartlett, M. R.: Reduction of postoperative pain by encouragement and instruction of patients. *New England Journal of Medicine, 270:*825-827, 1964.

Elder, G. H., Jr.: *Children of the Great Depression.* Chicago, University of Chicago Press, 1974.

Engel, G. L.: *Psychological Development in Health and Disease.* Philadelphia, W. B. Saunders Co., 1962.

— — —The need for a new medical model: A challenge for biomedicine. *Science, 196:*129-136, 1977.

Epstein, C. D.: Law partners and marital partners: Strains and solutions in the dual-career family enterprise. *Human Relations, 24:*549-563, 1971.

Erikson, K. T.: *Everything in Its Path: Destruction of the community in the Buffalo Creek Flood.* New York, Simon & Schuster, Inc., 1976.

Feldman, L. B.: Goals of family therapy. *Journal of Marriage and Family Counseling, 2:*103-113, 1976.

Feldstein, M.: Social insurance. *Public Policy, 25(1):*81-115, 1977.

Fienberg, E.: *The analysis of Cross-Classified Categorical Data.* Cambridge, Massachusetts, Massachusetts Institute of Technology, 1977.

Flaste, R.: Prevention of heart disease can start in childhood. *The New York Times,* 1977.

Fogarty, M. P., Rapoport, R., and Rapoport, R. N.: *Sex, Career and Family.* Beverly Hills, Sage, 1971.

Forssman, H., and Thuwe, I.: One hundred and twenty children born after application for therapeutic abortion refused. *Acta Psychiatrica Scandinavica, 42:*71-88, 1966.

French, J. R. P., Jr., Rodgers, W., and Cobb, S.: Adjustment as person-environment fit. In G. V. Coelho, D. A. Hamburg, J. E. Adams (Eds.): *Coping and Adaptation.* New York, Basic Books, Inc., 1974.

Freund, J. W.: The meaning of volunteer services in schools — to the educator and to the older adult. *Gerontologist, 11(3, pt.1):*205-208, 1971.

Gallup Poll, The New York Times, November 18, 1976.

Garfinkel, I., and Haveman, R.: Earnings capacity economic status, and poverty. In M. Moon and E. Smolensky (Eds.): *Improving Measures of Economic Well-Being.* New York, Academic Press Inc., 1974.

Garfinkel, I.: *Income Support Policy Where We Have Come Forward and Where We Should Be Going.* Discussion Paper 490-78. Institute for Research on Poverty. Madison, Wisconsin, University of Wisconsin Press, 1978.

Garland, N. T.: The better half? The male in the dual profession family. In C. Safilios-Rothschild (Ed.): *Toward a Sociology of Women.* Lexington, Massachusetts, Xerox College Publishing, 1972.

General Mills: *The American Family Report 1978-1979: Family Health in an Era of Stress.* Minneapolis, Minnesota, 1979.

Gerber, I., Wiener, A., Battin, D., and Arkin, A.: Brief therapy to the aged bereaved. In B. Schoenberg (Ed.): *Bereavement: Its Psychological Aspects.* New York, Columbia University Press, 1975.

Giordano, J.: *Ethnicity and Mental Health: Research and Recommendations.* National Project on Ethnic America of the American Jewish Committee, New York, 1973.

Goetzel, V.: Mental illness and cultural beliefs in a southern Italian immigrant family. *Canadian Psychiatric Association Journal, 18:*219-222, 1973.

Goodman, L. A.: A modified multiple regression approach to the analysis of dichotomous variables. *American Sociological Review, 37:*28-46, 1972a.

— — — A general model for the analysis of surveys. *American Journal of Sociology, 77:* 1035-1086, 1972b.

— — — Causal analysis of data from panel studies and other kinds of surveys. *American Journal of Sociology, 78:*1135-1191, 1973.

Gore, S.: *The Influence of Social Support and Isolated Variables in Ameliorating the Consequences of Job Loss.* Doctoral dissertation, University of Michigan. Dissertation Abstracts International 34:S330A-S331S (University Microfilms No. 74-2416), 1973.

— — — The effect of social support in moderating the health consequences of unemployment. *Journal of Health and Social Behavior, 19:*157-165, 1978.

Gove, W. R., and Geerken, M. R.: The effect of children and employment on the mental health of married men and women. *Social Forces, 56:*66-76, 1977.

Gove, W. R., and Tudor, J. F.: Adult sex roles and mental illness. *American Journal of Sociology, 78:*812-835, 1973.

Guerney, L. F.: Filial therapy program. In D. H. Olson (Ed.): *Treating Relationships.* Lake Mills, Iowa, Graphic Publishing, 1976.

Gurin, G., Veroff, J., and Feld, S.: *Americans View Their Mental Health.* New York, Basic Books, Inc., 1960.

Gurin, G., and Gurin, P.: Expectancy theory in the study of poverty. *Journal of Social Issues,* 1970.

Hackett, T., and Cassem, N.: Psychological management of the myocardial infarction patient. *Journal of Human Stress, 1:*25-38, 1975.

Haley, J.: Family experiments: A new type of experimentation. *Family Process, 1:* 265-293, 1962.

— — —*Strategies of Psychotherapy.* New York, Grune and Straton, Inc., 1963.

— — — Research on family patterns: an instrument measurement. *Family Process, 3:* 41-65, 1964.

Hall, D. T.: A model of coping with role conflict: The role behavior of college educated women. *Administrative Science Quarterly, 17:*471-486, 1972.

Halton, D. A.: *Understanding Cerebral Palsy: For Parents of the Cerebral Palsy Child.* Erie, Pennsylvania, Barber Center Press, Inc., 1976.

Handy, C.: The family: Help or hindrance? In C. L. Cooper and R. L. Payne (Eds.): *Stress at Work.* New York, John Wiley & Sons, Inc., 1978a.

— — — Going against the grain: Working couples and greed occupations. In R. Rapoport and R. N. Rapoport (Eds.): *Working Couples.* New York, Harper & Row Publishers, Inc., 1978b.

Hansen, D. A.: Personal and positional influence in formal groups: Propositions and theory for research on family vulnerability to stress. *Social Forces, 44:*202-210, 1965.

Hansen, D., and Hill, R.: Families under stress. In H. Christensen (Ed.): *Handbook of Marriage and the Family.* Chicago, Rand McNally, 1964.

Hansen, D., and Johnson, V.: Rethinking family stress theory: Definitional aspects. In W. Burr, R. Hill, I. Reiss, and I. Nye (Eds.): Contemporary Theories About the Family, Vol. I. New York, Free Press, 1979.

Haveman, H.: Poverty, income distribution and social policy: The last decade and the next. *Public Policy, 25:*3-21, 1977.

Hayghe, H.: Families and the rise of working wives: An overview. *Monthly Labor Review, 99(5):*12-19, 1976a.

— — — Research summaries: New data series on families show most jobless have working relatives. *Monthly Labor Review, 99(12):*46-48, 1976b.

Haynes, R. B., and Sackett, D. L.: *Compliance with therapeutic regimens — Annotated bibliography.* A symposium presented by the Department of Clinical Epidemiology and Biostatistics, McMaster University Medical Centre, Hamilton, Ontario, 1974.

Heckman, N. A., Bryson, R., and Bryson, J.: Problems of professional couples: A content analysis. *Journal of Marriage and the Family, 39:*323-330, 1977.

Hermalin, J. A.: *A Predictive Study of Schizophrenic Patient Rehospitalization.* Unpublished doctoral dissertation, Providence, Rhode Island, Brown University, 1976.

Hill, R.: *Families Under Stress.* Connecticut, Greenwood Press, 1949.

— — —Generic features of families under stress. *Social Casework, 39:*139-150, 1958.

— — —Modern systems theory and the family: A confrontation. *Social Science Information, 72:*7-26, 1971.

Hill, R., and Hansen, D.: The family in disaster. In G. Baker and D. Chapman (Ed.): *Man and Society in Disaster.* New York, Basic Books, Inc., 1962.

Hill, R., and Klein, D.: The family as a problem-solving group. In W. Burr, R. Hill, I. Reiss, and I. Nye (Eds.): *Contemporary Theories about the Family,* Vol. I. New York, Free Press, 1979.

Hill, R., and Rodgers, R.: The developmental approach. In H. Christensen (Ed.): *Handbook of Marriage and the Family.* Chicago, Rand McNally & Co., 1964.

Hill, R.: *The Strengths of Black Families.* New York, Emerson Hall, 1971.

Hobbs, D. F.: Parenthood as crisis: A third study. *Journal of Marriage and the Family, 27:*367-372, 1965.

— — —Transition to parenthood: A replication and an extension. *Journal of Marriage and the Family, 30:*413-417, 1968.

Hoffman, L. W.: Effects on child. In L. W. Hoffman and F. I. Nye (Eds.): *Working Mothers.* San Francisco, Jossey-Bass Publishers, 1974.

Holmes, T. H., Joffe, J. R., and Ketcham, J. W.: Experimental study of prognosis. *Journal of Psychosomatic Research, 5:*235-252, 1961.

Holmes, T. H., and Masuda, M.: Life change and illness susceptibility. In B. S. Dohrenwend and B. P. Dohrenwend (Eds.): *Stressful Life Events: Their Nature and Effects.* New York, John Wiley & Sons, Inc., 1974.

Holmes, T. H., and Rahe, R. H.: The social readjustment rating scale. *Journal of Psychosomatic Research, 11:*213-218, 1967.

Holmstrom, L. L.: *The Two-Career Family.* Cambridge, Massachusetts, Schenkman Publishing Co., 1973.

Hopkins, J., and White, P.: The dual-career couple: constraints and supports. *The Family Coordinator, 27:*253-259, 1978.

Hultin, M., and Ottosson, M. O.: Perinatal conditions of unwanted children. *Acta Psychiatrica Scandinavica, (Suppl) 221:*59-76, 1971.

Hunt, J. G., and Hunt, L. L.: Dilemmas and contradictions of status: The case of the dual-career family. *Social Problems, 24:*407-416, 1977.

Hunter, E. J., McCubbin, H. I., and Metres, P. J., Jr.: Religion and the POW/-MIA Family. In H. I. McCubbin, B. B. Dahl, P. J. Metres, Jr., E. J. Hunter, and J. A. Plag (Eds.): *Family Separation and Reunion: Families of Prisoners of War and Servicemen Missing in Action.* San Diego, California, Center for Prisoner of War Studies, Naval Health Research Center, 1974.

Illich, I.: *Medical Nemesis.* London, Calder & Boyars, 1975.

Indik, B., Seashore, S. E., and Slesinger, J.: Demographic correlates of psychological strain. *Journal of Abnormal and Social Psychology, 69:*26-38, 1964.

Jackson, E. F.: Status consistency and symptoms of stress. *American Sociological Review, 27:*469-480, 1962.

Jaffe, F. S., and Dryfoos, J. G.: Fertility control services for adolescents: Access and utilization. *Family Planning Perspectives, 8(4):*167-175, 1976.

Janis, I. L.: *Psychological Stress.* New York, John Wiley & Sons, Inc., 1958.

Jekel, J., and Klerman, L. V.: Adolescent fertility: An epidemic or endemic problem. *Studies in Family Planning, 10(3):*107-110, 1979.

Johnson, B., and Hayghe, H.: Labor force participation of married women. *Monthly Labor Review (March):*33-36, 1976.

Kahn, R. L., Wolfe, D. M., Quinn, R. P., Snoek, J. D., and Rosenthal, R. A.: *Organizational Stress: Studies in Role Conflict and Ambiguity.* New York, John Wiley & Sons, Inc., 1964.

Kantor, D., and Lehr, W.: *Inside the Family: Toward A Theory of Family Process.* San Francisco, Jossey-Bass, 1975.

Killorin, E., and Olson, D. H.: *Clinical Application of the Circumplex Model to Chemically Dependent Families.* Unpublished manuscript, 1980.

Kimmel, D. C.: *Adulthood and Aging: An Interdisciplinary, Developmental View.* New York, John Wiley & Sons, Inc., 1974.

Knowles, J. H.: The responsibility of the individual. *Daedalus, 106(1):*57-80, 1977.

Komarovsky, M.: *The Unemployed Man and His Family.* New York, Dryden Press, 1940.

Koos, E. L.: *Families in Trouble.* New York, King's Crown Press, 1946.

Lambert, K.: Agape as a therapeutic factor in analysis. *Journal of Analytical Psychology, 18:*25-46, 1973.

LaPorte, T. R., and Metlay, D.: Technology observed: Attitudes of a wary public. *Science, 188:*121-127, 1975.

Lazarus, R.: *Psychological Stress and the Coping Process.* New York, McGraw-Hill Book Co., 1966.

Lazarus, R. S., Averill, J. R., and Opton, E. M., Jr.: The psychology of coping: Issues of research and assessment. In G. V. Coehlo, D. A. Hamburg and J. E. Adams (Eds.): *Coping and Adaptation.* New York, Basic Books, Inc., 1974.

Lebel, J., and Lebel, M.: *The First Retrospective Evaluation of One Significant Intergenerational Experiment.* Lecture to 25th Annual Meeting of the Gerontological Society, San Juan, Puerto Rico, December 17-20, 1972.

Lee, D. H. K., and Kotin, P. (Eds.): *Multiple Factors in the Causation of Environmentally Induced Disease.* Fogarty International Center Proceedings No. 12. New York, Academic Press, 1972.

LeMasters, E. E.: Parenthood as crisis. *Marriage and Family Living, 19:*352-355, 1957.

Lenski, G.: Status crystallization: A non-vertical dimension of social status consistency and symptoms of stress. *American Sociological Review, 19:*405-413, 1954.

Levine, I., and Giordano, J.: *Informal Coping Systems and the Family.* Paper presented at Consultation on Strengthening American Families through the Use of Informal Support Systems, Wingspread Center, Racine, Wisconsin, April 19, 1978.

Levinger, G.: Task and social behavior in marriage. *Sociometry, 27:*433-448, 1964.

Levinger, G., and Senn, D. J.: Disclosure of feelings in marriage. *Merrill-Palmer Quarterly, 13:*237-249, 1967.

Levy, R. I.: Stroke decline: Implications and prospects. *New England Journal of*

*Medicine, 300(9):*490-491, 1979.

Lidz, T., Cornelison, A. R., Fleck, S., and Terry, D.: The intrafamilial environment of schizophrenic patients: II. Marital schism and marital skew. *American Journal of Psychiatry, 114:*241-248, 1957.

Lin, N., Simeone, R. S., Ensel, W. M., and Kuo, W.: Social support, stressful life events and illness, a model and an empirical test. *Journal of Health and Social Behavior, 20:*108-119, 1979.

Lindsay, J. S. B.: Balance theory: Possible consequences of number of family members. *Family Process, 15:*245-249, 1976.

Litman, T. J.: Health care and the family: A three-generational analysis. *Medical Care, 9(1):*67-81, 1971.

Lowenthal, M. F., Thruner, M., and Chiriboga, D.: *Four Stages of Life.* San Francisco, Jossey-Bass, 1976.

Lowenthal, M. F., and Haven, C.: Interaction and adaptation: Intimacy as a critical variable. *American Sociological Review, 33:*20-30, 1968.

Lowenthal, M. F., and Robinson, B.: Social networks and isolation. In R. H. Binstock and E. Shanas (Eds.): *Handbook of Aging and the Social Sciences.* New York, Van Nostrand Reinhold Co., 1976.

Mack, D.: The power relationship in black families and white families. *Journal of Personality and Social Psychology, 30:*409-413, 1974.

Mandelbaum, D. G.: Soldier groups and Negro soldiers. *Psychological Review, 66:* 267-277, 1952.

Mann, F. C.: *The Handling of Job Tensions.* Unpublished and undated manuscript, University of Michigan.

Marston, S.: *The Impact of Unemployment Insurance on Job Search.* Brookings Paper on Economic Activity, 1975.

Martin, T. W., Berry, K. J., and Jacobsen, R. B.: The impact of dual-career marriages on female professional careers: An empirical test of a parsonian hypothesis. *Journal of Marriage and the Family, 37:*734-742, 1975.

McAdoo, H.: Factors related to stability in upwardly mobile Black families. *Journal of Marriage and the Family, 40(4):*761-776, 1978.

――― Black Kinship. *Psychology Today,* (May):67-79, 1979.

McCubbin, H.: Integrating coping behavior in family stress theory. *Journal of Marriage and the Family, 41:*237-244, 1979.

McCubbin, H., Comeau, J. K., and Harkins, J.: *FIRM — Family Inventory of Resources for Management.* University of Minnesota, St. Paul, Minnesota, 1979.

McCubbin, H., and Dahl, B.: *Coping with Separation Inventory.* San Diego, California, Family Studies Branch, Naval Health Research Center, 1975.

McCubbin, H., Dahl, B., and Hunter, E. J.: *Families in the Military System.* Beverly Hills, California, Sage Publications, Inc., 1976.

McCubbin, H., Dahl, B., Lester, R., Benson, D., and Robertson, M. L.: Coping repertoires of wives adapting to prolonged war-induced separations. *Journal of Marriage and the Family, 38:*461-471, 1976.

McCubbin, H., Dahl, B., Lester, G., and Ross, B.: The returned prisoner of war: Factors of family reintegration. *Journal of Marriage and the Family, 37:*471-478, 1975.

McCubbin, H., Hunter, E., and Dahl, B.: Residuals of war: Families of prisoners of war and servicemen missing in action. *Journal of Social Issues, 31:*161-182, 1975.

McCubbin, H., Hunter, E., and Metres, P., Jr.: Adaptation of the family to the PW/MIA experience: An overview. In H. I. McCubbin., B. B. Dahl, P. J. Metres, Jr., E. J. Hunter, and J. A. Plag (Eds.): *Family Separation and Reunion: Families of Prisoners of War and Servicemen Missing in Action.* San Diego, California, Center for Prisoner of War Studies, Naval Health Research Center, 1974.

McCubbin, H., Joy, C., Cauble, E., Comeau, J., Patterson, J., and Needle, R.: Family Stress and Coping: A Decade Review. *Journal of Marriage and the Family, 42(4),* 1980.

McCubbin, H., McCubbin, M., Cauble, A., and Nevin, R.: *CHIP—Coping Health Inventory for Parents.* University of Minnesota, St. Paul, Minnesota, 1979.

McCubbin, H., McCubbin, M., Patterson, J., Cauble, A., Wilson, L., and Warwick, W.: *CHIP—Coping Health Inventory for Parents: An Assessment of Parental Coping Patterns in the Care of the Chronically Ill Child.* University of Minnesota, St. Paul, Minnesota, 1981.

McCubbin, H., Nevin, R., Larsen, A., Comeau, J., Patterson, J., Cauble, E., and Striker, K.: *Families Coping with Cerebral Palsy.* St. Paul, Minnesota, Family Social Science, 1981.

McCubbin, H. I. and Patterson, J.: *Systematic Assessment of Family Stress, Resources and Coping: Tools for Research, Education and Clinical Intervention.* St. Paul, Minnesota, Family Social Science, 1981.

McCubbin, H., Wilson, L., and Patterson, J.: *FILE—Family Inventory of Life Events and Changes.* University of Minnesota, St. Paul, Minnesota, 1979.

Mechanic, D.: *Students Under Stress.* New York, Free Press, 1962.

— — —Social structure and personal adaptation: Some neglected dimensions. In G. V. Coelho, D. A. Hamburg, and J. E. Adams (Eds.), *Coping and Adaptation.* New York Basic Books, Inc., 1974.

Meierowitz, J.: *Personal Communication.* Jerusalem, September 9, 1974.

Melson, G. F.: *Family and Environment.* An Ecosystems Approach. Minneapolis, Minnesota, Burgess Publishing Company, 1980.

Menaghan, E. G.: *The Effect of Family Transitions on Marital Experience.* Unpublished doctoral dissertation, Chicago, University of Chicago, 1978.

Menninger, W. C.: Psychiatric experience in the war 1941-1946. *American Journal of Psychiatry, 103:*587-593, 1947.

Merton, R. K.: Social structure and anomie. In R. K. Merton (Ed.): *Social Theory and Social Structure,* 2nd Ed. Glencoe, Illinois, Free Press, 1957.

Mindel, C., and Habenstein, R.: *Ethnic families in America.* New York, Elsevier, 1977.

Minuchin, S.: *Families and Family Therapy.* Cambridge, Massachusetts, Harvard University Press, 1974.

Minuchin, S., Montalvo, B., Guerney, B. G., Rosman, B., and Schumer, F.: *Families of the Slums.* New York, Basic Books, Inc., 1967.

Moen, P.: Family impacts of the 1975 recession: Duration of unemployment. *Journal of Marriage and the Family, 41:*561-573, 1979.

― ― ―Developing family indicators: Financial hardship, a case in point. *Journal of Family Issues, I (March)*:5-30, 1980a.

― ― ―Measuring unemployment: Family considerations. *Human Relations, 33(3)*: 183-192, 1980b.

Monat, A., and Lazarus, R. S.: *Stress and Coping: An Anthology*. New York, Columbia University Press, 1977.

Moos, R.: *Family Environment Scales and Preliminary Manual*. Palo Alto, California, Consulting Psychologists Press, 1974.

― ― ―*Human Adaptation: Coping with Life Crisis*. Lexington, Massachusetts, D. C. Health and Co., 1976.

Morris, N. M., Undry, J. R., and Chase, C. L.: Reduction of low birth weight rates by prevention of unwanted pregnancies. *American Journal of Public Health, 63*:935-938, 1973.

Movius, M.: Voluntary childlessness ― the ultimate liberation. *The Family Coordinator, 25*:57-62, 1976.

Murray, H. A., Barrett, W. G., and Hamburger, E.: *Explorations in Personality*. New York, Oxford University Press, 1938.

Narvon, L.: Communication and adjustment in marriage. *Family Process, 6*:173-184, 1967.

National Council on Employment Policy: The impact of employment and training programs. In M. Guttentag (Ed.): *Evaluation Studies Review Annual*. New York, Russell Sage Foundation, 1977.

Nelson, R.: The legal plight of the PW/MIA family. In H. I. McCubbin, B. B. Dahl, P. J. Metres, Jr., E. J. Hunter, and J. A. Plag (Eds.): *Family Separation and Reunion: Families of Prisoners of War and Servicemen Missing in Action*. San Diego, California, Center for Prisoner of War Studies, Naval Health Research Center, 1974.

Neugarten, B. L., and Hagestad, G. O.: Age and the life course. In R. H. Binstock and E. Shanas (Eds.): *Handbook of Aging and the Social Sciences*. New York, Van Nostrand Reinhold Co., 1976.

Nobles, W. W.: Toward an impirical and theoretical framework for defining Black families. *Journal of Marriage and the Family, 40(4)*:676-690, 1978.

Nuckolls, K. B., Cassel, J., and Kaplan, B. H.: Psychosocial assets, life crisis and the prognosis of pregnancy. *American Journal of Epidemiology, 95*:431-441, 1972.

Olds, S. W.: Young class in growing old. *McCalls, (July)*:26, 1973.

Olson, D. H.: Empirically unbinding the double bind: Review of research and conceptual reformulations. *Family Process, 11*:69-94, 1972.

Olson, D. H., Bell, R. and Portner, J.: *Family Adaptability and Cohesion Evaluation Scales (FACES)*. University of Minnesota, St. Paul, Minnesota, 1978.

Oppenheimer, V. K.: The life-cycle squeeze: The interaction of men's occupational and family cycles. *Demography, 11*:237-245, 1974.

Orden, S. R., and Bradburn, N. M.: Dimensions of marriage happiness. *American Journal of Sociology, 73*:715-731, 1968.

― ― ―Working wives and marriage happiness. *American Journal of Sociology, 74*: 382-407, 1969.

Palmer, J. L., and Barth, M. C.: The distributional effects of inflation and higher unemployment. In Eugene Smolensky (Ed.): *Improving Measures of Economic Well-Being*. New York, Academic Press, 1977.

Papenek, H.: Men, women, and work: Reflections of the two-person career. *American Journal of Sociology, 78:*852-872, 1973.

Parkes, C. M.: *Bereavement: Studies of Grief in Adult Life*. New York, International Universities Press, 1972.

Parkes, C. M., Benjamin, B., and Fitzgerald, R. G.: Broken heart: a study of increased mortality among widowers. *British Medical Journal, 1:*740-743, 1969.

Patterson, G. R.: Parents and teachers as change agents: A social learning approach. In D. H. Olson (Ed.): *Treating Relationships*. Lake Mills, Iowa, Graphic Publishing, 1976.

Pearlin, L. I.: Social and personal stress and escape television viewing. *Public Opinion Quarterly, 23:*255-259, 1959.

— — —Sex roles and depression. In N. Datan and L. Ginsberg (Eds.): *Life-Span Developmental Psychology*. New York, Academic Press Inc., 1974.

— — —Status inequality and stress in marriage. *American Sociological Review, 40:* 344-57, 1975.

Pearlin, L. I., and Lieberman, M. A.: Social sources of emotional distress. In R. Simmons (Ed.): *Research in Community and Mental Health*. Greenwich, Connecticut, JAI Press, 1979.

Pearlin, L. I., and Radabaugh, C. W.: Economic strains and the coping functions of alcohol. *American Journal of Sociology, 82:*652-66, 1976.

Pearlin, L. I., and Schooler, C.: The structure of coping. *Journal of Health and Social Behavior, 19:*2-21, 1978.

Perlmuter, L. C., and Monty, R. A.: The importance of perceived control: Fact or fantasy? *American Scientist, 65:*759-765, 1977.

Perrier: *The Perrier Study: Fitness in America*. New York, Great Waters of France, Inc., 1979.

Petersen, J. C., and Markle, G. E.: *Adjudication in Science: The Laetrile Controversy*. Paper presented at American Sociological Association, Chicago, September, 1977.

Phillips, D. P., and Feldman, K. A.: A dip in deaths before ceremonial occasions: Some new relationships between social integration and mortality. *American Sociological Review, 38:*678-696, 1973.

Pinneau, S. R., Jr.: *Effects of Social Support on Psychological and Physiological Strains*. (Doctoral dissertation, University of Michigan, 1975). Dissertation Abstracts International, 36:4239B-5366B. University Microfilms No. 76-9491, 221, 1976.

Plotnick, R.: Poverty and the public cash transfer system. In: *Poverty Reports — A Decade Review*. Madison, University of Wisconsin, Institute for Research on Poverty, 1975.

Poloma, M. M., and Garland, T.: The married professional woman: A study of the tolerance of domestication. *Journal of Marriage and the Family, 33:*531-540, 1971.

Portner, J.: *Impact of Work on the Family*. Minneapolis, Minnesota Council on Family Relations, 1978.

Powers, I.: National league of families and the development of family services. In H. I. McCubbin, B. B. Dahl, P. J. Metres, Jr., E. J. Hunter, and J. A. Plag (Eds.):*Family Separation and Reunion: Families of Prisoners of War and Servicemen Missing in Action*. San Diego, California, Center for Prisoner of War Studies, Naval Health Research Center, 1974.

Quinn, R. P., and Shepard, L. J.: *The 1972-73 Quality of Employment Survey*. Ann Arbor, Michigan, Institute for Social Research, 1974.

Radloff, L.: Sex differences in depression: The effects of occupation and marital status. *Sex Roles, 1:*249-265, 1975.

Rahe, R. H.: Life change events and mental illness: An overview. *Journal of Human Stress, 5:*2-10, 1979.

Raphael, B.: Preventive intervention with the recently bereaved. *Archives of General Psychiatry, 34:*1450-1454, 1977.

Rapoport, L.: The state of crisis: Some theoretical considerations. *Social Service Review, 36:*211-217, 1962.

Rapoport, R., and Rapoport, R. N.: *Dual-Career Families*. London, Penguin Books, 1971.

— — —*Dual-Career Families Re-examined*. New York, Harper & Row Publishers, Inc., 1976.

— — —*Working Couples*. New York, Harper & Row Publishers, Inc., 1978.

Rapoport, R. N., and Rapoport, R.: Dual-career families: Progress and prospects. *Marriage and Family Review, 1(2):*1-12, 1978.

Reid, D. D.: Some measures of the effect of operational stress on bomber crews, in Great Britain Air Ministry. *Psychological Disorders in Flying Personnel of the R.A.F.* London, His Majesty's Stationery Office, 1947.

Reiss, D.: Varieties of consensual experience. I. A theory for relating family interaction to individual thinking. *Family Process, 10:*1-27, 1971a.

— — —Varieties of consensual experience: II. Dimensions of a family's experience of its environment. *Family Process, 10:*28-35, 1971b.

Rice, D.: *Dual-Career Marriage: Conflict and Treatment*. New York, Free Press, 1979.

Richardson, J. G.: Wife occupational superiority and marital troubles: An examination of the hypothesis. *Journal of Marriage and the Family, 41:*63-72, 1979.

Ridley, C. A.: Exploring the impact of work satisfaction and involvement on marital interaction when both partners are employed. *Journal of Marriage and the Family, 35:*229-237, 1973.

Rodgers, R. H.: Toward a theory of family development. *Journal of Marriage and the Family, 26(3):*262-270, 1964.

— — —*Family Interaction and Transaction: The Development Approach*. Englewood Cliffs, New Jersey, Prentice-Hall, Inc., 1973.

Roland, A., and Harris, B.: *Career and Motherhood: Struggles for a New Identity*. New York, Human Sciences, 1979.

Rollins, B. C., and Cannon, K. L.: Marital satisfaction over the family life cycle: A re-evaluation. *Journal of Marriage and the Family, 36(2):*271-282, 1974.

Rollins, B. C., and Feldman, H.: Marital satisfaction over the family life cycle. *Journal of Marriage and the Family, 32:*20-28, 1970.

Rose, A. M.: Factors associated with the life satisfaction of middle class, middle-aged persons. *Marriage and Family Living, 17:*15-19, 1955.

— — —Factors in mental breakdown in combat. In A. M. Rose (Ed.): *Mental Health and Mental Disorder--A Sociological Approach.* London, Routledge and Kegan Paul, 1956.

Rosenberg, M.: *Society and the Adolescent Self-Image.* Princeton, New Jersey, Princeton University Press, 1965.

Rosenthal, R., Archer, D., DiMatteo, M. R., Koivumaki, J. M., and Rogers, P. L.: Body talk and tone of voice: The language without words. *Psychology Today, 8(3):*64-68, 1974.

Rosow, I.: Status and role change through the life span. In R. H. Binstock, E. Shanas (Eds.): *Handbook of Aging and the Social Sciences.* New York, Van Nostrand Rheinhold Co., 1976.

Ryder, N. B.: Contraceptive failure in the United States. *Family Planning Perspectives, 5(3):*133-144, 1973.

Ryser, C., and Sheldon, A.: Retirement and health. *Journal of the American Geriatrics Society, 17(2):*180-190, 1969.

Schvaneveldt, J. D.: Mormon adolescents: Likes and dislikes toward parents and home. *Adolescents, 8:*171-178, 1973.

Scott, R. D., and Askworth, P. L.: Closure at the first schizophrenic breakdown: a family study. *British Journal of Medical Psychology, 40:*109-145, 1967.

Shanas, E.: Family-kin networks in cross-cultural perspective. *Journal of Marriage and the Family, 35:*505-511, 1973.

Sherman, E. M., Brittan, M. R., and Friedelson, I. (Eds.): *A Plan To Span. U.S. Dept. of Health, Education, and Welfare.* School and Rehabilitation Service, Administration on Aging (Publication No. 190) June, 1970.

Sieber, S. D.: Toward a theory of role accumulation. *American Sociological Review, 39:*467-478, 1974.

Skidmore, F.: Welfare reform: Some policy alternatives. In S. Nagel, (Ed.): *Policy Studies Review Annual I.* Beverly Hills, Russell Sage Foundation, 1977.

Skinner, D., and McCubbin, H.: *DECS--Dual Employed Coping Scales.* University of Minnesota, St. Paul, Minnesota, 1981.

Spanier, G. B.: Measuring dyadic adjustment: New scales for assessing the quality of marriage and similar dyads. *Journal of Marriage and the Family, 38:*15-30, 1976.

Spanier, G. B., Lewis, R. A., and Cole, C. L.: Marital adjustment over the family life cycle: The issue of curvilinearity. *Journal of Marriage and the Family, 37:*263-275, 1975.

Speer, D.: Family systems: Morphostasis and morphogenesis, or is homeostasis enough? *Family Process, 9:*259-278, 1970.

Sprenkle, D., and Olson, D.: Circumplex model of marital systems III: Empirical study of clinic and non-clinic couples. *Journal of Marriage and Family Counseling, 4:*59-74, 1978.

Stack, C.: *All Our Kin: Strategies for Survival in a Black Community.* New York, Harper & Row Publishers, Inc., 1975.

Staples, R.: *The Black Family: Essays and Studies.* Belmont, California. Wadsworth Publishing Co., Inc., 1971.

Stein, H. F.: The slovak — American 'swaddling ethos: Homeostat for family dynamics and cultural continuity. *Family Process, 17:*31-45, 1978.

Stein, Z., and Susser, M.: Social factors in the development of sphincter control. *Developmental Medicine and Child Neurology, 9:*692-706, 1967.

Stierlin, H.: *Separating Parents and Adolescents.* New York, Quadrangle Books, Inc., 1974.

Stolz, L. M.: *Influences on Parent Behavior.* Stanford, California, Stanford University Press, 1967.

Stouffer, S. A.: An analysis of conflicting social norms. *American Sociological Review, 14:*707-719, 1949.

Straus, M.: Measuring families. In H. Christensen (Ed.): *Handbook of Marriage and the Family.* Chicago, Rand McNally, 1964.

Stryker, S.: Symbolic interaction as an approach to family research. *Marriage and Family Living, 21:*111-119, 1959.

Sussman, M. B.: The isolated nuclear family: Fact or fiction? *Social Problems, 6:* 333-340, 1959.

Sussman, M. B., and Burchinal, L.: Kin family network: Unheralded structure in current conceptualizations of family functioning. *Marriage and Family Living, 24:*231-240, 1962a.

Swank, R. L.: Combat exhaustion: A descriptive and statistical analysis of causes, symptoms and signs. *Journal of Nervous and Mental Diseases, 109:*475-508, 1949.

Sweet, J. P.: *Women in the Labor Force.* New York, Seminar, 1973.

Thomas, L.: On the science and technology of medicine. *Daedalus, 106(1):*35-45, 1977.

Tietze, C.: Mortality with contraception and induced abortion. *Studies in Family Planning, 1(45),*1969.

Tietze, C., Bongaarts, J., and Schearer, B.: Mortality associated with the control of fertility. *Family Planning Perspectives, 8(1):*6-14, 1976.

Titmuss, R. H.: *Problems of Social Policy.* London, H. M. Stationery Office, 1950.

U.S. Bureau of the Census: *Current population reports. Number, timing, and duration of marriages and divorces in the United States: June, 1975.* (Series P-20, No. 297). Washington, D.C., U.S. Government Printing Office, 1976.

— — —*Social and Economic Status of the Black Population in the United States and Historical View 1790-1978,* 1979.

U.S. Dept. of Commerce: *Bureau of the Census. Social Indicators III.* Washington, D.C., U.S. Government Printing Office, 1980. .

U.S. Department of Health, Education, and Welfare: *Physician Visits: Volume and Interval Since Last Visit, United States* — 1971, Series 10 (97). Rockville, Maryland, March, 1975.

— — —*The Measure of Poverty.* Washington, D.C., Government Printing Office, 1976.

— — —*Physician Visits: Volume and Interval Since Last Visit — 1975.* Series 10 (128). Rockville, Maryland, April, 1979a.

— — —*Smoking and Health, A Report of the Surgeon General.* Rockville, Maryland, 1979b.

U.S. Food and Drug Administration: *A Study of Health Practices and Opinions.* June, 1972.

Ventura, S. J.: Teenage childbearing: United States, 1966-75. *Monthly Vital Statistics Report, 26(5):*1-15, 1977.

Vincent, J. P., Weiss, R. L., and Birchler, G. R.: A behavioral analysis of problem solving in distressed and non-distressed married and stranger dyads. *Behavior Therapy, 6:*475-487, 1975.

von Bertalanffy, L.: *General Systems Theory,* rev. ed. New York, George Braziller, Inc., 1968.

Walker, W. J.: Changing United States life-style and declining vascular mortality: Cause or coincidence? *New England Journal of Medicine, (July 21):*163-165, 1977.

Waller, W., and Hill, R. L.: *The Family and Dynamic Interpretation,* rev. ed. New York, Dryden Press, 1951.

Wallston, B. S., Foster, M. A., and Berger, M.: I will follow him: Myth, reality or forced choice — job seeking experiences of dual-career couples. In J. B. Bryson and R. Bryson (Eds.): *Dual-Career Couples.* New York, Human Sciences Press, 1978.

Weiss, R. S.: *Marital Separation.* New York, Basic Books, Inc., 1975.

Weller, R. H.: Number and timing failures among legitimate births in the United States: 1968, 1969, and 1972. *Family Planning Perspectives, 8(3):*111-116, 1976.

Wertheim, E.: Family unit therapy and the science and typology of family systems. *Family Process, 12:*361-376, 1973.

— — —The science and typology of family systems II. Further theoretical and practical considerations. *Family Process, 14:*285-308, 1975.

Westoff, C. F.: The decline of unplanned births in the United States. *Science, 191:* 38-41, 1976.

White, R. W.: Strategies of adaptation: An attempt at systematic description. In G. V. Coehlo, D. A. Hamburg and J. E. Adams (Eds.): *Coping and Adaptation.* New York, Basic Books, Inc., 1974.

Wigginton, B. E.: *Foxfire Two.* New York, Anchor/Doubleday, 1973.

Wigginton, E.: *Foxfire Book.* New York, Anchor/Doubleday, 1972.

Winch, R. F., and Greer, S.: Urbanism, ethnicity, and extended familism. *Journal of Marriage and the Family, 30:*40-45, 1968.

Wittmer, J: Amish homogeneity of parental behavior characteristics. *Human Relations, 26:*143-154, 1973.

Wynne, L., et al.: Pseudo-mutuality in the family relations of schizophrenics. *Psychiatry, 21:*205-222, 1958.

Young, A. M.: Year-round full-time earnings in 1975. *Monthly Labor Review, 100(6):*36-41, 1977.

INDEX